Mother of the BBC

Mother of the BBC

Mabel Constanduros and the development of popular entertainment on the BBC, 1925–57

Jennifer J. Purcell

BLOOMSBURY ACADEMIC
NEW YORK • LONDON • OXFORD • NEW DELHI • SYDNEY

BLOOMSBURY ACADEMIC
Bloomsbury Publishing Inc
1385 Broadway, New York, NY 10018, USA
50 Bedford Square, London, WC1B 3DP, UK
29 Earlsfort Terrace, Dublin 2, Ireland

BLOOMSBURY, BLOOMSBURY ACADEMIC and the Diana logo are trademarks of
Bloomsbury Publishing Plc

First published in the United States of America 2020
This paperback edition published in 2021

Copyright © Jennifer J. Purcell, 2020

For legal purposes the Acknowledgements on p. viii constitute an extension of this copyright page.

Cover design by Eleanor Rose |
Cover photograph courtesy of BBC Photo Library, 1936

All rights reserved. No part of this publication may be reproduced or transmitted in any form or by any means, electronic or mechanical, including photocopying, recording, or any information storage or retrieval system, without prior permission in writing from the publishers.

Bloomsbury Publishing Inc does not have any control over, or responsibility for, any third-party websites referred to or in this book. All internet addresses given in this book were correct at the time of going to press. The author and publisher regret any inconvenience caused if addresses have changed or sites have ceased to exist, but can accept no responsibility for any such changes.

Library of Congress Cataloging-in-Publication Data
Names: Purcell, Jennifer, author.
Title: Mother of the BBC: Mabel Constanduros and the development of popular entertainment on the BBC, 1925-1957 / Jennifer J. Purcell.
Description: [New York: Bloomsbury Academic, 2020] | Includes bibliographical references and index. | Summary: "Demonstrates the immense influence exercised by Mabel Constanduros and early writers and performers, especially women, on the history of the BBC and popular entertainment" – Provided by publisher.
Identifiers: LCCN 2019050933 | ISBN 9781501346507 (hardback) | ISBN 9781501346538 (epub) | ISBN 9781501346514 (pdf)
Subjects: LCSH: Constanduros, Mabel. | Radio actors and actresses–England–Biography. | Radio authors–England–Biography. | British Broadcasting Corporation–Biography.
Classification: LCC PR6005.O43 Z68 2020 | DDC 828/.91209–dc23
LC record available at https://lccn.loc.gov/2019050933

ISBN: HB: 978-1-5013-4650-7
PB: 978-1-5013-8985-6
ePDF: 978-1-5013-4651-4
eBook: 978-1-5013-4653-8

Typeset by Deanta Global Publishing Services, Chennai, India

To find out more about our authors and books visit www.bloomsbury.com and sign up for our newsletters.

For Rob and Liam
In Memory of Anthea Duigan, Richard Constanduros and Malcolm Down

Contents

Acknowledgements viii
Abbreviations xi

Introduction 1
1 Comedy and the early BBC, 1922–9 15
2 Introducing the Buggins family 31
3 Early BBC celebrity: Negotiating morality, femininity and wireless celebrity 49
4 Variety and beyond: Evolving and cultivating career, 1930–9 71
5 The *Kitchen Front* and popular entertainment during the People's War 89
6 Mother of the BBC: Portraying the 'ordinary', family and femininity, 1936–45 109
7 Reimagining family and managing career in the post-war world 131
Conclusion 161

Notes 171
Bibliography 213
Index 226

Acknowledgements

For a project that spans nearly a decade, much gratitude is owed to many. First, I would like to thank my colleagues and students at Saint Michael's College for their support and assistance throughout this project. Many thanks are due to my colleagues in the history department, Susan Ouellette, George Dameron, Doug Slaybaugh, Kathryn Dungy and Roberto Saba, for their support, friendship and animated discussion; thanks especially to Susan for reading several early drafts of this manuscript. Without the hard work and heroic efforts of our library staff, I doubt this book could have been completed. In particular, I am indebted to Naomi King, Kristen Hindes, Steve Burks and John Payne. I am equally grateful to Saint Michael's College for Faculty Development and Summer Research Grants, which have enabled me to carry out research in the UK. Among my students, I would like to thank Sean Morrissey, whose research and experience contributed much to my understanding of amateur dramatics. The insights, critical questions and discussion imparted by students in the Spring 2018 British Sitcom course were of immense value in developing some of my thinking about situation comedy. Research assistants Casey Fratkin and Winter Royce-Roll have also contributed in important ways to this project. Lucy Curzon, Paul Deslandes, Brian Lewis and Christina Baade have heard many of the arguments set out in this book during annual meetings of the Northeast Conference on British Studies (NECBS). Over the years, members of the NECBS have been gracious with their time and insights, and been endlessly supportive. I owe much to many in the NECBS, and to the National Conference on British Studies (NACBS), for being a nurturing and welcoming intellectual community. I am deeply grateful to Gilli Bush-Bailey for so generously sharing her insights and research on Constanduros, and for her unstinting support and friendship along the way; to Leo Hollis for his endless patience, creative insight and encouragement from the very beginnings of this project; to Marjorie Levine-Clark for her support over the years; and to both Andrea Salter and Jenna Bailey for their continued friendship and moral support. To Claire Langhamer, I am deeply indebted for her wise counsel, sharp insight and sustained support, and for commenting on what must have seemed like countless drafts of this manuscript.

I would like to recognize Professor John Annette, president of Richmond University, the American International University, London, for his generous financial support of the Richmond University Annual Summer Fellows Program, and to extend my thanks especially to Professor Dom Alessio and the 2016 Summer Fellows for their intellectual support at a very critical moment in this project's evolution.

The staff at the BBC Written Archives Centre in Caversham Park have been generously and warmly accommodating throughout this project. In particular, I would like to thank Matthew Chipping for his insightful assistance, and his care and patience through much of this project. I also must thank Jeff Walden for his assistance in the very early days of this work. Louise North and Marion Fallon have been endlessly helpful, welcoming and kind. At the Sutton Local Archives, I would like to thank Kath Shawcross for helping me ferret out details about Constanduros's life in Sutton. Dick Bower graciously shared his history of the Sutton Amateur Dramatic Club (SADC) with me; I am especially thankful for the opportunity to attend a production of the SADC with him in 2016. I would also like to thank Jonny Davies for his invaluable assistance at the British Film Institute. Others who have generously offered their time, resources and/or advice at various junctures throughout the project include Leah Clark, Paddy Scannell, Stephen Laing, Carolyn Scott-Jeffs and Julia Taylor. Many thanks are due to Jonathan Hope and Lucy Marten at Advanced Studies in England for lively conversations on the topic of British sitcom. At Bloomsbury Academic, I thank my reviewers Kate Murphy, Maggie Andrews and Hugh Chignell for their careful reading and feedback, to Mary Al-Sayed for seeing value in this project, and to Katie Gallof and Erin Duffy for their patience, good counsel and support throughout.

I wish to thank the BBC Written Archives Centre for permission to quote BBC copyright material and the BBC Photo Library for permission to reproduce the cover image and Figure 1. Thanks to Getty Images for permission to reproduce Figure 2. Warm thanks to Stephanie Down and Celia Martin, daughters of Denis Constanduros, for permission to print the photograph in Figure 3. I am especially grateful to Stephanie Down and Celia Martin for sharing a photograph from their family collection. I also thank Taylor & Francis, Ltd., for permission to reprint sections of the following articles in Chapters 1 and 3: "'Enthusiasm, Experiment and Gallantry in Action': Developing Light Entertainment on the Fledgling BBC, 1922–1932', *Cultural and Social History*, 15:3 (2018) 415-32 and "'Behind the Blessed Shelter of the Microphone': Managing Celebrity and

Career on the Early BBC – Mabel Constanduros, 1925-57', *Women's History Review*, 24:3 (2015) 372–88, copyright © the Social History Society, reprinted by permission of Taylor & Francis Ltd, on behalf of the Social History Society, http://www.tandfonline.com.

This book began with a trip to Inverness, Scotland, and a warm reception from Mabel Constanduros's grandchildren, Anthea Duigan and Richard Constanduros. Richard and his wife, Kathleen, generously shared their family archives with me, while Anthea kindly opened her home and shared memories of her grandmother. Through Anthea, I was introduced to the family of Constanduros's writing partner and nephew, Denis. Over the years, Anthea and Stephanie and Malcolm Down have been enthusiastic and generous supporters of this project, sharing family stories, documents and photographs along the way. Members of the Constanduros family, including Robert Constanduros, have also been kind and generous in their time and support. It has truly been an honour and a delight to have been so warmly embraced by Mabel Constanduros's family over the course of my work on this book. I only wish that I could share the finished book with Anthea, Richard and Malcolm Down, and dedicate the book in their memory.

My family is the foundation on which this book rests. To my brother and sister, Bill and Kim, and to Doug, thanks for your encouragement over the years. To my mom, Diane, thank you for unconditionally loving and supporting the three of us no matter what we got/get up to, and to mom and Doug, thanks for being Mummum and Poppop and caring for Liam as I researched and wrote this book. Words are not enough to express the gratitude I feel for my son, Liam, and my husband, Rob, for making my life rich and my heart soar, and for always reminding me what is truly most important. Without Rob and his constant patience, selfless support, love and friendship, this book would never have been possible. Thank you.

Abbreviations

BBC	British Broadcasting Corporation
BBC WAC	British Broadcasting Corporation Written Archives Centre
EFR	*English Family Robinson*
FLF	*Front Line Family*
GFP	General Forces Programme
ITMA	*It's That Man Again*
KF	*Kitchen Front*
MO	Mass-Observation
MOF	Ministry of Food
TIFH	*Take It from Here*
VRC	Variety Repertory Company

Introduction

Sometime in January 1957, Mabel Constanduros wrote to Val Gielgud, then head of BBC Drama, petitioning him to broadcast several plays and adaptations that were accepted by the BBC, but had yet to be produced. Constanduros was in the hospital, recovering from a severe heart attack, and was worried that she would be unable to work while she recovered. She hoped the income from broadcasting her adaptations of Elizabeth Gaskell's *Wives and Daughters* and Ernest Raymond's *We, the Accused*, as well as an original play she had written, would bridge the gap until she could write once again. Reminding Gielgud that the BBC, and he in particular, had been good to her over a career that spanned more than thirty years, Constanduros humbly apologized at the end of the letter for calling in this favour. This was the final letter Constanduros sent to the BBC. Though friends and family were hopeful about her recovery, Constanduros died in hospital on 8 February 1957.

Tributes to Constanduros underscored her importance as a pioneer radio writer and performer, arguing that her works were the 'forerunners of all of the "air families" in this country', placing her popular radio family, the Bugginses, at the head of a lineage that included the Dales, the Archers and the Groves.[1] Some highlighted her commitment to amateur theatrics and successful forays into the London theatre scene and post-war cinema. She was, however, a 'born broadcaster' and her career was fundamentally entwined with the BBC. Radio critic and close friend Collie Knox argued that she was the first to 'study the then new medium at all seriously', adding that 'her brilliant range of character studies, of whom perhaps Grandma Buggins is the most famous, and her incredible flow of output as a writer for radio, the films and the stage testify to one whose work was her life'.[2] To contemporaries, Constanduros was as important and popular as early radio legends Tommy Handley and Robb Wilton.[3] Yet, while Handley and Wilton are firmly situated in the popular mind – reruns of their performances still air regularly on BBC radio and the two feature prominently in popular and academic histories of the BBC or studies of British comedians – Constanduros rarely achieves notice as a cultural force on par with her male contemporaries. Indeed, within a decade of her passing, even Constanduros's own family underrated her significance when they made the decision to destroy her personal diaries and documents to save space; by then, they felt her works were old-fashioned.[4] Given her love for writing and the prolific canon she left behind, Constanduros's personal documents must have filled a room – or, more likely, rooms. What remains, however, are scores of published material – novels, children's books, Samuel French acting editions and a short autobiography – along with a few recordings of Buggins family sketches, reams of radio scripts and thick folders filled with contracts, correspondence with BBC staffers and internal memoranda housed at the BBC's Written Archives Centre.

The book that could have been written with her personal documents would have been different than what is presented here. With Mabel's personal reflections at my disposal, this book would have read like a standard biography: intriguing questions that remain about her marriage and working relationships with male collaborators may have been answered. More importantly, Constanduros's personal papers may have given us the opportunity to witness the behind-the-scenes, private struggles and triumphs of a female writer and performer carving out a long and fruitful career at the BBC. What emerges from the extant record is instead a biography of Constanduros's working life, as well as a history of early BBC light entertainment. The history of light entertainment written here is rarely told from the institutional or policy level, as in Asa Briggs's magisterial five-volume history of the BBC or, more recently, in Martin Dibbs's fine study of early BBC Variety, but rather from the personal and relational perspective of a popular, jobbing writer and artist.

David Hendy has persuasively argued that biography can enrich our understandings of the BBC; in particular, he suggests that biography helps us understand that 'the BBC is best conceived as one of Barbara Rosenstein's emotional *communities* – a place where the stress is … more on "systems of feeling," the nature of affective bonds between people, the modes of emotional expression that they expect, encourage, tolerate and deplore'.[5] Mabel's correspondence with the BBC reveals these emotional communities, sketching out the network of 'affective bonds' she nurtured with producers, staffers and performers within the BBC and with those outside the institution (like critic Collie Knox), which made it possible for her to entertain audiences for thirty-two years. While broader institutional policy serves to contextualize Constanduros's career, her correspondence provides insights into how both policy and these emotional communities functioned within the BBC to develop programming and to cultivate artists and writers. As Kate Murphy has shown in her groundbreaking work on women staffers, biography also provides important insights into women's professional experiences at the early BBC. Murphy's reconstruction of the lives of women who worked for the institution in the early days reveals a BBC 'burst[ing] with women';[6] in reconstructing Constanduros's working life, a vast array of women writers and performers lost to the past, but well known to and beloved by audiences at the time, has been further illuminated. While the emphasis of this book is firmly situated in Constanduros's work and correspondence, where her work intersects with other writers, performers and staffers – both women and men – they are worked into the narrative. As with staffers, the early BBC provided numerous opportunities for many women to build a professional life; equally, women writers and artists were essential to the listening landscape of the early BBC.

More research is necessary to understand the full extent to which women writers and artists influenced (and continue to influence) the evolution of BBC entertainment, as well as the opportunities and challenges presented by these women's involvement with the BBC. It is hoped that by delving deep into the working life and art of Mabel Constanduros, this book will demonstrate how important reconstructing the lives and work of women writers and artists on the BBC is to creating a more inclusive, diverse and complex history of the BBC. As Gilli Bush-Bailey has highlighted, the 'patriarchal assumptions about class and gender difference' embedded at the heart of the BBC has resulted in a 'careless masculinity that has made and continues to make histories that marginalise or simply forget women, and forgets their role in laying the foundations of today's broadcasting'.[7] As will be seen, Constanduros pioneered important and enduring entertainment techniques and paradigms for situation comedies and soap operas in Britain. Such revelations contest the standard histories of popular entertainment in Britain, which have argued that both genres are essentially American innovations.[8] Furthermore, reconstructing the working lives, the public performances of self and the cultivation of career in which early BBC women artists and writers engaged offers opportunities to explore women's management of celebrity, their negotiations of professionalism, and the ways in which these performers and writers participated in broader cultural and national discourses.

While the presence of female writers and performers from the very beginnings of the BBC does not mean that all of them were engaged in 'domesticating the wireless', research into Constanduros's working life provides insights into the ways in which BBC programming became more female oriented and domestically focused earlier than has been imagined. Maggie Andrews has argued that the domestication of the BBC took place in the 1930s, but Constanduros's popular comedy sketches and revues of the 1920s reveals that this domestication has roots in some of the earliest BBC entertainment.[9] In her 1925 BBC debut, Constanduros delivered monologues as both working- and middle-class female characters; more importantly, the Buggins family sketches (also 1925) were oriented towards the family, the feminine and the everyday. For over thirty years on air, Constanduros consistently presented the feminine and the family (both middle- and working-class) as sites of humour and popular entertainment.

Considering the ways in which the popular, and in particular the feminine popular, have been discounted, dismissed and denigrated, it is perhaps unsurprising that Handley and Wilton are well remembered while Constanduros is not. Soap opera, which Constanduros has long been credited with introducing British audiences to, has always carried the taint of the feminine and the popular, and has become a cultural shortcut for 'bad drama'.[10] This is particularly significant in Britain, where fears over the creeping emasculation of the national institution that is the BBC have held sway since the 1930s and where the public-service orientation of broadcasting has consistently shunned the popular as mindless, inauthentic, commercial and American.[11] Long-time head of BBC Drama, Val Gielgud, articulated this critical mentality when he traced the origins of soap opera in Britain back to Constanduros and himself:

> How many people remember Mabel Constanduros was lineal predecessor to Mrs Dale when she appeared as the main character in *The English Family Robinson* in 1937? For the introduction of this first of the soap-opera-style serials into British broadcasting I must accept full responsibility, and I confess that it weighs upon my conscience to do so. It was a time when we were perhaps more influenced than we should have been at Broadcasting House by trends and fashions in American radio. ... For the soap-opera in the general, and for *The Dales* in particular, I can only blush and bow my head. I made no secret of my opinion that such programmes were aesthetically contemptible and sociologically corrupting. They tied up actors, producers, and writers alike in the equivalent of a chain-gang, offering the bait of security and regular employment, while simultaneously squeezing all virtue out of them by the process of a remorseless routine, demanding neither talent not personality, merely application. In particular, certain actors became so identified with the characters they played that they became almost useless in any other capacity. From the point of view of the listener, the persisting drip-drip-drip of such programmes destroyed

all possibility of criticism. The audience was gradually drugged into belief in the reality of a dream-world ruled by bogus values, entirely occupied with trivialities.[12]

Here, Gielgud rehearses the usual criticism regarding the destructive, inauthentic, popular forces of soap opera: the 'aesthetically contemptible' drama that corrupted performers, writers and producers; the 'drip-drip-drip' of the popular that 'drugged' audiences; and the essential American-ness of the genre. Gielgud's dismissal of soap opera's dramatization of what he called 'trivialities' is echoed in his criticism of *Mrs. Dale's Diary* that the serial 'was [too] detached from public life, thus lacking social responsibility'.[13] Once the BBC brought in Basil Dawson as a writer intended to develop the 'male angle' in *Mrs. Dale's Diary*, the series shifted focus away from the purely private to include public and current affairs, earning higher status within the BBC.[14] The tension between the popular and the worthy seen in these discourses can be further detected in the BBC's designation of the department most associated with the popular as '*Light Entertainment*' (in contradistinction to *serious* broadcasting).

The deep cultural disdain that exists in Britain towards middle-class suburbia is another significant reason for the minimization of Constanduros's efforts to dramatize the everyday, domestic world of middle-class suburbia in *English Family Robinson (EFR)*. Orwell's searing invective on middle-class suburban life in *Coming Up for Air* (1939) is but one example of a cultural and intellectual phenomenon that has considered suburbia and suburban domesticity, in particular, to be 'stultifying and degrading'.[15] Andy Medhurst has observed similar strains in his exploration of the depiction of suburbia in twentieth-century British cinema and television: suburbia in these genres is often portrayed as 'a trap, offering nothing but drab conformism and frigid respectability'; further, women are usually implicated in this state of affairs, creating, accepting or representing the domestic 'routine and rut' from which men feel compelled to escape.[16]

Further deepening Constanduros's perceived irrelevance to British culture are her comedic works, which also trade in the female and the domestic. Women's humour has a long tradition of being sidelined, especially in Britain. J. B. Priestley's famously pompous retort that Jane Austen's humour amounted to little more than 'small potatoes', Regina Barreca has argued, 'illustrates the accepted critical position with regard to women's humor … a view so traditional and so unenlightened as to be of help in determining why women's comedy had gone unrecognized'.[17] The insidiousness of this assumption has played out in the ways in which women have traditionally been typecast as 'straight (wo) men' to 'funny men' in British situation comedies, where, for instance, Prunella Scales's acerbic Sybil counterbalances the zany antics of Basil in *Fawlty Towers* (1975, 1979) or Dandy Nichols's near silence as Else Garnett plays up Alf's verbal tirades in *Til Death Us Do Part* (1966–75) – or more recently played out in the relational dynamics between Barbara (Sue Johnston) and Jim (Ricky Tomlinson) in *The Royle Family* (1999–2012). Frances Gray has noted that women in British sitcom typically represent the 'status quo, providing a commonsense context in which (male) eccentricity and anarchy can bloom'.[18] This situation is further exacerbated by the dearth of female writers of British situation comedy – a genre in which only a few writers, such as Carla Lane, Victoria Wood, Dawn French, Jennifer Saunders, Caroline Aherne and Miranda Hart, have managed to leave an impression in the popular British mind – and then only since the 1970s.[19] Women writers of comedy represent significant transgressions against the cultural norm, for, as Barreca reminds us, 'women are not meant to give utterance: when they do, they "step out of their function as sign". When they create comedy, they are stepping out of their "destined communication" and are deviating from it in order to transform their position'.[20] Long before Carla Lane's *Liver Birds* (1969–78, 1996) and *Butterflies* (1978–83) debuted on television, Mabel Constanduros's radio and stage works privileged the perspective of women and the feminine laughter of their everyday struggles.

Finally, Constanduros's early contributions to BBC entertainment were largely lost in the wake of the Second World War. As Val Gielgud reflected in the 1960s,

> One of the effects of Hitler's War was to make much of what happened before it blurred, unreal, or simply forgotten. I am surprised, looking back at the records, to find that so much which was hailed as original in post-war broadcasting had already appeared in slightly different forms between 1932 and 1939.[21]

Further complicating the recovery of interwar BBC history and the contributions of early radio pioneers is what Lance Sieveking called 'the ghastly impermanence of the medium', in which early live performances were literally lost to the ether and recorded performances were often erased to enable the recording of subsequent programming.[22] Exacerbating the ephemerality of early radio is the fact that documents were rarely preserved before the establishment of BBC Written Archives in 1932.[23] Perhaps the greatest force wiping away much of the interwar BBC, however, is the advent of television. Artists and writers who did not manage the transition to post-war television, such as Constanduros, seem to be further relegated to the shadows of broadcasting history. Thus, this is a work primarily of recovery: the recovery of Constanduros's contributions to British popular culture and of the development of popular ('light') entertainment in the pre-television era. It is, however, an incomplete recovery that necessitates further research into early BBC programming, the emotional communities of the BBC and of the vast contributions women have made to the listening (and viewing) landscape of BBC entertainment. A review of *Radio Pictorial* and *Radio Times* in the interwar period will demonstrate that women entertainers and writers were not the rare, 'one-off' exception to the assumed rule that only men can deliver quality entertainment (especially comedy).[24]

'Secret ambitions – heaven knows where they came from'

Mabel Constanduros was born in South London in 1880. Born to Richard and Sophia Tilling, she was the eldest daughter of seven. Richard was the son of Thomas Tilling, who started the Tillings Omnibus Company in 1850 and was famous for revolutionizing bus service by introducing timed schedules.[25] Mabel grew up in Peckham, South London, and attributed much of her later radio Cockney characterizations to her experiences there. In a 1929 *Radio Times* article, she explained that from an early age, she enjoyed listening to and imitating her grandfather's employees, the children she met while volunteering in Lambeth and the colourful characters she met in the streets. She also drew inspiration from the Dickens novels that the family read aloud and performed for enjoyment.[26]

In her 1946 autobiography, *Shreds and Patches*, Constanduros remembered her thrill in entertaining others, even as a child. As early as seven years of age, she wrote and acted in plays for her family and learned to recite various rhymes and poems. Her 'stock piece' was Lewis Carroll's 'The Walrus and the Carpenter', which she played 'very dramatically with different voices for the Walrus, the Carpenter and the oysters'.[27] When she grew older, she spent her days writing, organizing and performing in plays and variety shows with friends and siblings. The pages of her 1899 diary, when she was nineteen, are crammed with efforts to put on a variety show at the Surrey Masonic Hall and the ecstasy of being told that well-known opera singer Iver McKay thought highly of her acting.[28]

She dreamt of nothing else than to train as an actress, but her parents refused to pay for her to attend dramatic school; they felt it was a 'craze' of all young girls that passed when the 'Right Man came along'.[29] Her father offered to send her to Girton instead, but her mother insisted she stay at home to help with the family. 'Poor Mother!' Constanduros wrote in *Shreds and Patches*, 'She wanted to make me into a pattern housewife like herself, but I had secret ambitions – Heaven knows where they came from.'[30] Young Mabel remained at home acting as her father's secretary – a job she preferred to domestic work – until she married. Mabel married Athanasius ('Ath') Constanduros in 1907 and moved to Sutton, in London's burgeoning suburbs.[31]

Shortly after their marriage, both Mabel and Ath joined the Sutton Amateur Dramatic Club (SADC), where the two seem to have been active members for over a decade. Places in productions were purportedly competitive, and early veterans of the Club include Leslie Howard, Gladys Young (whose brother, William co-founded the Club), Helen Haye and Jack Warner.[32] Mabel and Ath often appeared together on stage during that period, but it was Mabel who was cast in the significant roles and it was Mabel who tended to receive notice in reviews of the productions.[33] They also appeared on stage together in a Lloyd's Dramatic Society production of *French Leave* in 1922. Mabel's last SADC productions were in 1925, after which, there is no record of her association with the Club until the 1950s when she became honorary vice-president along with other star SADC veterans.[34] Ath continued to appear on stage after his wife's departure until his death in 1937.[35]

At some point in 1919, Mabel sought out voice training with Elsie Fogerty at the Central School for Speech and Drama. With Fogerty, Mabel honed her writing and monologue skills, and found her voice. A student at CSSD remembered how Fogerty's work with Constanduros transformed a 'little woman … who struggled with lovely lyrics, which her strangely husky voice just did not suit' into a 'great little artiste [who], once in command of her own voice' had the students 'helpless with laughter' or 'could reduce us to tears just as easily'.[36] Further evidence of Fogerty's mentoring exists in the fact that her 1920s SADC appearances warranted far more positive and substantive reviews than she had received previously.[37] It is unclear who specifically encouraged Mabel to audition for the BBC – most accounts mention someone who saw her perform and urged her to try out – but Mabel does credit Fogerty for giving her the 'courage to go through the door of Broadcasting House'.[38]

When Mabel Constanduros began her acting and writing career on the BBC in 1925, the BBC was less than three years old and was in search of its identity and relevance within British culture. It was an institution in the making;

specializations had yet to crystalize, and opportunities abounded for enterprising individuals to develop material and techniques specific to the new medium, as well as to influence the evolution of programming. Constanduros first appeared on the BBC at the age of forty-five, as an actress in the First BBC Repertory Company, and was still performing and writing on radio thirty-two years later, long after the BBC had established its credentials as a national institution.

Spanning such a long and critical period during the history of the BBC, Constanduros's lengthy career offers superb opportunities to view BBC's institutional and programming history not from the top-down institutional, departmental or policy documents, but rather bottom-up, through the lens of the performer/writer. This methodology affords us different perspectives through which new insights are gained into the evolution of popular entertainment from its early beginnings on the BBC. Additionally, the 'star' status that Constanduros enjoyed from her earliest solo performances on the BBC opens up spaces for the analysis of the social, cultural and performative aspects of radio celebrity, from the beginnings of radio in the 1920s to its eclipse by television in the 1950s. The performance of female celebrity also brings up the ways in which gender impacts the exploration of what is knowable in the historical record, and emphasizes the essential silences that were cultivated by women as they sought to carve out a career while negotiating their public identities in the early to mid-twentieth century.

Chapter 1 looks at Constanduros's experiences on the early BBC and considers how the fluid nature of the early institution opened up spaces for amateurs, such as herself, to not only become professionals but also impact the entertainment offerings of the BBC. The chapter sketches out a picture of the BBC in its exciting and uncertain beginnings, following staffers and performers in their efforts to understand the medium and to provide a service worthy of the lofty values set out by its first general manager and later its first director general, John Reith. This discussion demonstrates how – much as the start-up tech companies of today – early staffers found themselves wearing numerous hats in order to learn the business, develop and understand the technology, and keep the organization – and its limited set of programmes – running. Beyond the frenzied excitement and hectic working schedules of the staffers, decisions made by programming executives underscore the exciting possibilities of sound, firmly situating the early BBC within the larger societal context which saw increased popular interest in spiritualism and unseen phenomena, as well as popular psychology, in the wake of the First World War.

During its first decade, the BBC faced numerous challenges in attracting well-known stage professionals to the microphone, not least because the microphone required them to adapt visual stage acts for an aural medium. As a result, the BBC had to turn to amateurs to provide talks and entertainment. Amateur performers, like John Henry (the first popular comedian of BBC radio) and Constanduros, proved willing to adapt their material to suit both the medium and its domestic audience. The innovations developed by these early radio entertainers became important seedlings for popular entertainment on both radio and television.

Chapter 2 introduces the Buggins family as a case study for understanding the origins of situation comedy on the BBC. During the first year of her work on the BBC, Constanduros experimented with bringing staged monologue and duologue to the microphone. Unhappy with these forms on radio, and anxious to distinguish her work from other early radio comedians, Constanduros created comedy that was centred on the day-to-day domestic intrigues of a working-class Cockney family. Moving away from the popular cross-talk routines of early radio variety, Constanduros crafted short situational sketches more theatrical in style than the typical music hall turns found on radio at the time, thus eschewing direct forms of audience address by introducing the fourth wall into radio comedy.[39] At the same time, the Bugginses became the first comedic family in Britain, beating out America's first radio family, the Goldbergs, by a year. In creating the first radio family, Constanduros provided a foundation for situation comedy that has proved remarkably enduring and popular.

Analysis of early Buggins radio sketches in the second chapter also reveals how writers and artists experimented with, and learned to craft, entertainment which exploited the aural medium in order to successfully engage the imaginations of their listeners. Further, the chapter considers audience responses to the Buggins sketches, demonstrating the ways in which listeners interacted with and interpreted early radio programming. Finally, the humour of the Buggins family sketches is analysed within the context of early twentieth-century British history and the ways in which the working classes were represented on early BBC radio are discussed.

Chapter 3 addresses the evolution of radio celebrity in the interwar period, beginning with an analysis of Constanduros's radio appearances in the 1920s and the 1930s. Set within the context of rapid technological innovation at this time, the analysis reflects on the ways in which listeners negotiated the programmatic landscape without the aid of seriality or fixed-point scheduling in order to shed light on the ways in which listeners became familiar with popular programming and entertainers. Fan magazines, such as *Radio Pictorial*, were also integral to the construction of celebrity in this period. Expanding beyond these considerations, I explore the contours and experiences of early BBC radio celebrity, especially as it relates to gender, and consider how celebrities cultivated silences and carefully constructed a publicly consumed private life.

Chapter 4 discusses the evolution of BBC Variety entertainment in the 1930s, and how artists like Constanduros responded to the shifting landscape of radio entertainment in the period in order to advance their careers at a time when other early radio humourists, such as Helena Millais, were rapidly becoming obsolescent. The chapter also demonstrates how Constanduros used her celebrity to open up opportunities that expanded her reach beyond the microphone; in particular, I look at her unsuccessful foray into music hall, her more successful attempts at writing and acting for the 'legitimate' and amateur stage, and the translation of her radio families and their worlds into novels. Here we can perceive how BBC writers and performers engaged in the cross-fertilization of multiple media in ways that both strengthened career opportunities and enhanced audience experience.

Because Constanduros sought to represent both working- and middle-class life, and because the classed profile of listeners changed so drastically during her career (from a largely middle-class audience in the 1920s to a more representative listenership by the mid-1930s), we can also analyse crucial dimensions of class in the representation of national identity through popular media. Constanduros's lengthy career and expansive oeuvre affords insights into the manner in which the BBC sought to represent the nation and appeal to listeners at critical moments across the mid-twentieth century. Further, through her efforts to cultivate her radio career and broaden her cultural reach, we can also consider representations of family and nation on the stage, in literature and in the cinema. This attempt to reach beyond radio also reveals intersections that existed between these media in the era before television became the primary cultural medium.

Chapter 5 looks at the efforts of both Constanduros and the BBC to entertain audiences during the Second World War. Alongside the wartime history and development of BBC popular entertainment, this chapter discusses Constanduros's efforts to remain relevant during the Second World War. Using programming information, scripts and contracts, it specifically details the early efforts of the BBC to respond to the conflict and to present popular entertainment to the nation.

The majority of this chapter focuses on the way in which People's War rhetoric drove artists and writers like Constanduros to participate in the war effort through their art. In particular, I focus on the Ministry of Food's (MoF) relationship with the BBC to analyse the ways in which both the Corporation and the artists supported governmental propaganda efforts. Taking the immensely popular Buggins family *Kitchen Front (KF)* sketches as a case study, I analyse wartime scripts and correspondence with the BBC to discuss the role of popular entertainment on the *KF* programme. Further, detailed analysis of the scripts provides insight into the evolution of propaganda on the programme; specifically, I chart how Buggins family characters evolved over the course of the war, especially in their relation to the societal expectations of the People's War. This analysis will also demonstrate the propaganda value of the Buggins family wartime sketches and will consider the ways in which the Buggins family represented wartime working-class interests, thus creating possibilities to draw the working classes into the national fold.

In Chapter 6, I discuss the BBC-constructed version of an 'ordinary' British family as depicted by *English Family Robinson (EFR)* (1938). I then follow the programme (which is considered the first British soap opera) into wartime, as the Robinsons hold up a mirror to the nation and help redefine the 'ordinary' during the People's War. In addition to tracing the evolution of *EFR* through the 1940s, I also discuss the ways in which Constanduros continued to write 'ordinary' families, both dramatically and humorously, in wartime through fruitful collaborations with her nephew, Denis Constanduros, and with Howard Agg. Exploration of *EFR* and these collaborative ventures outlines the early developments of realism particular to British soap opera and comedy, as well as to British cinema.

Additionally, the chapter analyses the ways in which both gender and class were represented on the BBC in the 1930s and the 1940s. Specifically centring on Constanduros's radio writing and correspondence with the BBC, the analysis not only unpicks popular depictions of gender and class on radio but also illuminates how societal assumptions about gender might be deployed behind the scenes at the BBC in efforts to build a successful career on radio. In particular, Constanduros's leverage of gendered assumptions illustrates how she became the mother of the BBC in her promotion of numerous actors' and writers' careers on the BBC.

In Chapter 7, I follow the complex cultural shifts evident in the reconstruction of a national sense of the 'ordinary' as the nation moved from a wartime to a peacetime footing. The main part of this analysis will be reflected through consideration of the Robinsons (from *EFR*) on stage in *Acacia Avenue* (1943) and in its cinematic adaptation, *29 Acacia Avenue* (1945), as well as the changing onscreen fortunes of the Huggett family, another Constanduros creation. After their first appearance in the hit post-war film *Holiday Camp* (1947), the Huggetts (starring Jack Warner and Kathleen Harrison, as well as a young Petula Clark) featured in three further films and spawned a popular radio series in the 1950s. Both movie families (produced by a famous cinematic couple, Sydney and Muriel Box) not only offer fascinating insights into the post-war reconstruction of the 'ordinary' British – in particular the 'ordinary' British family – but also enable fruitful examinations of the intersections between radio and cinema. The chapter continues the overall framework of the book by situating Constanduros's career within the broader history of the changing BBC, charting challenges presented by major shifts in audience expectations and experiences brought on by wartime experiences and the rising fortunes of television.

The book concludes with Constanduros's efforts to remain relevant and to nurture her career in the final years of her life. In these endeavours, Constanduros continued to foster relationships with staff on an ever-shifting BBC, adapting novels, appearing on nostalgia programmes and becoming a regular contributor to the popular post-war programme *Woman's Hour*. Constanduros also tried her hand at television, but she remained firmly a radio professional, and thus the chapter considers the ways in which radio pioneers and professionals, such as herself and Val Gielgud, regarded the advent of television. Finally, I reflect upon the ways in which the Second World War and television have rendered many early radio pioneers largely invisible in histories of the BBC and British entertainment, and underscore the vital importance of women as writers, staffers, producers and performers in the BBC since its very inception.

1

Comedy and the early BBC, 1922–9[1]

On a dreary February morning in 1925, Mabel Constanduros paced up and down the Embankment, nervously awaiting her audition with the BBC (then called British Broadcasting Company) at Number 2 Savoy Hill – a building situated alongside the Thames and pieced together rather haphazardly for broadcasting into a 'rabbit warren of offices, rehearsal rooms, studios, libraries, laboratories and stores'.[2] Historian Raphael Samuel's evocative description of the area surrounding the BBC offices colourizes the district Constanduros entered on that February morning: 'It looked across to the back of the Savoy Hotel … . Circled by eating-houses and pubs … shadowed by theatreland and Covent Garden (then an all-night market) on one side and the down-and-outs of the Embankment on the other, this was a distinctly raffish part of London.'[3]

Once inside, Constanduros made her way to an anteroom just outside the 2LO *Children's Hour* studio. Others in the anteroom seemed 'old and rather shabby' to Constanduros, in desperate need of work because of the flagging economy and hoping to try their hands at something new.[4] Though she would soon foster a close relationship with the programme that would last for the entirety of her long career with the BBC, Constanduros had never heard the popular *Children's Hour* programme until that day; in fact, she had never 'listened in' herself. She was invited to audition, having been recommended to the BBC staff by someone who had seen her perform on the amateur stage.[5]

Constanduros wrote in her biography that as she waited, her nervousness was nearly overwhelming, and she contemplated slinking unnoticed out of the building. She remained, however, and when her name was called, awkwardly fumbled with her umbrella before being swept into an alien landscape of broadcasting. The room was as drab as the weather she had come in from: 'There were no windows and the room was hung and carpeted with grey, the colour of cobwebs.'[6] Despite the presence of two grand pianos, some furniture and a microphone, an odd-looking box standing alone in the middle of the room which reminded Constanduros of a 'meat safe', the studio felt cavernous.[7] Alone and bewildered, a disembodied voice asked her to begin speaking. Constanduros hesitated, realizing that she had forgotten the Shakespeare, Scottish ballads and speeches she had practised; instead, the Cockney character monologues she had written to entertain family and friends flowed forth. Convinced the audition was an utter failure, she recalled feeling surprised to learn that her performance was considered the best of the day and was thus offered a place on the newly formed London Radio Repertory Company. Constanduros was one of only two women in the Company: her counterpart was Phyllis Panting, who would later become editor of *Woman and Beauty* magazine.[8] Other members of the Company included Ashton Pearce, Herbert Ross and Henry Oscar.[9]

When Constanduros was offered the place on the London Radio Repertory Company in 1925, radio was an emergent technology and the BBC was a fledgling institution. She came into an organization that was less than three years old and was brimming with possibility and excitement as both its identity and the technology developed in tandem. Constanduros was thus well situated to experiment with the new technology and became an important pioneer in developing techniques and content specifically for radio entertainment.

Constanduros's first documented radio appearance was in *A Dweller in the Darkness*, a one-act horror play written specifically for wireless by Reginald Berkeley (author of *French Leave*, in which Constanduros had appeared twice on the amateur stage before coming to radio) and performed by the London Radio Repertory Company in April 1925.[10] The half-hour play was broadcast on 2LO, and was sandwiched between a lecture about Milton and a William Hurlstone quartet in E minor.[11] The experimental play used an 'innovative soundscape' of mysterious noises to heighten the terror of the plot, in which an evil spirit haunts sceptics at a séance. The play also set off a firestorm of controversy as some BBC executives pressured Berkeley to change the last line of the play – one of the first instances of censorship on the BBC.[12] Constanduros would appear in several groundbreaking wireless plays, including the first broadcast of Tyrone Guthrie's *Squirrel's Cage* (1929) and her own experimental mystery play, *The Survivor* (1928), written and performed with Michael Hogan.[13] Hogan, whom Constanduros met while performing with the London Repertory Company, would become an important early writing partner, collaborating on numerous Bugginses projects until 1934, when he left to become a screenwriter in Hollywood.[14]

Regular broadcast service in Britain began in February 1922 from Marconi Company's Writtle Experimental station, and their London station, 2LO, began broadcasting later that year. As a result of talks between wireless manufacturers and the Post Office that summer, the station was taken over by the newly formed 'broadcasting syndicate', the British Broadcasting Company, which began broadcasting in November 1922.[15] An initial staff of six was set up rather hastily in a 30-foot-by-15-foot room in the General Electric Company's Magnet House, Kingsway.[16] Cecil Lewis, the original organizer of programming, remembered how they were 'confronted with new and difficult problems on every side, with no precedents of past experience to go upon – and even without an office to work in!'[17] The accommodations at the 2LO Marconi House studio were equally sparse: according to the first director of music, Stanton Jefferies, the studio was so cramped they had to 'broadcast with the door open in case the cellist should fracture his elbow!'[18] By March 1923, the staff, which had now grown to twenty-eight (thirty if one counted the then general manager, John Reith, and the office boy, Pell), moved from the tiny room at Magnet House into more permanent accommodations at Savoy Hill; two months later, the studio at Marconi House also made the move to Savoy Hill.[19]

Memoirs written by the early BBC staff indicate the fluid, entrepreneurial nature of the organization in its first decade. The British Broadcasting Company, which was reorganized as a public corporation in 1927, did not ossify into the formalized, deeply bureaucratic structure associated with the Corporation until well into the 1930s. Instead, the BBC of the 1920s was organic, exciting, experimental and eminently 'modern'. For instance, the early BBC prided itself on embracing qualified and able young women into its ranks. As Kate Murphy has shown, the BBC initially had no restrictions on the employment of married women; only in 1933 did they implement a marriage bar – the mark, she argues, of 'cultural orthodoxy', signalling the 'Corporation's sense of conformity and respectability'.[20] This transformation towards 'orthodoxy' largely began when the BBC moved to the grander premises of Broadcasting House in 1932 – a moment that marked the advent of the 'Stuffed Shirt Era', with its caricatured image of the 'prim official with a black hat and a rolled umbrella', according to managing editor of the *Radio Times*, Maurice Gorham.[21]

Kate Murphy highlights what she calls the 'adhoc' nature of the early organization, while Asa Briggs has pointed to the 'delightful informality' that reigned at the time.[22] As an example of this informality, Briggs cites the day in 1923 when Reith rang Music Director Stanton Jefferies and asked him to play a piano solo on air because the Archbishop of Canterbury, who was listening with Reith at the time, wanted to hear one.[23] 'Before broadcasting was armoured in

Reithian principles' and wrapped in bureaucracy, Charlotte Higgins notes in her recent history of the BBC, 'it was first a technology'.[24]

Radio was an emergent technology in the 1920s, and the workplace milieu of the BBC office is strikingly reminiscent of computer and internet start-ups in their earliest phases. Recollections of early BBC staffers in many ways parallel those of pioneering Microsoft workers in the 1970s and the 1980s. Throughout the 1920s, the BBC staff grew organically and nearly exponentially through chance meetings, networking and want ads – many original staffers (including Reith) answered job advertisements or agreed to take a position through personal contacts, with little to no idea of the business to which they were applying; the earliest Microsoft employees also confess ignorance when they applied for their positions.[25] Further, the 'maniacal work ethic'[26] that reigned in the early days at Microsoft can also be seen in the BBC employees, who exhibited similar excitement about working with an emerging technology, as well as a deep commitment to learning their craft. Peter Eckersley, chief engineer of the BBC until 1929, recollected fondly 'the sense of pioneering a fascinating new development'.[27]

Eric Maschwitz, who joined the Company in 1926 and would later become the director of Variety, recalled,

> The medium was new, exciting and, above all, friendly … . Savoy Hill was like a small, excited club whose members came in to work in the early morning and stayed on until Big Ben chimed midnight – for the very good reason that there was always something interesting afoot![28]

Roger Eckersley, who started in Engineering with his brother Peter, moved on to the role of the outside broadcast director, and then onto that of the director of programmes within the space of three years, remembered the 'charming, undepartmental spirit of the place. The staff was in its tiny beginnings … . Everyone was ready to do everyone else's job'.[29] The fluid and exciting nature of the business in the early days, argues Kate Murphy, 'provided unique opportunities for women', possibilities of which Constanduros took full advantage.[30]

When Constanduros made her first appearance on radio in 1925, broadcasting was still very much in its infancy, but it was on the verge of a meteoric take off. At the end of 1924, the BBC boasted a little over 1.1 million licences.[31] However, it has been estimated that perhaps the figure for actual listeners may be five times that number.[32] The main regional stations dictated by the Wireless Sub-Committee of the Imperial Communications Committee, whose work in 1922 established the BBC, were also operational: London (2LO), Manchester (2ZY), Newcastle (5NO), Cardiff (5WA), Glasgow (5SC), Birmingham (5IT), Aberdeen (2BD), Bournemouth (6BM), Sheffield (6SL) and Belfast (2BE), as well as a number of relay stations, which were also in operation by spring 1925.[33] By that summer, the BBC proudly boasted the world's largest broadcasting station at Daventry (5XX), enabling 85 per cent of the population to have access to wireless even with cheap sets.[34] Wireless sets were only just becoming important commodities, especially for the middle classes; that year, costs for a crystal set with two headphones ran between £2 and £4, while a valve set (which increased reception) went for as low as £5.[35] For considerably more money, one could buy a wireless set hidden by 'cabinet-work in any period' and choose to have a loudspeaker 'cunningly incorporated' into the cabinet.[36] However, tuning in was still very much a craft and a thriving amateur wireless constructor community kept up with technological advancements in station transmission and developments in set components through popular wireless magazines such as *The Wireless Constructor* and *Popular Wireless Weekly*. Simply hearing *anything* over the air was enough to excite radio enthusiasts in the 1920s, where *Popular Wireless and Wireless Review* magazine offered free wireless schematic patterns similar to how women's magazines distributed free knitting patterns in their periodicals. Among innumerable advertisements for valves, transformers and batteries, *Popular Wireless* subscribers and authors alike swapped secrets of their technical feats snatching distant sounds out of the air.[37]

The early BBC was shaped by a pioneering spirit and the excitement of creating something new. It was also, as David Hendy has argued, very much a part of a '"psychologising" age ... coincid[ing] historically with the popularisation of psychology within "the culture, the social fabric, and the mentality of the era"'.[38] Many BBC staffers were veterans, and Hendy further points out the fact that the war developed in its combatants an 'alertness to sound – or more specifically, an alertness to the rich set of meanings various sounds were capable of conveying',[39] or 'sonic mindedness', as Yaron Jean has termed it.[40] This shift in the emotional significance of sound and, especially, silence would also impact the way in which wireless technology and the content of programmes developed during the interwar period.[41]

Programming on the early BBC at once reflected this new significance of sound (and silence), the excitement of experimental technology and the psychologizing age. Silence (sometimes up to fifteen minutes' worth) was built into the programming day,[42] and when the BBC broadcast a nightingale's song, Reith's rationale was that the song brought 'something of the silence which all of us in the busy world unconsciously crave and urgently need'.[43] Beyond the nightingale, various sound experiments and programme ideas were floated during weekly Programme Board meetings: in early 1925, the Board suggested broadcasting sounds from a Sheffield Coal Mine, a Cunard Liner departing port and the human pulse. All of these suggestions made it on air: the coal mine being broadcast for half an hour![44] The psychologizing age is further made clear in other programming suggestions: one made by the director of programmes, Arthur Burrows, in the first week of 1925 outlined a 'thought transference' experiment that would test the abilities of a psychic to pick up the thoughts of the radio audience. The audience would be instructed to 'concentrate' on the same thing, such as Nelson's Column, at the same moment, and the psychic – unaware of the instructions to the audience – would 'state the thought upper most in his mind'. The Board thought the idea had publicity value and could test 'the power of mass thinking'. Celebrity expert in spiritualism Sir Arthur Conan Doyle was to be called on for what they considered a 'thoroughly scientific experiment'.[45]

The Programme Board's experimental mindedness reflects a larger cultural fascination with technological and scientific experimentation seen by social and cultural historians/commentators Robert Graves and Alan Hodge in their 1940 history of the interwar period. They note as examples that held the public's fascination attempts in August 1924 to pick up signals from Mars with huge twenty-four-valve wireless sets, medical discoveries such as insulin treatment for diabetics and x-ray treatment for cancer, and the development of a 'death-ray' which could supposedly 'set fire to anything inflammable, wreck aircraft and destroy life'.[46] They also comment on a thriving interest in spiritualism during the period.[47] As Jay Winter has argued, those who were willing to entertain the possibility of communication with the deceased pointed to the unseen forces that brought wireless entertainment into people's homes. If the unseen, but proven, phenomena of electricity, magnetism and radio waves existed, so too might 'thought waves or other forms of human feeling or expression'.[48]

By 1926, the BBC Programming Board was fielding requests by scientists and researchers to use airtime for experimental purposes. Manchester psychologist, T. H. Pear, was given local airtime in 1926 to broadcast a myriad of different voices in order to analyse subject assumptions about class, age and character based on voice.[49] Dr. Wooley of the Society for Psychical Research suggested an experiment where some people would be cut off from all communication and the audience would be instructed to think 'at them' for twenty minutes. The Board 'approved' the suggestion 'in principle', but it was made clear that Wooley would take full responsibility for the programme *and* it was stipulated that the programme must be aired later in the evening, at 11 pm.[50] This last note underscores the increasing 'sophistication' of programmatic thinking in the pre-Corporation days:[51] on the eve of incorporation in 1927, programming had evolved from one-off sound interests like the coal mine and thought experiments to more structured airtime and considered programme development. During that time, the programming department also underwent a major restructuring. Arthur Burrows left in early 1925 to become secretary general of the first international broadcasting organization, the Union Internationale de Radiophonie in Geneva, and Roger Eckersley replaced him as the organizer of programmes in September[52]; Rex Palmer became head of a newly created central booking department.[53] Nonetheless, experimentation and 'stunts' still continued: in May 1926, the BBC broadcast the Changing of the Guard for the first time, and in July of that year, they broadcast a diver at the bottom of the Thames.[54]

Recruiting talent to the early BBC

While early engineers and executives attempted to figure out the potentialities of the technology, the BBC suffered from what Val Gielgud, director of drama (1929–63), called an 'inferiority complex' when it came to talent, especially in regards to professional entertainers.[55] Reith was notoriously opposed to 'pure entertainment' on radio and thought 'so great a scientific invention for the purpose of "entertainment" alone … a prostitution of its powers and an insult to the character and intelligence of the people'.[56] Entertainment on early wireless was thus largely a means to test the technology. At the Writtle Experimental station in 1922, for example, engineer (soon to become chief engineer at the BBC) Peter Eckersley sang opera arias and interjected humorous comments throughout the 'programme' himself.[57] Peter's brother, Roger, who came to the BBC in February 1924, remembered how he had

> played the piano interlude for which Sophie Dixon will be remembered, and it wasn't that I played the piano well. … Any of us who could sing, or play the piano would unblushingly put on a variety revue which would be broadcast to a long-suffering public.[58]

Eric Maschwitz, who eventually became the director of BBC radio Variety in 1933, remarked that when he joined the BBC in 1926, 'programmes had an air of lively improvisation; the Chief Engineer figured in the Children's Hour, while certain of the revues were written, even acted, by my humble self, the Assistant Director of Outside Broadcasting'.[59]

Maschwitz also recalled how difficult it was to recruit entertainers to the fledgling BBC. He wrote,

> Part of our job was to gather theatre and music-hall people into the broadcasting fold. To-day, when broadcasting is an integral part of 'show business', it seems almost incredible that until the early 1930's, it was largely shunned, even boycotted, by the Profession, some people still regarding it as a dangerous rival, others dismissing it as an unprofessional toy.[60]

In his survey of British radio drama, published in 1957, Gielgud offered his explanation for the distinct reluctance of theatre professionals to take radio seriously in the early days. The BBC in the 1920s and the early 1930s was, he lamented, run by amateurs who were more interested in technology than in programme content. The BBC at the time, 'hardly knew their own business, and', he argued, 'were learning it at the expense of actors who had learned theirs'.[61]

While some stage professionals must have recoiled at the prospect of working with a troupe of amateurs who were only just beginning to understand their craft, other factors contributed to the dearth of professional talent on the early BBC. In addition to the inevitable learning curve required in developing a new technology, the medium's untried nature scared off talent who feared that radio would be a short-lived fad. On the other hand, theatre and music-hall owners were fearful that if radio did indeed last, it might undermine their box-office receipts. Many artists were thus specifically banned from going on radio by their contracts, or outright intimidated into avoiding radio.[62] The BBC estimated that in the 1920s nearly 50 per cent of established stage artists, like George Robey and Ted Ray, were prevented from broadcasting due to contractual prohibitions.[63] BBC propriety might also militate against music-hall artists making the leap to radio, or at least staying on air. Since, as McKibbin notes, the BBC circumscribed '95 per cent of English humour, it was … all too easy for comedians brought up in a music hall tradition to cross that line'.[64]

Artists, both professional and amateur, came to Marconi House and Savoy Hill through various informal mechanisms. In the mid-1920s, for instance, Roger Eckersley trawled English seaside resorts Margate and Eastbourne looking for acts that might translate well on radio. When he found them, he set up recording equipment in the venue to capture the performance and its atmospherics.[65] He also recruited among the various acts he found while broadcasting the future King George VI's disastrous speech from Wembley Exhibition in 1925.[66] Always on the 'look out' for fledgling BBC artists, George Grossmith Jr., light entertainment adviser in the 1920s, regularly named performers he had recently seen on stage as potential radio acts. Others gained auditions on the strength of personal connections.[67] Music-hall comedienne and film actress Helena Millais became the first female entertainer on the BBC in 1922 due to a chance conversation with a director and Constanduros recruited talent from her amateur dramatic club in Sutton.[68]

Further, wireless presented challenges to artists used to performing in front of a live audience. Joseph Coyne, a well-known 1920s stage comedian, explained these in a 1926 *Popular Wireless and Wireless Review* article: 'To make laughs on a warm stage, with a buoyant audience sitting out beyond the lights, waiting to be tickled to death – that's hard enough at times in all conscience', Coyne admitted.

> But to make an invisible audience of umpteen millions start chuckling and then laughing, and then throwing headphones to the dickens and rolling around regardless of the consequences – why, that's a very different matter … the help we get from an audience, when we are acting on the stage proper, is withheld from the broadcasting comedian. He must *imagine* the effect he is creating on the huge audience he cannot see.

The prospect of performing on air, he confessed, was positively 'frightful'.[69] Constanduros echoed this feeling in *Shreds and Patches*, but stated that broadcast rehearsals were worse than the actual performance:

> Broadcasting humorous material in cold blood in an empty room to a microphone is bad enough, but it is nothing to the pain of rehearsing it at a morning rehearsal on a bare stage with the producer standing watch in hand, timing you, and the orchestra sitting behind you talking and making little roulades on saxophones and 'plonks' on strings that orchestras apparently cannot help indulging in. By the time you have read through eight minutes of new material in these circumstances, your spirits have reached the lowest level. After the first page you are convinced that nothing you have said is funny. By the time you reach the end you know your turn will be a failure. The prospect of broadcasting the dreadful stuff to millions of listeners is abhorrent and you would rather go home quietly and die.[70]

If a performer was willing to adapt their material for an aural medium *and* learn to perform in a cold, lifeless studio with no immediate audience response, the professional had then to accept that their material would die a quick death.⁷¹ Whereas a comedian could tour the halls for a year or two successfully using the same jokes day in and day out, their material had an incredibly short shelf life on radio. At a BBC Programme Board meeting in June 1926, it was suggested that perhaps the BBC could hire writers as a way to overcome this challenge; this was quickly dismissed as a possibility, however, since it was believed that the big artists already had teams of writers and would therefore not want BBC writers. A better option, it was thought at the time, was to ask *Punch* for material which could be adapted for broadcast purposes. It does seem that the Board subsequently fostered a relationship with the magazine, as several well-known *Punch* humourists appeared on air subsequently.⁷² L. Du Garde Peach was one such *Punch* writer who established a deeply respected and long-term presence on the BBC.⁷³ Peach initially worked in short broadcast comedies and eventually drama, but became legendary for his historical pageants. Giddings and Selby attribute to him pioneering efforts in reconstructing the past through sound effects as well as his creation of 'convincingly natural everyday speech for characters from the past which replaced the conventional "Tushery" of Wardour Street English'.⁷⁴

In the 1920s, the BBC Programme Board, and even hobbyist magazines like *Popular Wireless*⁷⁵, ruminated over enticing established celebrities to the microphone. Extant Programme Board's meeting notes from the Company period suggest an ongoing attempt to entice well-known entertainers to the microphone.⁷⁶ For instance, throughout June 1926, the Board tried in vain to convince American diseuse Ruth Draper, who was delivering her popular monologues nightly at the Garrick Theatre that month, to perform on the BBC.⁷⁷ While ultimately unsuccessful with Draper (she wouldn't broadcast on BBC radio until 1939), the Board was happy to sign relative newcomers to London's musical-comedy scene, Flotsam and Jetsam, who broadcast for the first time in September.⁷⁸

To further complicate matters of recruitment, the BBC simply could not afford to pay its artists as well as theatre or commercial radio. Gielgud remembered early professionals dismissing the BBC artist fee as no more than 'cigarette-money'.⁷⁹ Indeed, popular singer Clara Butt argued in 1926 that the radio licensing fee should be raised from 10s to £1 in order to pay 'star artists adequate fees'.⁸⁰ Maschwitz remembered that there was so 'little money to spend on actors and less than little for the employment of authors' that BBC staffers were obliged to write and perform on radio themselves, some launching their own careers in entertainment and eventually catapulting out of BBC staff positions and into wider fame, as indeed was the case for Maschwitz.[81] As late as 1953, even after the BBC had won over professional entertainers, one BBC governor noted the massive financial gulf that existed between American and British entertainment coffers, stating that the United States 'spends more on two top level shows than the total of £700,000 per annum spent by our Variety Department in producing one hundred shows a week'.[82] Beyond these obstacles, some stage humour simply could not translate to radio, especially the physical humour of music hall, which relied on visual cues and audience rapport for laughs.[83]

Andre Charlot, the well-known British revue impresario, was one of the first established theatre managers willing to test radio's potential advertisement value for promoting his stage Variety revues, and agreed to air them from *The Prince of Wales* theatre in 1925.[84] But some on the Programme Board complained that certain stage humour did not translate well to wireless; further, it was noted that audience laughter in the theatre annoyed and alienated listeners who could hear frivolity, but could not see the visual gags.[85] Hilda Matheson, director of talks from 1927 to 1932, would reflect on this concern in her 1933 volume, *Broadcasting*:

> Excerpts from musical comedies and from theatres, relays from music halls, suffered from certain drawbacks which sometimes aroused irritation and resentment. The funny man of the stage was somehow less funny when one could not see his face, and his jokes seemed poorer when one heard the audience laughing but could not laugh oneself. Acoustic difficulties made the patter of a musical comedy difficult to follow.[86]

Added to the annoyances of listening in on visual gags, George Grossmith, Jr. struck a note of concern about the 'doubtful language' of the revue and recommended carefully censoring it in future.[87] As Eckersley would argue, the BBC had to maintain stricter standards with regards to propriety. 'We are caterers for all and sundry', he argued, 'and have to be correspondingly careful and it's true enough that a jest in doubtful taste heard in the parlour, within the bosom of the family, has a different effect from the same joke heard by a lot of happy people in the atmosphere of the Music Hall.'[88]

Charlot addressed many of these concerns in 1928, when the BBC contracted twelve shows under the title of *Charlot's Hour*. In this revue, Charlot catered specifically for a listening audience: talking directly to them as an 'Uncle' and involving them in contests to write music or sketches for the programme.

Charlot even engaged in what had by then become a well established form of radio humour: a cross-talk routine with an onstage character named Jane.[89] The BBC would continue to broadcast Charlot's revues well into the 1930s, and relays from Sir Oswald Stoll's *Alhambra* and *The Coliseum* began in 1929,[90] but staged entertainment of this nature was still largely visual and could not provide the basis for strictly aural programming.

In addition to the problems of relaying stage performances to the wireless, Matheson outlined the challenges of using seasoned stage professionals on air:

> The actor or actress trained for stage work has been trained for something differing in almost every respect from microphone conditions. The production of his voice, his articulation, enunciation and rate of speech, the degree of gesture in his voice – upon the rightness of these for broadcasting depends the real success of the broadcast play. Yet the untrained performer may have learned too little of voice and breath control, may be insufficiently supple and plastic for a producer's purpose, and the stage actor may have to be the choice in the end.[91]

Gielgud recalled that many stage actors had to re-learn their technique and realize that even though the audience was the largest they had ever played to, 'it was unnecessary for them to project their voices and their personalities as if they were playing in some super-equivalent of Olympia'.[92]

The London Radio Repertory Company that Constanduros joined in 1925 was an early attempt to address ways to train and retain actors to perform specifically over the wireless. It was also expedient at a time when the BBC was faced with the challenge of attracting actors to the wireless. As early as 1923, regional radio stations turned on several occasions to well-respected local repertory theatre companies to broadcast dramatic programmes. For instance, in November 1923, the vaunted Birmingham Repertory Company performed Shakespeare for 5IT, and 5NO (Newcastle) benefited from a relationship with the Newcastle Repertory Theatre in the first half of 1924.[93] It has been suggested that R. E. Jeffrey, the first dramatic director at 2LO, was a proponent of radio repertory companies and was perhaps the inspiration behind the 2BD (Aberdeen) Repertory Players, whose first performance is listed in February 1924.[94] Nonetheless, many regional repertory companies were well established on air before the first documented performance of the 2LO Repertory Players in May 1924.[95]

Few potential microphone comedians or actors, professional or amateur, were turned away without an audition from the BBC in the 1920s and the 1930s. As early as 1924, the BBC felt it had too many musicians on hand

and thus prioritized musicians' auditions based strictly on experience and professional credentials.[96] Drama auditions were never closed, however; it was noted as policy that 'Mr. [Howard] Rose sees practically all artists who apply for an audition, although if they sound quite unsuitable they are refused a test'.[97] In 1931, Variety auditions were staged twice a week for two and a half hours, except in summer or if the list of artists had grown to a sufficient number.[98] However, few who auditioned were considered talented, and of those, fewer still were suitable for radio.[99] As will be seen in the next chapter, the lack of good microphone variety and dramatic talent would continue to plague the BBC throughout the decade.

Once the BBC secured good talent, especially humourists, they were careful not to lose them. Early on, the Programme Board attempted to protect their best entertainers with a contract that gave the Company an option on their time and, though it did not bar artists' appearance beyond the BBC, it required them to specify 'Courtesy of the BBC' when appearing elsewhere. Some artists were amenable to this agreement, but Constanduros flatly refused to sign such a contract. The Board was not, however, unduly concerned about Constanduros's attitude as they believed she was ultimately loyal to the BBC, as indeed she proved to be over the course of her long career.[100]

Amateurs and early broadcasting entertainment

Since so few established professionals came to the microphone in the 1920s, amateurs like Constanduros were integral to early BBC entertainment. Constanduros and other erstwhile amateurs took advantage of the absence of seasoned writers and stage professionals on air and participated in the 'delightful informality' of the period by experimenting with various microphone and writing techniques, content and genres to establish themselves as radio professionals. Like Maschwitz, and other BBC staffers, some performers also embraced the fluidity of the fledgling BBC. Constanduros remembered how 'one had to be prepared to do anything and everything in those Savoy Hill days; we learned how to use the microphone and to be quick-witted'.[101] Experimentation was a hallmark of the early BBC, and while the historiography tends to focus on the technological experimentation of the period, little has been said about experimentation with successful microphone strategies and genres, or the development of what Scannell and Cardiff have called 'radiogenic' entertainment.[102]

It is generally believed that BBC radio entertainment in the 1920s largely consisted of 'relaying shows' from the theatres or music halls or attempts at simply 're-create' those shows.[103] Indeed, it has been argued that the BBC did not get 'serious' about entertainment until the creation of a separate Variety department in 1933, under Maschwitz.[104] However, at the very beginnings of BBC radio, much experimentation occurred in writing radiogenic material, in learning the art of the microphone and in performing entertainment specifically for radio that went far beyond the confines of the halls or theatres. Time-tested practices that worked in traditional theatres rarely translated to the wireless. Gielgud, for example, noted how drama producers had to learn how to use incidental music throughout a programme instead of simply broadcasting music before the play, as was done in the theatre.[105]

Experimentation with sound effects also began in the 1920s: Constanduros remembered a roller skate gliding across a tin bath substituting for the sound of a moving train, and in 1924, R.E. Jeffrey 'spent the first few hours firing a shotgun over the banisters into the well of the staircase', much to the consternation of BBC staff and with little success, as the anticipated gunshot 'sounded like flat champagne' over the air.[106] The sound of seagulls crying was created using elastic bands and a rainstorm was reproduced by dropping sand on paper.[107] But, as Hilda Matheson asserted, the use of sound effects was only one aspect of successful radio technique; ideas, impressions and insinuation were also key. 'The obvious secret of [radio drama]', she wrote, 'has been to make every use of impressions, effects and suggestions which the microphone was peculiarly fitted to convey – rapid change of aural "scene", suggestions of infinite distance and infinite closeness, and the general fluidity of time and space.'[108] The early amateurs who were willing to experiment with their material and effectively evolve according to the unique needs of the medium and its audience became the first big radio celebrities of the 1920s.

Helena Millais, the first female entertainer on the BBC, was effective in transferring her stage routine of popular music-hall and sentimental songs, peppered with humorous monologues, to wireless. She became known affectionately as 'Our Lizzie', a Cockney charwoman whose 'Fragments from Life' like 'Lizzie Goes Shopping' were popular staples of her routine.[109] Millais underscored the importance of being mindful of her radio audience in a 1938 *Radio Pictorial* article. 'I always', she told the magazine, 'remember that my unseen audience is conjuring up a picture of me from my voice and intonation. I am careful to exaggerate nothing, thus giving them a natural miniature instead of a vulgar cartoon.'[110] Millais's routine worked well both on stage and microphone, and after a three year contract with the BBC in the mid-1920s, she returned to the stage touring with renewed national success.

Tommy Handley, who would become one of the biggest radio stars of the BBC with his lead role in the 1940s' hit, *It's That Man Again* (*ITMA*), reinvigorated his waning stage career by appearing on 2LO's first attempt at translating theatre revue to radio in *Radio Radiance* (1925-6).[111] Others – like Clapham and Dwyer, who first appeared in early 1926, and Gert and Daisy (1927) – successfully brought their cross-talk stage routines to the air, becoming immensely popular on-air comedians and cementing their popularity for decades to come. Indeed, many on the early BBC believed cross-talk routines were ideal for the particularities of the broadcasting studio.[112]

Norman Clapham (known as John Henry on air) was the first amateur-turned-professional on the BBC who wrote and performed 'radiogenic', aural humour. Henry made his debut on the BBC in October 1923, but very little is known about his pre-BBC career, as the earliest BBC artist files are missing. Clapham performed to Canadian troops during the First World War and, thereafter, became a clerk at the Board of Trade, where he was '"discovered" when entertaining at a smoking concert' put on by his department.[113] Clapham was indicative of many variety entertainers on the BBC during the 1920s and the 1930s: Briggs argues that '"local" comedians … engaged mainly in appealing to small intimate audiences in provincial after dinner shows or summer holiday audiences on the pier at seaside resorts'.[114] This experience can be seen in the casual, armchair style with which John Henry addressed his audience, an intimate approach well-suited to the domestic space of radio listening.

Many early commentators noted radio's intimacy and realized that harnessing it was crucial to success with audiences. The epitome of radio success, Roger Eckersley explained to the *Daily Mail* in 1932, required one to 'approach the microphone with the idea of sitting down in the best armchair and talking interestingly'.[115] Gielgud believed that 'the microphone exposes ruthlessly the insincere and the stupid. Its impact is so intimate, its approach so subtly close, its capacity of exaggeration so immense, that no tricks, however skilled, can hope to get by'; however, he continued, 'This extreme intimacy is to be exploited, not to be feared … . Story, argument, dramatic effects, must all be directed to the individual or the small group in the domestic setting.'[116] Matheson stressed that radio's intimacy made it nearly impossible for music-hall comedy to make the leap to radio: 'The family circle side of broadcasting, and the isolated intimacy of a voice in one's own room ... may cause remarks which would pass unnoticed in a music hall to sound like monuments of bad taste in a drawing-room or a kitchen.'[117]

In the 'My Wireless Set' sketch, Henry describes how he built his wireless; throughout, he name drops celebrity BBC staffers like Chief Engineer Peter Eckersley and makes inside jokes only wireless enthusiasts would understand. For instance, on the difference between outside and inside aerials, Henry deadpans, 'inside ones are cheaper. 10 shillings cheaper ... that's the favourite joke of the Post Office'. (10 shillings, of course, being the cost of a radio licence.) Joking about the differences between valves, Henry gets his digs in on BBC programming; there are two types of valves, he states, 'bright ones and dull-emitters ... the bright ones are for use when there's a popular programme being broadcast and the dull ones are for symphony concerts'. His on-air wife, Blossom, makes an appearance in the sketch, and the two have fun with early sound effects as they try to 'tune' the wireless.[118] Here, Henry and Blossom capitalize on the aural, drawing on sound effects and developing linguistic slapstick ideally suited for microphone entertainment. John Henry's sketches thus exploited audience 'knowingness' by poking fun both at the BBC and the emerging technology, illustrating the earliest use of what Cardiff has called 'a self-reflexive style of comedy that became one of the hallmarks of British broadcasting'.[119]

Michael Bailey and others have commented on the gendered nature of early BBC radio, whose technology and hobbyist tinkering may have appealed more to men than women.[120] Indeed, Henry's humour was often aimed at a masculine audience, with frequent jokes about nagging and overbearing wives. At the same time, Henry's armchair domestic joshing suggests that the 'domestication of the airwaves', which Maggie Andrews has argued took place in the 1930s, can be seen in the earliest popular comedy act on the BBC.[121] Mabel Constanduros further domesticated the wireless with the innovative, family-centred comedy she developed in 1925, her first year on the BBC.

2

Introducing the Buggins family

The radio comedy that Mabel Constanduros perfected in the 1920s was not the intimate, armchair address of John Henry's, nor was it the music-hall monologue clowning of other early BBC comics. Instead, Constanduros wrote and performed theatrical comedy steeped in situational humour and character development. Astutely aware of her domestic audience, her humour privileged the female perspective, and her comedy was rooted in the everyday happenings of the household and the relational dynamics of the extended family.

No official record exists regarding which comedic monologues Constanduros slipped into during her audition in 1925, but it seems entirely possible that one of the characters who appeared that day was a Cockney housewife much like Mrs. Buggins, the character (and her family) that would catapult her into stardom later that year.[1] Constanduros's first documented solo appearance was in June, billed with comic acts John Henry, Blossom and Joe Murgatroyd.[2] Aside from a few titles in the *Radio Times* listings, no internal BBC memoranda or contracts exist regarding the content of her earliest broadcasts. Based on the extant titles in the listings, it seems that her earliest radio performances were probably monologues or duologues. For instance, on 3 August, Constanduros wrote and broadcast on 2LO 'In the tram, a comedy dialogue of low life' with Frederick Collier. Later that month, she penned and delivered 'Mrs. Smythe Browne Buys a Book' on 5XX, a monologue and a popular one at that, as it was aired again a few days later on 29 August on Glasgow's station (5SC) and was published in the Samuel French Monologue series.[3] This was also the first documented Buggins radio appearance, and the title suggests another monologue: 'Mrs. Buggins Chooses a Hat.'[4] Mrs. Buggins became the lynchpin of the Buggins family sketches for which Constanduros is best remembered. Though her initial stardom was largely founded on working-class characterizations like the Bugginses, other monologues in the early days, like 'Mrs. Smythe Browne Buys a Book', poked fun at the suburban middle classes, a theme to which she would return successfully later in her career.

Mundy and White argue that the BBC's comedic output was 'scarce before the creation of a separate "revue and vaudeville" section … in 1930'.⁵ Certainly, John Reith was notoriously ambivalent about entertainment; while Reith allowed that the purpose of wireless was 'to entertain, to interest, to enlighten', the emphasis fell largely on the enlightenment and uplift of audiences, and policy was driven by a strong sense of what Martin Dibbs has called 'cultural paternalism'.⁶ Nevertheless, by the time Constanduros came to the microphone in 1925, she felt that the field of established comic artists performing monologues and duologues was already quite crowded. In addition to John Henry and Blossom and Helena Millais as 'Our Lizzie', Constanduros shared the microphone with other entertainers who were doing what the BBC called 'dialect' entertainment in the same vein as her own work. Within this context, Constanduros

> was convinced that if you wanted your public to listen to you, you must give them well-defined characters which could be recognised easily, and very individual voices. One voice is apt to become tiresome on the air if it goes on for a long time, so I invented my cockney family … being several people at once enabled me to do sketches, which I think are more entertaining than monologues.⁷

Here we can see the mindful inception of the first radio family. Constanduros's Buggins family was thus, on the one hand, formulated specifically for a radio audience and, on the other, an intentional attempt to differentiate herself from other established radio comics.

The creation of the Buggins family represents a significant milestone for radio as it was the first radio family on either UK or American radio, beating out the first American radio family, the *Goldbergs*, by four years.⁸ In 1939, then director of Variety, John Watt, recognized that 'her creation of the Buggins family was a historic achievement'.⁹ According to Tim Crook, the Bugginses were 'the forerunner of virtually every soap and sitcom family that's ever been'.¹⁰

Beyond her invention of the radio family, Constanduros's sketches have proved influential models of situation, narrative and characterizations in British sitcom across the twentieth and into the twenty-first century. As Brett Mills has argued, 'as genres develop over time, characteristics of them are lost to the past. While this highlights the problems in concretely defining genres, it also shows that genres are a process that exist in the developing relationship between the text, its producers and its receivers'.¹¹ Scott Banville has termed the process by which this occurs as 'remediation'.¹² Character types and situations from Buggins sketches have been worked and reworked innumerable times through this process of remediation into later sitcoms. Irascible mother-in-laws like Grandma Buggins – from Gran (Nancy Roberts) in the 1950s television Grove Family to Catherine Tate's Nan – quickly became commonplace.[13] Carl Giles's *Express* cartoon grandma is deeply resonant of Constanduros's grandma: 'beastly, disillusioned, debunking, and basically benign ... the malevolent matriarch'.[14] Further, Constanduros's characterizations can be detected in later female sitcom leads such as Ria in *Butterflies* and Ma Boswell in *Bread*.[15] Though not nearly as rough or shocking to our contemporary senses, Father Buggins's abusive drunkenness, bluster and selfishness resonates in similar working-class fathers from Alf Garnett in *Til Death Us Do Part* (1966-1975) to Frank Gallagher in *Shameless* (2004–13). Finally, the chaos that befalls sitcom families on outings beyond the home echoes in sketches like 'The Buggins's Day Out' and 'The Bugginses at the Zoo', as well as numerous Buggins scenes at the train station, in which the children and/or Grandma inevitably get lost.[16]

Beyond the creation of the first radio family, which itself was an innovation that both exploited the domestic setting of radio listening and used multiple voices to engage listeners' interest, extant recordings of Constanduros's sketches make clear how she experimented with and learned to exploit the aural nature of radio. Initially, Constanduros worked in monologue or dialogue, next she created and gave voice to a cast of distinct characters, and finally she introduced sound effects. Where television or theatre supplies both the visual and the auditory dimensions of the experience, the radio audience must use their imaginations to invoke the visual scene and characterizations for themselves. Numerous radio critics and theorists have described the complexity of this phenomenon, resisting the idea that radio is a 'blind' medium.[17] As Cecil Lewis argued in 1929,

> the limitations of actions and *mis en scene* are bounded only by the imagination of the listener himself. The stage author deals in scenes and situations which can be presented to the eye. The wireless author may make use of practically any scene or situation which can be conceived by human thought or imagination.[18]

Constanduros's 1930 sketch 'Father Sweeps the Chimney' illustrates how she activated the imagination of the listener by employing several voiced and non-voiced characters, dialogue and sound effects to help audiences imagine the visual scene of chaos and destruction that ensued when father (played by Michael Hogan) tries to use the wireless aerial to clean the chimney. When the aerial gets stuck in the chimney, the family attempt to pull it out:

> **Father:** Heave! 'eave I tell ya!
>   All *grunt in effort*
> **Father:** 'eave!
>   *Crashing while father hollers out 'oh!'*
> **Mrs. B:** *sadly* Oh father, need you upset right in the china cabinet? Alfie, get up out of the coal. Emma! That's baby you're sitting on. *With feeling:* There, there ducky, don't cry.

While the sound effects help the listener's imagination fill in the action, Mrs. Buggins's line is crucial in depicting the scene. Mrs. Buggins helps the audience visualize the consequences of the crash: the mangled china cabinet and the dusty children in the coal heap. While none of the children utter a sound throughout the scene, Constanduros ably turns the listener's 'eye' first to a filthy, coal-blackened Alfie and then to the baby by announcing Emma's position and shifting from an authoritative tone to a soothing one.

At the end of the sketch, father gets stuck in the chimney and the rest of the family attempt to free him. After pulling on his legs unsuccessfully, they try another method:

> **Mrs. B:** We shall 'ave to pry him out with the poker. Draw'r in your breath, Father dear, and make your 'ead as thin as you can. Now, Emma [place] the poker up between 'is 'ead and the wall.
>   *(Muffled, as if from inside the chimney) Father screams in protest*
> **Mrs. B:** Goodness Emma! You've got the poker up 'is 'ostril!
>   *(Muffled) Father screaming in agony*
> **GMA:** Well, you can't leave 'im there, we shall want the fire. Poke 'im about a bit. It's them ears of his, they always was obnormal. Fetch a sharp wrench, we'll 'ave one of those long ears.
>   *(Muffled) Father screams protests*
> **Mrs. B:** Oh be careful, Grandma, you'll 'ave one of them off!
> **G'ma:** Well, it seems to me, it's a one eared 'usband or no 'usband at all.
> **Mrs. B:** Father, dear? We're going to make an last effort. If you down come down this time, we shall 'ave to wait til you've starved yourself thin enough to drop. Now then, one, two, three. Pull! 'e's coming, 'e's coming, 'e's coming!
>   *Father screams Oh! as if he's falling.*

Mrs. B: Oh, father, I'm glad yore safe. But I do wish you 'ad'nt swept the chimney with yore head![19]

This sketch demonstrates how Constanduros exploited the possibilities of an aural medium. Constanduros regularly took advantage of the fact that the audience could not see radio performers and often voiced numerous characters without the knowledge of the audience. In this sketch, she performed four characters, but was capable of voicing up to seven characters in one sitting; she did this so well that audience members were convinced that her sketches included a large cast of actors.[20]

In her radio work, Constanduros conjured the visual through a masterful use of what Susan Douglas has termed 'linguistic slapstick'.[21] This form of auditory slapstick, as Mundy and White have suggested, usually 'emphasiz[es] ... word play, puns, jokes and punch lines', tactics that were peppered throughout her comedic radio sketches. As is demonstrated in 'Father Sweeps the Chimney', however, much more is involved in successful radio slapstick. Gordon Lea, an early critic of radio drama, believed that writers of radio should employ the 'self-contained method', a style of writing that was

> self-explanatory in every detail ... . It will indicate scenery, character, costume, all action – everything in fact which is necessary to the complete mental vision of the play, in the text of the play itself, with such additional help as may be required from music and sound-effects.[22]

This style of writing and performance engaged the listener's imagination, enabling the listener to create the imagined scene (and characters) based on their own experiences, thus 'see[ing] the play in its ideal setting'.[23] In his exploration of radio drama, Tim Crook refers to the listener's imagination as the 'fifth dimension' or the 'imaginative spectacle', and argues,

> This dimension can create anything. It has visual spatialisation in the imagination of the listener. The imaginative spectacle has the power to create a full sensory spectrum of experience: colour and visual depth; olfactory perception; touch and texture; imaginary sound and taste.

'Father Sweeps the Chimney' demonstrates the ways in which Constanduros and other early radio artists and writers developed the 'self-contained method' and engaged the 'fifth dimension' of their audience, leveraging word play but going further, employing auditory cues, dialogue and sound effects in order to aurally evoke the slapstick physicality of their comedy.

Laughing at/laughing with the working class: Interpreting Buggins humour

Given the highly individualistic audience interpretations possible in radio listening, and because BBC audience research did not exist until 1936, more than a decade after her debut[24], it is nearly impossible to be certain why the Buggins family remained popular over the course of Constanduros's long career. Some clues do exist, however. In the later period, it is clear from Listener Research that nostalgia was the primary reason for their popularity: the Bugginses were by then familiar voices. Two intriguing sources survive from the early period, however, to give us some insight into early audience reception of Constanduros's work; they also underscore quite clearly the polysemic nature of radio broadcasts.

T. H. Pear, the Manchester psychologist mentioned in chapter one who requested airtime from the Programming Board in 1926, published the results of his radio experiment and other voice experiments in 1931. The majority of Pear's book explained and analysed the radio experiment, which considered how subjects interpreted character based on the speaker's voice alone. Included in the book is also an experiment conducted at the University of Manchester that tested listeners' reactions to a gramophone recording of the popular BBC sketch, 'The Bugginses Make a Christmas Pudding'. This experiment provides the only specific data regarding audience reactions to Constanduros's early radio comedy.

Pear's panel consisted of forty-eight staff and students at the University, and twenty-eight Worker's Educational Association (WEA) students, many of whom were mature students.[25] While Pear does not discuss the class status of his panel, the profile suggests a mix of middle- and working-class subjects. If it is assumed that the staff and traditional students are generally representative of the middle class, while the WEA students are likewise representative of the working class, the ratio between the two classes in this experiment roughly mirrors what is thought to be the class composition of the BBC listening audience in the 1920s and the 1930s. Thus, the results of the experiment enable some insight into the possible interpretations of BBC listeners at the time.[26]

The experiment demonstrated that most listeners found the Walworth dialect of the characters to be entertaining and authentic, and most thought the sketch amusing and fast-paced. The various character voices performed by Constanduros were, according to Pear, easily distinguishable from one another. Additionally, some found the working-class dialect humorous, while others found it 'annoying'. Nonetheless, Pear asserted that all subjects reacted to the sketch and the dialect in 'some marked manner'.[27]

Subjects' reactions to the sketch underscore the diversity of possible interpretations of radio entertainment. Pear reported that nearly 61 per cent of listeners in the study had an emotional response to the sketch and felt it 'authentic'; 38 per cent felt it 'artificial or mechanised'.[28] Of those who reacted emotionally to the piece, some were positively moved, expressing 'amusement, interest, admiration, affection, sorrow [or] sympathy'. Others responded negatively with emotions such as 'dislike, annoyance [or] distaste'.[29]

Pear also queried listeners' response to the South London working-class dialect and found that, despite many of the respondents being from Lancashire or Yorkshire, some enjoyed the dialect while others loathed it. Reasons for this disparity are rooted in the primacy of listener experiences and imaginations discussed earlier. Some, like Pear himself, reported positive memories of trips into London or interactions with people with similar accents; others recalled negative experiences associated with London or the accent, and still others found it 'foreign' sounding.

Pear listed out the responses, with little to no analysis of them, but the responses fell roughly into two categories: reaction to the intonation or the accent itself and the listener's own emotive response to the accent and/or the sketch. It is instructive to consider most of the responses here, as it signals the incredible complexity involved in discerning audience reaction and popularity. Negative responses included:

> Somewhat insincere (possibly heard at theatres); associated with people disliked; slightly nasal ... drawling; pitched too high in the female; resembling a squeak when pitched too high; too conceited; a deviation from normal intonation; appearing to affect superiority; 'oi' instead of 'i'; vulgar; jars on ears; associated with living in London (disliked) ... popularly associated with costermongers, etc.; shrill, connected in my mind with pathos; sounds too much distorted; associated (*Punch* and *Humourist* blamed for this) with a shallow self-complacent type ... connect with rather bad comedy; with wireless stout women; not Standard English ... whining ... not full and rich; not musical; like nothing on earth; sometimes difficult to understand.[30]

In contrast, the following positive responses were recorded:

> Ugly but friendly; familiar; pleasant for a short time, when not used too strongly; pleasantly inflected; associated with people living in London; clear;

makes play seem all the more vivid ... a refreshing change, better than Yorkshire or Lancashire ... amusing; novel and seldom heard; consonant with listener's Southern birth and feeling; associated with resourceful type of person; can always be recognised ... every vowel contains about five different shades of emotion in it; associated with early childhood; connected with a music-hall comedian; fascinatingly smooth, suggesting better education; unusual and humorous ... associated with Mabel Constanduros's and Michael Hogan's sketches ... a more enjoyable caricature of good English than the Lancashire accent ... associated with books containing Cockney humour; humorous and naïve (in children); a change; clearly distinguished from another local accent which I definitely dislike ... bright; cheery; business-like; rather interesting to a student of philology and phonetics; friendly even towards a stranger.[31]

Pear's list evokes a mosaic of possible listener reactions, and the diversity of opinions regarding the same sketch is striking. Some of the technical observations were clearly a result of his use of university students on the panel, some of whom were studying philology. Some respondents were familiar with the work of Constanduros and Hogan, and thus appreciative of the recording because of the performers' established celebrity and style.

The emotive responses of Pear's panellists help us to understand how Constanduros's working-class characterizations might have been interpreted by BBC listeners. Unfortunately, Pear does not seem to have followed up on the reasons for particular responses. Clearly, however, class was central to many of them.

While some respondents' technical observations about pitch or quality of voices might be associated with their academic interests, quite possibly, these responses might be rooted in either a negative identification with or an instinctive dislike of working-class accents or working-class populations in general. This could be true of the individual who disliked the accent because it was 'not Standard English'. Negative responses to the vulgarity of the sketch or specifically to the association with costermongers may suggest a dislike of working-class individuals or working-class comedy. Given the profile of some of the subjects in Pear's sample, it is possible that some working-class subjects recoiled at the use of the accent because of an attempt to distance themselves from their working-class origins through education.[32] On the other hand, some of the positive responses appreciated the characterizations for their friendly and bright nature, while others simply appreciated the novelty of the London accent.

Some listeners, like the individual who found the sketch 'conceited', seemed troubled by what might be interpreted as classed superiority in Constanduros's portrayal of the working classes. The respondent who blamed popular magazines *Punch* and *Humorist* for their interpretation is suggestive that, at least for some listeners, Constanduros's comedy was linked to the laughter of middle-class superiority found in these periodicals. Sitcoms often employ the superiority theory of humour, relying on stereotypes to mock others and thereby 'uphold power structures within society', acting as 'a useful tool for normalising the demonisation of certain social groups'.[33] Yet, the diversity of responses in Pear's study supports the fact that audiences can engage in the laughter of superiority in unexpected ways and from unexpected subject positions.[34]

Filson Young, radio critic and consultant for the BBC, devoted an entire chapter to radio humour in his 1933 tract on British broadcasting. Roger Eckersley considered Young's criticisms of BBC entertainment 'pungent and usually right'.[35] The Bugginses occupy the majority of Young's attention in the chapter, giving us yet another early insight into interpretive possibilities of Constanduros's radio work. Young was clear that he generally disliked the state of comedy on the BBC, which he believed was too closely associated with music hall and too London-centric. His negative reaction to the accent might help elucidate some of the responses found in Pear's experiment. In Young's view, the accent represented 'a compound of squalor and cruelty', and music-hall Cockney acts presented

> a world where everything is essentially cruel and derisive; where sympathy or kindness is looked upon as a weakness; where drunkenness or any other human frailty, including the most atrocious crime, is regarded as amusing and as a fit subject for laughter. This bitter field is sown with sarcasm rather than with irony; with harshness rather than with severity; with a vocal and intellectual stridency which hurls itself upon everything that simple people regard as true and genial and honourable in life, and tears it to pieces.[36]

Young's negative depiction of working-class music-hall comedy is suggestive of his own middle-class position, but also echoes Victorian critics of music halls, such as William Archer, who derided the entertainment as 'the art of elaborate ugliness, blatant vulgarity, alcoholic humour and rancid sentiment'.[37] Perhaps fearful of the destabilizing potential of this rough comedy, Young attacks these acts as an outsider beyond the audience who are called into alliance together by the 'knowingness' of the everyday life experiences depicted in them. As Peter Bailey has argued,

> It is knowingness that … pull[s] the crowd inside a closed yet allusive frame of reference, and implicat[es] them in a select conspiracy of meaning that animates them as a specific audience. This flattering sense of membership is the more so since music-hall performance suggested that such privileged status was not so much conferred as *earned* by the audience's own well-tested cultural and social competence.[38]

The competence was not just about knowledge of, or familiarity with, music-hall comedy, but rather lived experience. 'Performers', Bailey suggests, 'were applauded not just for their naturalistic re-creation of a shared world but for their authority in the actual business of living in that world'.[39]

As opposed to some of Pear's respondents who found resourcefulness and cheerfulness in the sketches, Young found nothing but 'malice' at the heart of each of Constanduros's characters:

> The funniest figure in Miss Constanduros's little gallery is 'Grandma' – an embodiment of complete selfishness and malice, and so mean and squalid in her habits as to be physically revolting. Who are the others? There is 'Father', an abusive lout who quarrels with everyone, nags at his wife, and beats his children. There is Alfie, a sinister miniature of his parent, who displays a precocious virtuosity in malice and unveracity. There is the wife and mother, the humour of whose conversation consists largely in the ingenuity of the punishments with which she threatens her offspring, and the general unloveliness of her relations with her mother-in-law.

Even the inarticulate baby 'contribut[ed] its fair share to the general squalor and discomfort' of the sketches.[40] Though repulsed by Cockney humour in general and by the Buggins family in particular, Young nonetheless felt Constanduros was the 'solitary example known to me in which the microphone has evolved a Cockney humour which is unfailingly funny'.[41] It was not, however, a 'happy laughter'.[42] Instead, he found himself continually shocked by the depths to which Grandma would sink, and he ultimately felt that Constanduros had created such despicable characters that one derived a grim satisfaction when catastrophe befell the family. 'Whatever [the reason for his laughter] there is undoubtedly humour in it. I do not deny that', Young conceded, 'but what I do know is that it is humour of an essentially unlovely and ill-natured kind, springing, not from the well of love in our hearts, but from the well of bitterness.'[43] Similar tension has been worked into some of the best sitcoms ever since. For instance, Phil Wickham noted the presence of 'darkness underlying the laughter' in the popular *The Royle Family* (BBC2/BBC1 1998–2012); beneath the sitcom lies 'an undercurrent of bullying, neglect and disappointment [that] runs through that front room but, as [Caroline] Aherne has said, there is a lot of love there too.'[44]

It is entirely possible that Young responded positively to Constanduros's portrayals because they presented a sanitized, drawing-room version of the popular Cockney acceptable to BBC policymakers and middle-class audiences. While Young disparaged music-hall humour for its mirth for misfortune, he revelled in the misfortune of the Bugginses and their circumstances. While Young was repulsed by what he felt was the malice with which the characters acted towards one another and by the squalor of their situation, he nonetheless delighted in the laughter of superiority.

The Buggins characters, their situation and their relationships could be seen as caricatures of middle-class expectations of working-class families and living conditions. In this way, Constanduros might be seen as leveraging 'class-based contempt' for the working classes by adhering to certain stereotypes that resonate with a middle-class audience.[45] These caricatures might then constitute a middle-class knowingness, calling middle-class listeners into league with one another, as against the working classes at whom they laughed. Middle-class audiences in the 1920s and the early 1930s may have quailed at laughing at working-class misfortunes when they confronted them on the streets, but in the comfort of their armchair, they might revel in the 'bitterness' of their situation: a classed laughter heightened by anxieties brought on by the spectre of class conflict shaded by the 1926 General Strike and the depression.

Yet, as has been argued in recent discussions of working-class caricatures, to see this type of humour as wholly one-sided is to miss the 'complexities inherent in comedic discourses'.[46] As Barry J. Faulk has argued, 'cultural messages get scrambled in transmission; they face resistance, appropriation, and acclaim. Performance forms meet and miss their intended targets, lose and find new constituencies, over and over.'[47] In her analysis of servants' use of humour, Lucy Delap reminds us, 'What one finds funny is highly context-dependent, and this makes it hard for a historian to judge the success of comic performances and texts. Comic discourse is richly unstable, and sometimes escapes the intentions of the author or performer.'[48] Some working-class audiences might smirk with the same superiority as middle-class audiences, feeling certain they were more respectable than the radio family. As Peter Bailey has pointed out, while some performers' acts suggested that the world was '"overwhelmingly peopled by fools", it is almost certain that the manner of performance reassured [the] audience that they weren't among them.'[49] At the same time, audiences might identify with the situations presented in the sketches and appreciate the humour in them. Brett Mills reminds us that a 'variety of audience positions' exist in relation to a comedy text: 'to laugh with Alf [in *Til Death Us Do Part*] is to enjoy jokes which position him and the viewers as superior to those he castigates; to laugh at Alf is to find your own views more civilised and informed than those he espouses.'[50]

Publicly, Constanduros stated that she did not wish to divide audiences, but rather hoped audiences might laugh *with* the family, sympathize with their situation and recognize their good-natured resourcefulness.[51] The characters, she told audiences, were composites of people she had known from her childhood, or from working-class people she had met or heard on the streets of South London. Constanduros told *Radio Times* readers that father was constructed from childhood experiences with a hairdresser who was cruel to both herself and her sisters. The inspiration for daughter Emma came from a group of eighty working-class schoolchildren from Lambeth with whom she volunteered as a young lady. 'My horrid little smug Emma Buggins', she wrote, 'is drawn from one of these children, who had a "company face" which she put on for our benefit and a perpetual grievance.'[52] But while Filson Young believed Mrs Buggins equally despicable, revelling in the punishment of her children and ungenerous towards Grandma, Constanduros's expressed intentions were far more sympathetic. Mrs. Buggins was meant to be 'the typical London working woman – patient, hard-working, and amazingly optimistic and gay'.[53] In a 1937 *Lancashire Daily Post* article, Constanduros explained:

> The English working-man's wife is the salt of the earth. I try with Mrs. Buggins to give a faithful picture of how good these people are; how they manage so marvelously in adverse circumstances. They are more important than any other class of beings in England.[54]

Clearly, Constanduros signalled her class position vis-à-vis her comedic family in her use of 'these people', and perhaps, by using this phrase, calls into being an audience of middle-class readers. Yet Constanduros also leveraged complexity by drawing on both negative and positive stereotypes of the working classes: 'the salt of the earth' versus malevolent working-class caricatures. By employing the family as a site of humour, Constanduros could thus place these caricatures side-by-side to create an equivocal and perhaps more sympathetic portrayal of the working classes than monologue or duologue comedy might successfully depict.

Further, situating her working-class characters within the family group, and often in the domestic setting, could soften the threat that middle-class audiences felt towards the working classes at a time of heightened class conflict. Extant recordings and scripts of 1920s and early-1930s sketches suggest that the Bugginses rarely came into conflict, or indeed, contact, with others beyond their family or their class: conflict existed only within the family or within the working-class neighbourhood.[55] Father may bluster and blow in his home, but his threat was safely contained within his home. Further, he was not always evident in the sketches; he is either entirely absent or silenced by characters making references to a voiceless father. The Buggins sketches not only contained the working-class threat but were also dominated by women and children: the main Buggins family often welcomed other female neighbours or relations into their fold, but only rarely did men darken their door. Finally, Mrs Buggins's main priority was to keep up appearances and maintain respectability: chiding father to put a collar on or berating Emma in a brisk, authoritative tone for getting her best clothes dirty.

Some of Constanduros's portrayals adhere to the stereotypes in a way that mark the working classes out as outsiders, foreigners. Her sketches of working-class life are imbued with the same humanity and pathos often found in Victorian literature, voicing their plight (while simultaneously maintaining the stereotypes), as in Constanduros's story of the homely Emily Ogboddy, whose closest chance at marriage materializes in the smooth-talking boarder who ultimately runs off with Emily's money – given freely by a desperately lonely woman to a man she knew to be a blackguard and suspected burglar.[56] Slapstick scenes carry an unmistakable sense of the violent, as when Bert roughly scrubs his wife's face with carbolic soap in order to rid her of a botched makeover in a sketch entitled 'Saving Her Face'.[57] Or when Father Buggins forces his children to eat sawdust or squirts them in the face with ink, all in the spirit of Christmas fun in *Santa Claus at the Bugginses*.[58] Constanduros's working-class humour can thus be situated within a longer tradition of depicting Cockney caricatures in popular culture as rough and even violent, but nonetheless 'compatible with middle-class desire' and ultimately unthreatening.[59]

The Buggins sketches are representative of any number of British radio and television working-class families who offered audiences a glimpse into working-class lives. This 'cultural tourism'[60] is best demonstrated in the opening of *The Bugginses*, a 1928 novel about the famous family and its neighbours, which carefully points out the hard life of her protagonists:

You did not complain of sulky tempers and sharp words in Halcyon Row. There were so many worse things you might have had to bear. There was poor Mrs. Evans at No. 8, for instance, who fled from a drunken husband's violence to the silent sympathy of Emily and Ag nearly every Saturday night. Mrs. Biggs at No. 20, who was working herself literally to death to support an idle husband and six delicate children. No, there were worse things to put up with than those one found at No. 17.[61]

In the *Radio Times* article mentioned earlier, Constanduros tells readers about various friendships forged with working-class Londoners and suggests that her ability to listen and sympathize with others' stories lends authenticity to her work. 'I am always listening to other people's points of view', she wrote, 'and always learning, and while they are talking to me every trick of voice and manner is registering itself upon my mind.' These experiences with London's working classes, she stressed, comforted her 'that the Buggins family has not lived in vain'.[62]

Identification between producer and consumer is critical in dictating popularity in mass media, as has been argued by LeMathieu in *A Culture for Democracy*.[63] The popularity of the Bugginses may rest in this constructed identification between Constanduros and her audience. Indeed, focusing the sketches on the family group held rich possibilities for cross-class identification: generational and marital struggles being the core of human existence, regardless of class. In professing her connection with and knowledge of everyday Londoners, she also asserted authority to represent working-class life, echoing the editor of the *Sunday Chronicle's* belief that, to be successful, 'an editor [or writer] must first and last know people, the great mass of people, happy and unhappy, who work for a living'.[64]

Certainly, Constanduros was familiar with South London's working classes. In their research for *The Bugginses* novel, Constanduros told readers that she and writing partner Michael Hogan went on 'excursions' through the streets of Walworth picking up sayings and storylines from the people they met.[65] This information signals a knowingness that established superiority vis-à-vis the working classes and enabled her to become a bridge between working-class life and (largely) middle-class audiences of early BBC radio. Like the female visitors and social explorers of the late-nineteenth and early twentieth centuries who attempted to depict a sympathetic portrait of the lives of the working classes they encountered for middle-class readers, Constanduros's Buggins family was also largely sympathetic.[66] Indeed, Constanduros's early understanding of the working classes was founded on similar experiences: as mentioned earlier, Emma Buggins derived from her work with Lambeth schoolchildren ('social work' required of herself and her sisters by her parents), and Constanduros often visited Tilling employees' families in their homes when she was a young lady.[67] Similar to the female social workers and visitors mentioned previously, Constanduros also relied upon the aural for her knowledge of the working classes, but in contrast to those earlier explorers who used the written word, Constanduros worked through the aural, inviting middle-class audiences to take an 'excursion' with her through the streets of Walworth, hearing and imagining working-class Londoners for themselves.[68]

Constanduros often claimed that her interest in the human condition was inspired by Dickens and that her ability to voice numerous characters also derived from her family's love of Dickens. As Denis Constanduros (Mabel's nephew and writing partner) remembered, the family often gathered around the table in the evening to read Dickens: each family member being given a speaking role to recite.[69] Further, Constanduros's rendering of the Cockney accent also seems to be influenced by the literary rendering of Cockney that Dickens, Mayhew and Thackeray employed in their novels. For instance, her consistent use of 'nothink' as a substitute for 'nothing' in her working-class sketches is suggestive of nineteenth-century literary Cockney with which middle-class BBC listeners would have been familiar.[70] A resident of Walworth in the 1930s later remembered 'nothing' pronounced as 'nofink' when he grew up.[71] Dialectologist William Matthews did note the tendency to replace 'f' or 'v' with 'th' in his 1938 work *Cockney Past and Present*, yet he conceded that 'this habit is not consistent'.[72] Further, Matthews's examination of Cockney in the 1930s was based on experience of the dialect in North London and, therefore, since the accent Constanduros performed was South London Cockney, it is difficult to be certain of its authenticity.[73] Nonetheless, John Watt thought Constanduros's 'understanding of Cockney ways and turns of phrase unsurpassed',[74] and T.H. Pear pointed out that hers was 'generally believed' to be an excellent rendering of the Walworth accent.[75] Most certainly, Constanduros spent time in Walworth, and her accent and turns of phrase likely were a hybrid of middle-class sensibility and working-class contact.

While intended to create a sympathetic and authentic image of the working classes, Constanduros's humour was nonetheless deeply ambivalent: shaded as it was by classed cross-dressing and paternalism. The Tilling family were known for their beneficence towards employees: none of Tilling's drivers, for instance, came out in the rancorous 1891 bus strike, and her grandfather was often cited as the model employer, so it is possible that this same paternalism factored into Mabel's relations with and depictions of the working classes.[76]

Growing up solidly upper middle class, Constanduros remembered fondly servants who not only cared for and nurtured her as a child but also became close friends.[77] Ellen, whose 'people had lived with ours for about a hundred years', seemed a kindred spirit who shared and encouraged Mabel's youthful exuberance for acting by learning and reciting 'long poems by heart … our favourite being a dreadful piece of mawkishness called "Tracy de Vore and Hubert Gray", from the poetical works of Eliza Cook'.[78] This fifteen-page gothic revival 'piece of mawkishness' may well underscore Constanduros's feeling that her relationship with Ellen was one that transcended the boundaries of class: in the tale young Tracy, a baron's heir, and Hubert, the herdsman's son, are so close that when Tracy becomes ill and dies, so too does Hubert.[79]

But while childhood enthusiasm may well have overcome class, Denis Constanduros remembered in his 1948 biography of Mabel's father how very different Mabel and Ellen's worlds really were. In the chapter significantly entitled 'Upstairs/Downstairs', Denis provides some insight into the inspiration for Mabel's working-class characters:

> To our generation the whole careful relationship of deceit and artificiality, of partial kindness and generosity on the one side and of partial devotion on the other seems so natural as to be almost unnoticed. It seemed quite normal for us that as soon as the door was closed behind them – or even before – we should repeat stories of their amusing mispronunciations ('Good enough for *Punch*, my dear!'), while we knew quite well that downstairs they were laughing at us and probably entertaining their friends at our expense.[80]

As Delap has argued, 'jokes at the expense of servants can be read as a form of disciplining mockery …. It was a useful means of establishing social distance and "place"'.[81] Though fraught with inequity and 'artificiality', relationships between servants and masters were nonetheless intimate, sometimes affectionate and often tempestuous, their lives intertwined in ways that on occasion upended the master/servant power structure.[82] While friendships forged in the nursery may have dissipated as children 'progressed downstairs',[83] Mabel always spoke fondly in her autobiographical writing of servants and her father's employees. Still, jokes and songs meant to entertain large audiences were meant to 'amuse and not to provoke'; therefore, Lucy Delap argues, 'the material context of their production can limit the meaning that can be read into them'.[84]

While often sympathetic, Buggins humour made liberal use of middlebrow 'knowingness'. Laughter in the Buggins sketches was reminiscent of the amusement middle-class readers of *Punch* enjoyed in their portrayals of servant mispronunciations and 'attempts to imitate middle-class speech and accent', as well as their 'desire for a social life, for contact with other workers, or for social activities such as reading literature or playing music'.[85] Constanduros's characters also display middle-class assumptions about the urban working-class: a hatred (or ignorance) of the countryside, a morbid and insatiable fascination with murder in the yellow press, and xenophobia. They also exhibit a laughable superstition of all things modern or scientific, as in the 1927 sketch entitled, 'Aunt Maria's Wireless'.

In this sketch, Mrs. Jenkins is initially superstitious of the newly installed radio that was purchased to convince Aunt Maria to live with her, in the hope that she might leave her inheritance to the Jenkinses when she died. At first, Mrs. Jenkins refuses to touch the set, because she thinks it will electrocute her. Mr. Jenkins believes his wife has been hoodwinked into buying a defective set because he cannot figure out how to turn it on. When he finally does, he puts on earphones and starts to converse with an unseen woman he hears over the wireless, throwing Mrs. Jenkins into fits of jealousy. However, she soon figures out the wireless, and the two enjoy some good old-fashioned Reithian entertainment: 'Sympathy in a Miner' (Symphony in A Minor). Upon hearing the title of the piece, Mrs. Jenkins exclaims, 'Pore things! I'm glad someone 'as sympathy for 'em. Always underground!'[86] The two sit entranced for hours, listening to various talk and music programmes. Thus distracted, their rich Aunt Maria chokes on a fish bone. Meanwhile, their competition for the inheritance, 'Emmer-leen', comes to the rescue, and Aunt Maria (and her money) goes away with her. Here we see several important elements of a middle-class, middlebrow and distinctly BBC humour. Like John Henry, Constanduros evokes wireless laughter by engaging with a radio audience knowledgeable with the technology. We also see some of Constanduros's brand of humour in the malapropism of the symphony – true to Reithian concerns, the working classes are depicted as being ignorant of classical music. Further, there is a critical laughter had at the expense of the Reithian mission of educating the working classes (can we *really* expect them to be trained up?). And finally, as the couple succumb to the attraction of the wireless, there is a criticism that both echoes Reithian concerns regarding lazy listeners and prefigures the mass appeal of the 'idiot-box', dramatized so brilliantly in *The Royle Family*.

As in the symphony, a further source of humour in Constanduros's working-class comedy is the perceived ignorance of the British literary canon, which would elicit the knowing laughter of the educated British middle class, and, crucially, outline significant barriers of entry into the middle-class ranks. Indeed, all of Constanduros's works are peppered with literary references from British and American classics. Names are drawn from literature, such as Mr. d'Arcy Fanshawe, with allusions to both Jane Austen and Nathaniel Hawthorne. Shakespearean references are perhaps her favourite, however, such as Mrs. Ogboddy's distortion of Ophelia's 'Rosemary for remembrance' as 'Rosemary for 'er membranes', a blunder which twists cultural intelligence into sauciness.[87] The quick-witted malapropisms that are peppered throughout Buggins humour are ideal wordplay for an aural medium, where 'words themselves are used to create humour'.[88] There are so many embedded references to classic literature, twists of phrases, puns and word play that it is clear that love of language rested at the heart of Constanduros's writing. For instance, one has to appreciate the logophile in Constanduros, who puns the word 'winkles' (or cockles) by playing on the common cockle reference as well as the lesser-known slang for bayonet, 'winkle-pin', which also nudges one to make a rather blue leap; and let's face it, the word 'winkle' in and of itself is quite funny.[89]

Deep ambivalence resides at the heart of Buggins humour. Middle-class stereotypes of the working classes and superior, middlebrow laughter is embedded in a paternalistic sympathy for the difficulties of their lives. Of course, cultural knowingness was not the sole province of the upper and middle classes and the very fact that the BBC prided itself on developing such cultural awareness in working-class listeners suggests further cross-class appreciation, rendering the working-class characters in Constanduros's sketches outsiders beyond a culturally knowledgeable working-class elite. While her sketches may have appealed to a largely middle-class audience, Constanduros's humour was multivalent, and the 'conspiracies of meaning' embedded in her cultural references and malapropisms potentially cut across class.[90] Thus, as Bush-Bailey has observed, while such characterizations and humour might 'simply re-inscribe conservative class values', they also have the potential to 'disturb and re-evaluate the old categories of "them" and "us" that preoccupy the middle class in the ongoing project of establishing class position and defining the all-important hegemonic "we"'.[91]

3

Early BBC celebrity[1]

Negotiating morality, femininity and wireless celebrity

When the BBC made Constanduros a star in 1925, she also gained celebrity status as her voice became increasingly well known to audiences across the United Kingdom. Technological constraints of wireless in the mid-1920s meant that audiences initially became familiar with Constanduros on regional stations, as she travelled widely across the country on broadcasting tours; by the end of the decade, broadcasting tours had all but ceased, but Constanduros was by then a national celebrity. Wireless celebrity was an altogether new experience: distinct from the stars of the silver screen, early BBC radio stars had to learn to negotiate the meaning and nature of wireless celebrity. While Reithian puritanism and societal prescriptions prevailed upon the public performances of wireless celebrities, early BBC stars soon learned that the intimate address of wireless often made the boundaries between themselves and their audience maddeningly, and sometimes dangerously, porous.

Early radio celebrity

As only a handful of BBC documents relate specifically to Constanduros's career prior to 1935, an analysis of *Radio Times* and *Times* broadcast listings during the first decade of Constanduros's career is necessary to understand how her audience became familiar with her work in the first decade of her career; it also reveals the development of BBC programming during this period.[2] Due to the technical constraints of early radio transmission, as well as the edifice of BBC regional and national broadcasting, Constanduros was most often heard on provincial stations during the first three years of her career. While most of her solo broadcasts during this time were from 2LO, the London regional station, she became nationally known on 'broadcast tours' to regional stations in the Midlands, Wales, Scotland and Northern Ireland.[3] For instance, London heard Constanduros solo performances sixteen times in 1926, but she also appeared on 6BM (Bournemouth) four times, and went on a broadcast tour to stations at Newcastle, Aberdeen, Glasgow, Belfast, Birmingham, Cardiff and Plymouth in the summer. She appeared only once that year on 5XX (Daventry), the national station. With the creation of the Corporation in 1927, Constanduros received more national airtime, with several 2LO performances also going out on 5XX; but she continued to perform in the regions, including Bournemouth, 6LV (Liverpool) and 5WA (Cardiff) multiple times in the year. When appearing on these stations, she was often billed by herself, offering 'selections from her repertoire' several times across the broadcasting day, suggesting that she and her work were now familiar to audiences. Though sometimes appearing solo in the provinces, when on 2LO she was more often billed in a 'Variety' or 'Vaudeville' programme with other performers, or in revues or burlesques written by herself. Other early comedic performers like John Henry and Helena Millais had similar broadcast experiences to those sketched out here. It is clear, however, from an analysis of *Radio Times* listings, that by 1927 Constanduros's radio presence was steadily eclipsing theirs. This is most likely due to the fact that both Henry and Millais had begun to turn their backs on wireless in favour of the more lucrative music-hall circuit. In contrast, Constanduros remained committed to the BBC and expanded her radio audience beyond that of her comedic colleagues by becoming a regular on *Children's Hour* that year. Indeed, the 30 July 1927 listing for *Children's Hour* announced that Constanduros had become 'firmly established in the hearts of a host of listeners', polling second in the programme's request week.[4] According to the *Children's Hour* board meeting minutes in mid-1928, she had slipped somewhat: the Buggins family sketches now polled fourth out of twenty, behind 'Farmyard Stories with Noises', *Children's Hour* staff programmes, and 'The Dicky-Bird Hop' by Ronald Gourley. The same analysis stated that Constanduros was ranked seventh among eighteen of the most popular performers on the programme.[5] These rankings are impressive since Constanduros is listed in the *Radio Times* as having performed only nine times on the daily programme from mid-1927 to mid-1928, whereas acts ranked above hers were regulars on *Children's Hour*. Her appearances on the programme increased into the 1930s, and she would build a strong relationship with the programme and its staff over the course of her long radio career.

By 1928, regional broadcast tours ceased. New artists, like Doris and Elsie Waters, who debuted in 1927, are not listed in the *Radio Times* as making the rounds to regional stations like the more seasoned veterans of wireless comedy had in the past. Constanduros herself now broadcast more nationally, sixteen of seventeen 2LO performances being heard on 5XX, with some performances going out several times on the experimental 5GB station. She still performed beyond London, however, making multiple appearances on 6LV, 5PY (Plymouth), 2ZY (Manchester) and 5NG (Nottingham), but never in the back-to-back performances that were the hallmark of earlier broadcast tours. In 1929, she broadcast only four times on provincial stations; the rest of her twenty-six appearances for the year were broadcast on 5XX or 5GB.[6]

1929 was a pivotal year in the implementation of the BBC's 'regional scheme' and was marked by increased 'centralisation', whereby London incrementally took over both regional and national broadcasting.[7] Chief Engineer Peter Eckersley's plan of 'alternative' programmes saw older, low-wave stations dismantled under the Corporation and consolidated to 5GB, which would eventually become the regional programme in March 1930.[8] For instance, 5IT (Birmingham) was dismantled in August 1927, and its listeners moved to 5GB, though many 5GB programmes were produced in the Birmingham studio; 2LO was removed from service at the end of 1929.[9] Constanduros's 1930 appearances demonstrate this movement towards the national and regional structure, which became the main listening experience of the 1930s in Britain: after March, when the regional programme went on line, she appeared almost exclusively on regional or national programming. Some regional stations did persist into the 1930s, and Constanduros did perform on them; for instance, she appeared on Cardiff and Plymouth stations in 1931. Nonetheless, these broadcast to a much smaller audience than the regional programme out of London.[10]

From twenty-eight performances (across all stations) in her debut year of 1925, Constanduros's presence steadily increased to its height in 1928 at fifty-two total broadcast appearances. By 1930, however, that number was down to twenty-one, though it rebounded somewhat to twenty-six in 1931. This downward trend does not necessarily reflect a decrease in popularity; certainly, a 1932 *Radio Times* article declared Constanduros one of the most popular wireless celebrities.[11] Rather, centralization, policy decisions and the evolution of BBC attitudes towards light entertainment contributed to the diminishing number of Constanduros's appearances from 1929 onwards. The creation of the Revue and Vaudeville section of the productions department in 1930 and the establishment of the Variety department in 1933 signalled a more competitive atmosphere in the realm of light entertainment, with new and established talent as well as new programming ideas vying for airtime against well-known wireless acts. At the same time, the BBC often limited exposure of some of its most popular artists. Martin Dibbs argues that, 'despite requests from the public, the [Variety] Department's policy was to restrict engagement of the most popular artists in order that listeners would not tire of them'.[12]

BBC celebrity

In her autobiography, Constanduros remembered how early on in her career, fans 'crowded round the car … waving and shouting at [Michael Hogan and herself]', and once, the two were crushed by a crowd of fans and the police had to be called in to help.[13] Much of this attention was due to the aural nature of her celebrity: the Bugginses had 'caught the imagination of the listener', and many of her fans were so intimately familiar with her voice that they were naturally curious about her appearance.[14] A similar mystique grew up around BBC announcers, whom Reith initially required to remain anonymous and unseen in order to 'create a sense of the BBC's collective personality' in the minds of listeners.[15] But as Maggie Andrews has noted, 'The general public was … fascinated with the personal and intimate details of those who worked in both Broadcasting House and Alexandra Palace.'[16] The nature of wireless, in which performers and announcers adopted a conversational tone to address people in their homes, contributed to a desire to better know these radio companions.[17] This familiarity imbued BBC celebrity with an aura of ordinariness that in many ways was distinct from the celebrity of film stars.

The 1930s fan magazine, *Radio Pictorial*, capitalized on the curiosity of listeners who were 'intrigued by the disembodied voices which came floating into their rooms' and contributed to the development of the celebrity status of wireless performers and staffers.[18] The pilot numbers of the magazine addressed the audience desire to simply connect the voice of their favourite radio personality with a face. These initial issues consisted of little more than a scattering of small publicity photographs of several radio performers and a brief sketch of upcoming programmes; the second number of the magazine is dominated by a full-page black-and-white headshot of Constanduros, with no supporting interview or narrative.[19]

By the time of its national launch in January 1934, *Radio Pictorial* had evolved into a full-length colour fan magazine in which readers could enjoy intimate access to BBC artists and staffers through interviews and portraits of BBC personalities at home, as well as insider views of the BBC, complimented, of course, by loads of celebrity pictures. The pictorial nature of the magazine

Figure 1 Photo of Mabel Constanduros. Publicity photos of radio artist in character helped audiences connect the voice with a face. These photos also aided audience imagination as they listened in. Photo credit: BBC.

also underscores the ongoing feminization of wireless during this period. Julia Taylor notes contemporary anxieties about the feminization of the media, which commentators believed led to the 'creeping spread of graphics and illustrations in newspapers'. This trend was thought to be particularly emasculating: one contemporary worried that 'when men think pictorially they unsex themselves'.[20]

The first national number of *Radio Pictorial* promised their readers that the magazine would be

> full of personalities and full of pictures; on every page something about the people who work behind the microphone. A great invisible world that talks to you from countless stations, a world that has existed, so far, for your ears alone – is now made visible for your eyes to dwell upon and to add pleasure to your listening.[21]

Moving away from the amateur wireless magazines of the 1920s that focused on the technology and made celebrities of engineers, *Radio Pictorial* shifted to the 'social side of broadcasting' and promised to complement the aural imaginations of countless listeners, feeding their desire to get to know the personalities that informed and entertained them by the hearthside.[22] Tim Crook has argued that images and film of radio artists and announcers can impact the imaginative process of listening; thus photographs from *Radio Pictorial* and other fan magazines intermingled with the purely fictionalized representations conjured in listeners' 'theatre of the mind'.[23] At the same time, the magazine sought to enhance the sensuality and enjoyment of the listening experience by providing the means by which fans might gaze upon their favourite radio companions as they listened in.

From the 1930s onwards, fan magazines began to depict film stars in a casual manner, playing in the back garden with family or enjoying a 'frugal breakfast' in an ordinary kitchenette. Embedded in these articles is a 'ubiquitous narrative principle of the "inside" journey into the "real lives" of celebrities, lives much like the readers'.[24] *Radio Pictorial* offered its readers a similar image of radio personalities: the magazine often ran series on BBC stars' homes and families that gave readers access to the 'inside' lives of celebrities, which also underscored and promoted a sense of ordinariness. Nonetheless, radio and television celebrity differs considerably from that of film stars, who are 'marked by their "specialness", not only in terms of their talent, but also because they are more attractive, more interesting, more exciting than us'.[25] The argument that Brett Mills has made in regards to television stars applies equally to radio stars: 'the success of many people who appear on television rests on their being "like us", and the relationship we have with them is one quite different to that for film stars.'[26] Indeed, television and radio artists are often called on to perform more roles that depict ordinary characters than do film actors.[27]

As has been discussed previously, radio and television method is necessarily intimate and domestic, and as the BBC gradually began to appreciate the domestic setting of their audience, announcers 'develop[ed] a "conversational" rather than "declamatory" tone [that was] intimate rather than intimidating'.[28] At the same time, broadcasting enables the cultivation of audience familiarity with celebrities over a long period of time through a process of '"routinization" which makes their performance of personality familiar to the audience'.[29] Additionally, BBC artists and announcers actively performed ordinariness in the public eye, both on and beyond the microphone.

Through interviews, autobiographical writing and radio talks, Constanduros adopted a tone of 'pseudo intimacy and personalization' consistent with numerous BBC radio celebrities who became an extension of listeners' own family or social circle.[30] Constanduros was careful to foster a sense of approachability and ordinariness throughout her autobiographical narratives, a style indicative of BBC radio celebrity, which David Cardiff notes, 'flattered [the audience] with the illusion of direct, informal contact'.[31] *Radio Times* numbers often featured articles that facilitated this relationship between BBC personalities and readers. Articles such as 'Famous Broadcasters Give Their Views on the Best Way to Spend Bank Holiday' or 'Their Memories of Home' included brief (approximately 100–250 word) personalized recollections or opinions written by BBC celebrities in a chatty, conversational manner meant to underscore intimacy and ordinariness. For instance, Constanduros's memories of home elicited late-Victorian gas-lit nurseries and Mother, while her ideal Bank Holiday included enjoying time with friends and finishing the evening 'peacefully in the garden to watch the moon rise'. Famous disc jockey Christopher Stone wanted nothing more than to spend time alone, reading books and playing with the children on his Bank Holiday. Other celebrities used these articles as opportunities to perform their usual character roles or work out new material: Arthur Askey's response to the memories of home question was a comic piece about the interference of the telephone. 'Home Sweet Home – except for the "phone!". That doesn't quite rhyme', he wrote, 'but it's so true. Do you know playmates … oh, excuse me – I'm wanted on the "phone."'[32]

The experience of Tommy Handley, star of the wildly popular 1940s programme *ITMA*, underscores both the construction of BBC celebrity ordinariness and the implications of it. By the time *ITMA* went on air, Handley was an established and well-known star who had been on radio for nearly twenty years; yet it was not until several years into the hit radio show that he felt compelled to ask for a private telephone line because of the number of prank callers ringing up with lines from his hit show: after a particularly good episode of *ITMA*, Handley could receive up to fifty or sixty phone calls a night.[33] Constanduros also mentions receiving phone calls from fans in her autobiography.[34] Even though telephone ownership in the United Kingdom at this time was largely contained to the upper and middle classes, and even at that was not widespread, it was nonetheless a possible means of connecting with BBC celebrities, and it certainly seems as though many availed themselves of this opportunity.[35] Thus, boundaries between public and BBC radio celebrity in the early years could be porous: the telephone-owning public had direct access to Handley and other BBC celebrities via private telephone, as they would any of their friends or family.

The intimate and informal relationship that existed between audience and radio celebrity can also be seen in fan letters. Early in her career, Constanduros recalled receiving 'letters of appreciation' or 'my applause by post', which offered such praise as '"Your turn last night was immense".... "Thank you for your clever and intensely amusing impersonations" [and] "I never laughed so heartily in my life."'[36] Soon, she remembered, the letters became 'more personal': in addition to letters of 'applause', she received requests from people hoping she would help them break into radio, photographs of men interested in marriage and numerous 'begging letters' from individuals with hard-luck stories, to whom she often sent money because she was 'distressed' by their situations – until a consultation with the Charity Organisation Society informed her that some were scam artists.[37] Celebrity can make stars easy targets for con artists, but the intimate, relational performance of BBC celebrity might work both ways: adding to the celebrity's sense of being personally connected and obligated to their listeners.

Early BBC celebrities had to learn to negotiate boundaries and construct walls to shield them from the public in order to preserve both privacy and safety. The loss of privacy could be shocking for early BBC celebrities, all the more so because it was so new and unexpected.[38]

While they might cultivate a sense of familiarity and accessibility, celebrities also had to learn to be guarded in their interactions with the public. In *Shreds and Patches*, Constanduros confides that early on in her career, she gave her address to an admirer who later subsequently showed up at her residence, and over the course of a fearful two hours, threatened to strangle her. This experience became part of Constanduros's story of fame and its consequences, told multiple times over the course of her career. In this version of the story, she was alone and saved only by an insistent taxi driver demanding his fare. In an earlier telling of the story in *Radio Pictorial*, Constanduros does not give out her address: the stalker simply shows up at the door and is let in by a maid, but when her young son Michael comes home, the maid asks the taxi driver for help in defusing the situation.[39] As is discussed later, the *Shreds and Patches* version is consonant with an autobiographical performance meant to highlight her maternal qualities, and thus necessitates the absence of Michael in a precarious situation brought on by her celebrity (and naiveté). The absence of Bina, her housekeeper, increases the dramatic effect of the story.[40]

Constanduros's autobiographical performances demonstrate the 'combination of familiarity and extraordinariness' that rests at the heart of celebrity.[41] While often steeped in a sense of ordinariness, her narrative was balanced by examples meant to mark out her talent and experience as something altogether *out* of the ordinary. In autobiographical writing and radio talks, Constanduros often discussed her Victorian childhood, evoking happy memories of a close-knit family and a golden age of London city life filled with colourful costers and omnibuses. In these nostalgic walks through the past, Constanduros invited audiences to collectively remember and experience the past with her and thus 'operated as a celebrity, personifying something of [her] time which resonated with audiences'.[42] On the other hand, recollections about fan behaviour, name-dropping of other well-known celebrities as intimate friends and behind-the-scenes access to the BBC invited audiences into an exotic world that otherwise they might never experience.

Performing celebrity: Morality and femininity

BBC radio celebrity during the Reithian period often demanded the strict appearance of moral uprightness. Well-established celebrities, fan favourites and staffers could be easily sacked or rested for moral transgression. The vexed question of artist morality was broached early on when Daisy Kennedy, a skilled and popular violinist, divorced in 1924.

Kennedy was married to the highly acclaimed concert pianist, Benno Moiseiwitsch, but in 1924 she left Moiseiwitsch for writer J. D. Drinkwater.[43] At this time, adultery was the only allowable offence for divorce in Britain: the 1857 Matrimonial Causes acts established the right for husbands to dissolve marriage on the grounds of adultery, while the 1923 Act gave wives the same right.[44] After returning from a tour of the United States in January 1924, Moiseiwitsch found an empty house and a letter imploring him to petition for divorce; Kennedy and Drinkwater used the 'Brighton quickie' method to provide evidence of Kennedy's adultery and ensure a successful case. The commonly employed 'quickie' was described in A. P. Herbert's 1934 fictional tale, *Holy Deadlock*, a novel which supported divorce reform that allowed 'divorce by consent', as the following:

> As a rule, the gentleman takes the lady to a hotel – Brighton or some such place – enters her in the book as his wife – shares a room with her, and sends the bill to his wife. The wife's agents cause inquiries to be made, and eventually they find the chambermaid who brought the guilty couple their morning tea.[45]

In this case, it was Moiseiwitsch's agents who made inquiries, and a waiter who gave evidence of Kennedy's presence with Drinkwater at the hotel.[46]

Kennedy's contract with the BBC had recently expired, and its renewal was briefly held up while Reith and other BBC executives wrestled with the problem of exposed indiscretions in the private lives of its artists. Organizer of Programmes Cecil Lewis wrote to the Controller (Carpendale): 'The Managing Director [Reith] wishes me to bring to your notice the question of whether artists, who are in the public eye, should be allowed to broadcast from our Stations at a time when some incident in their private lives is being drawn attention to in the press.' Lewis continued that Reith, 'inclines to the view that we should not allow private circumstances to make any difference in this case, but he admits that this is opportunism and says that if we had a number of other very fine violinists he would not favour a renewal'. Lewis himself felt that private matters should not undermine the career of someone in the public eye, unless that person's actions elicited 'general odium from their fellow creatures'.[47] In the event, her contract was set aside and she was rested. Peter Black, in his 1972 memoirs of the BBC, remembered Reith having said that she was taken off air 'because we can't have a divorced woman performing'.[48]

Yet, this exchange suggests a situation more complex than the question of simply putting a divorcee over the air. If Reith was adamantly opposed to divorcees, Kennedy's BBC career should have ended in 1924. Nonetheless, after a brief rest of no more than five months, Kennedy continued to perform regularly on the BBC well into the 1930s.[49] This internal memo thus demonstrates a pragmatic ambivalence towards moral transgression not only on Reith's part, but also on the part of other BBC staffers like Lewis, which unsettles the paragon of respectability so often ascribed to Reith and his BBC.[50] Certainly it seemed as if artists (especially the talented ones) might have a chance to escape the sack for impropriety. Staffers, however, were held to higher standards – at least in public. In his 1948 autobiography, Maurice Gorham was highly critical of his time at the BBC and exposed the early BBC days as decidedly less than the paragons of morality; he remembered:

> People dressed respectably but they didn't behave respectably .... I never knew an office where sex played so large a part, where so many people lived with their secretaries, where the hunters and the hunted were so conspicuous as they went about their sport. And there was another side to it, too, which the BBC of the late-twenties shared with the theatre, the ballet, and the book business. It was not always the men who did not chase secretaries who were the most moral.[51]

The ambivalence described in the case of Daisy Kennedy was problematic for contemporaries who perceived hypocrisy at the heart of BBC policy. Radio critic Sydney Mosley believed that since the BBC was a public institution, it had an obligation to maintain high moral standards. In his 1935 tract, *Broadcasting in Our Time*, he argued,

> Here is a great monopoly controlling the most formidable instrument for good or ill. Are we not entitled to demand that the men that wield this power should be men of the highest possible principles and of unsullied reputation? The Corporation professes this ... faith, and, indeed, any 'public' scandal, even if it be no more than a divorce, brings dismissal in its train. Sometimes this has been a real hardship which has evoked my sincere sympathy, but perhaps it is better for the Corporation to err on the strict side, *providing it is consistent in its treatment of delinquents – which it is not.*[52]

Perhaps when Mosley wrote this, he had in mind the case of Chief Engineer Peter Eckersley. By the late 1920s, Eckersley was more than a staffer – he was a celebrity. Eckersley cultivated an armchair familiarity with the public similar to that discussed earlier, often explaining the complex technology of broadcasting in understandable terms for the British public, and radio magazines in the 1920s treated him, and other engineers who conjured voice out of the air, as star material. In 1929, at the height of the BBC's execution of Eckersley's Regional Scheme, the

Chief Engineer was forced to resign his post due to his being a co-respondent in a divorce case involving the wife of a staffer in the Music Department.[53] Despite Eckersley's importance to the organization, he was sacked, while Kennedy, who was similarly implicated in her divorce case, saw little damage to her BBC career. What looked like hypocrisy to the outside world, however, might be sound practice in the eyes of the BBC. Briggs notes that in the latter half of the 1920s, Reith and the Board distinguished between 'BBC staff, who were not to seek the limelight, and the broadcasters from outside who were often to have thrust upon them notoriety if not fame', and staff were told explicitly to avoid 'personal publicity'. Briggs contends that this policy was integral to the 'institutionalization of the BBC'. While Eckersley was an 'exception to the rules' and was allowed to maintain his celebrity status, a staffer so closely tied to the Corporation could not ultimately withstand the publicity of indiscretion when it threatened to stain the institution's reputation.[54]

Though BBC artists may have been treated with less rigidity than BBC staffers, the circumstances surrounding the death of popular BBC comedian John Henry serve to underscore the perils of celebrity scandal. In May 1934, the British public were saddened to learn of Henry's suicide; more shocking, though, was the revelation of the scandalous double life that led to his demise. Only a few weeks beforehand, Henry's comedy partner, Gladys Horridge, died in childbirth. Horridge had lived with Henry for several years, and though the two never married, Henry swore at the inquest that she was his wife. However, when the news broke of Horridge's death, his estranged wife of nearly thirty years came forward to demand maintenance payments owed her. While he escaped prosecution for providing false evidence about Horridge, he was now required to appear at Somerset House to face charges pressed by his estranged wife. Fearful that the scandal had 'upset these stern moralists at Broadcasting House' and concerned that public exposure of his indiscretions would do irreparable harm to his career, a despondent Henry took his life.[55] The newspapers published extracts from the coroner's inquest and the six suicide letters Henry left behind.

The papers, even the normally staid *Times*, presented a tragic, cautionary tale of celebrity. Henry had lately been out of the public eye, the story ran: having tried his luck on the music-hall circuit and lost, he was desperately attempting a radio comeback, that, according to one paper quoting Eric Maschwitz, would have been 'magnificent'.[56] Indeed, Henry had just performed with Constanduros, Millais and other early radio favourites in a Variety show tracing 'The First Twelve Years of Radio' only weeks before. The press presented an ambivalent picture of Henry: on the one hand, publishing extracts from the suicide letters that demonized his estranged wife, who Henry said was bent on revenge and so mercilessly hounded him; at the same time, however, providing inquest testimony from his twenty-three-year-old son that Henry never paid maintenance. Finally, the press deepened the melodrama of Henry's failure to regain his radio celebrity with a star-crossed love story, publishing his final wish to be buried with Horridge and his confession of undying love for Horridge, stating that he could no longer live without her, so he was 'going to see his girl'.[57]

Outside the BBC, marital indiscretion in interwar Britain could potentially destroy an entertainer's career. According to Graves and Hodge, the nation experienced 'remarkable change' towards divorce in the 1920s, adopting the 'American view' that marriage was a 'social habit, rather than a sacrament'. To support their observation, they cite celebrity parties by famed playwright and composer Ivor Novello, where divorced couples and their new love interests socialized together, and quote statistics revealing a substantial increase in *decrees nisi* by 1928.[58] Nonetheless, such trends did not assuage the deep social disapprobation of divorce during the period: Graves and Hodge register the somewhat surprisingly (in their view) widespread and 'curiously old-fashioned ... puritanical attitude to divorce' during the Abdication Crisis of 1936.[59] Indeed, until 1952, divorce cases were heard alongside criminal proceedings in magistrates' courts, and details of the cases were often published in the press.[60] Those in the public eye were keenly aware of the damage such negative publicity might wreak upon their careers. Comedienne and actress, Beatrice Lillie remembered in her 1972 autobiography, 'Getting a divorce in London [was] comparable to signing your own death warrant.'[61]

Jessie Matthews was a young, up-and-coming film and stage star when her career was nearly shattered by an affair with actor Sonnie Hale, in which she was demonized for breaking up Hale and singer Evelyn Laye – the celebrity super-couple of the age. Matthews's first marriage ended in divorce due to her husband's adultery, but this, according to Matthews, caused little sensation at the time. The 1930 Laye-Hale divorce was altogether different. 'The hunt was on, the hounds were after me, and the whole British public was going to be in at the kill', Matthews remembered forty years later:

> It hit all the headlines. It was one of the first show business marriages to end in a show business type divorce. Even the Judge showed what a bit of drama can do for the Law Courts. He spared neither Sonnie or myself. We were the villains of the piece ... . Had we been criminals I don't think the Judge could have done a

better job. And we were just two young people who had fallen in love. That day in court marked me .... For days I sat at home and wept, quite sure that I was the most hated woman in England. I had done the unforgivable, taken the husband of the golden girl of song.[62]

To avoid the damage of such public scandal, celebrities often found themselves performing the public role they imagined was demanded of them. When Beatrice Lillie found herself trapped in a loveless marriage, she did not seek a divorce, but rather threw herself into her work – taking to the stage for months at a time both in the United Kingdom and the United States.[63]

Hermione Gingold, who endured a particularly devastating and abusive marriage to publisher Michael Joseph, largely escaped public opprobrium for her divorce from him. Yet, few knew the details of her abuse, the affair with Eric Maschwitz that ended that marriage, revelations about less-than-maternal feelings towards her children or the numerous abortions she sought, until the publication of her 1980s tell-all memoir.[64] Prior to the 1988 autobiography, Gingold published three autobiographical works from 1945 to 1963, all of which deviate from autobiographical narrative into fantastical surrealism that unsettles and misdirects the reader away from Gingold's life story when (we subsequently learn in the 1988 memoir) she lost her beloved fiancé in the First World War.[65] In 1988, we also learn from Gingold that both she and Eric Maschwitz consciously tried to avoid the public scandal of their own divorce. Not long into their marriage, Gingold learned of Maschwitz's serial philandering, but the two continued the charade of marriage for more than a decade, living in the same flat, but occupying separate bedrooms and living separate lives.[66] In another instance of autobiographical revisionism, a 1938 *Radio Pictorial* series about Gingold conveniently writes Michael Joseph and her wartime fiancé completely out of her life, replacing them both with the by then estranged Maschwitz.[67] Maschwitz and Gingold did not seek a divorce until 1941, nearly fifteen years after Gingold first learned of his indiscretions, and several years after Maschwitz departed the BBC.[68]

Gingold's literary gymnastics in her mid-century autobiographies were perhaps more extreme than other celebrities' attempts at shielding themselves from intense public gaze or public scandal, but many celebrities employed well-placed silences, misdirection, and amplification of socially acceptable values and norms as they carefully constructed their publicly consumed private lives. Though not inclined to the fantastical divergences from her life story such as

Gingold employed, Constanduros nonetheless misdirected her autobiographical readership through 'a shifting, patchwork narrative lacking chronological certainty' and filled with silences.[69] In *Shreds and Patches*, Constanduros adheres closely to traditional tropes of femininity, amplifying a socially acceptable image of femininity while simultaneously muting personal details that might disturb that image. The glare of celebrity complicated societal expectations of feminine humility, and domestic femininity, especially motherhood, sat uneasily with the demands of a successful radio career.

Constanduros navigated these tensions between femininity, career and celebrity by employing a chameleonic approach, shifting her performance according to audience expectations. Denis Constanduros remembered his aunt Pix (as she was known in family circles) as an expert at playing to her audience:

> Vivacious and sociable, her desire to please and astonish would often dismay her more literal-minded sister [Norah]. If the vicar called, [Norah] would be amazed to hear Pix deeply engaged in a discussion of the efficacy of prayer – though she never went with her husband to church – and the poor parson would go away convinced that he had made a convert. If the caller was a woman she would be suitably domestic. 'I always give my fruit cake a good hour and a half in a slow oven', she would say, regardless of the fact that she never went near the kitchen. 'Pix's cakes' became another family joke.[70]

Though illustrative of her social interactions, this comment is particularly instructive in understanding the ways in which Constanduros managed her career and celebrity. As has been seen in her development of radio technique, Constanduros was a consummate reader of her audience. In order to strengthen her celebrity status and promote her career, Constanduros constructed a life story to suit a desirable image of acceptable femininity, adhering to the expectations of her reading audience. While the book is steeped in tropes of traditional femininity, Constanduros nevertheless subtly pushed the edges of those boundaries to broaden the possibilities for women. This chameleonic performance suggests a useful strategy women might employ to successfully navigate the inherent gendered conflicts celebrity presented in the first half of the twentieth century.

Constanduros's career produced certain challenges to the construction of a believable image of acceptable femininity. Radio performance offered a relatively benign public stage, shrouding the female body from public view; but fame and ambition are problematic for women, to be met with humility in order to escape ridicule.[71] Further, broadcast tours in the early days of radio complicated the delicate balancing act of the working and career-minded mother. A gruelling travel schedule such as this might beg the question of Constanduros's commitment to family obligations. To address this concern, Constanduros dedicated a short chapter in *Shreds and Patches* to her faithful housekeeper, Bina, without whom she stated, 'I could never have a home'.[72] Constanduros further stressed that she waited to begin her career until Michael was eight and Bina was firmly enmeshed in the rhythms of their family life.[73] Bina was instrumental in providing domestic cover both at home and in Constanduros's autobiographical narrative; as Gilli Bush-Bailey has argued, 'Constanduros's professional success … was made possible by the presence of another woman taking the weight of the domestic duties'.[74]

Much of her autobiographical performance is moored to a safe, though undoubtedly authentic, maternal identity. It is clear both from the memoir and from correspondence with family, that Constanduros had a close relationship with her only son, Michael. In *Shreds and Patches*, Constanduros confided to her readers that her first son, Tony, died at the young age of four, and the grief of this loss, though not discussed in depth, is palpable in her autobiography.[75] In a brief biographical sketch of Constanduros, radio critic and personal friend Collie Knox revealed this 'deep sorrow … that sadness that has made her so golden hearted a woman'. Constanduros told Knox that 'it was a deep grief … . I was stunned. I shall never forget that misery. How I hated the sunshine. It seemed to mock me … . And the world seemed full of little girls and boys – strong, vigorous little boys – of four years old.'[76] Published one year after *Shreds and Patches*, Knox's brief sketch is the only deeply personal, public account of the grief Constanduros endured with the loss of her eldest son. Knox states that, after the death of Tony, it was only natural for her 'only surviving son Michael … to be the be-all and end-all of his mother's existence'.[77]

Threaded throughout the narrative, Constanduros makes clear that Michael's needs and desires always took precedence over her career ambitions. As with Bina, Constanduros also dedicates a chapter to Michael, which discusses his youthful relationships, career decisions, family life and wartime service in India. Additionally, the book includes reassuring images of mother and son, as well as a cosy family portrait of herself alongside Michael and his wife, Hilda. In case any doubts remained in the minds of her readers, she pointedly addressed the problem of working motherhood: 'I've always been torn between my work and my home … my career suffered, however, not my home or Michael … many

Figure 2 This Wills cigarette card image is illustrative of early BBC celebrity and adheres to Constanduros's constructed femininity. Photo Credit: Getty Images.

times I have rushed between a BBC rehearsal and transmission to say good night to him.'[78] This prioritization of motherhood over career and fame is a common trope that has changed little over time, for, as Brenda Weber has noted of recent female celebrities, 'the famous mother must make clear that if asked to choose between family and fame, she would give up her career instantly'.[79]

More problematic than motherhood, and nearly silent in the memoir, is Constanduros's marriage. Constanduros employed the common practice of married female entertainers by using the title 'Miss' in her artistic work, and thus, her marital status was publicly unclear. In stark contrast to her son, Athanasius's ('Ath') presence in Constanduros's life story is fragmented and uncertain.[80]

Throughout her patchwork memoir, Constanduros employed a disjointed narrative that shifts back and forth across time – a strategy that successfully deflects the reader's gaze away from too close an examination of her marriage. Further, Constanduros rarely offers much detail about her marriage or her husband. When Constanduros finally tells the reader explicitly of Ath's death, the fact does not stand on its own but rather is intertwined within her son's life story: in the book, Michael's struggles to find a suitable career are resolved by Ath's death, which left Michael the family insurance brokerage. Constanduros provides little insight into when or why Ath died, nor does she attach much emotion to his passing. Indeed, a casual reader could be forgiven for having thought Ath dead in the early stages of Constanduros's career. Statements throughout the memoir, such as '[the] carefree and happy life that we lived, Michael and I', which effectively write Ath out of her life before his death, are suggestive of a frayed marriage.[81] This active silencing of Ath is not fully apparent in the text, and careful chronological analysis of the book must be done to discern this narrative trick. Such analysis indicates that the period referred to in the aforementioned statement occurs fully five years *before* Athanasius's death. In choosing to emphasize a 'we' explicitly limited to her son, she effectively removed Ath from her day-to-day autobiographical life. Indeed, Collie Knox's biographical sketch further supports the narrative absence of Ath. In his discussion of Michael, Knox writes, 'Fate decreed she would have to bring [Michael] up alone'; Michael, however, was twenty-two when his father died.[82]

Intriguingly, given the memoir's focus on Constanduros's career, there is no mention that Ath performed in the Sutton Amateur Dramatics Club (SADC), the same club where Mabel cut her acting teeth. Indeed, the two often appeared together in productions from 1909, when they joined the club as a married couple, until the SADC went on hiatus at the outbreak of war in August 1914. Prior to the war, the two performed together in five productions and apart four times (the club regularly gave two performances a year).[83] Ath was also present at the 1920 meeting that re-established the SADC, and the two appeared together in several subsequent plays; they also appeared in two productions of *French Leave* with Lloyd's Amateur Dramatic Society (Ath was an insurance broker with Lloyds).[84]

Once Mabel became a star in 1925, the two never again performed on the same stage. Mabel's last performance with the SADC was in January 1925, only a few weeks before her BBC audition. Interestingly, Mabel's connections to the SADC seem to dissolve afterwards. Although the SADC excitedly and regularly touted Jack Warner, another of their members who climbed from amateur obscurity to radio fame in the late 1930s, no evidence exists of the Club recognizing Mabel's rise to stardom – until she was tapped to become an honorary vice-president of the Company (along with other star veterans of the SADC) during its Golden Jubilee year celebrations in 1952, well after Ath's death.[85]

After Mabel began her career on the BBC, Ath continued regular appearances with the SADC until his death in 1937, and reviews of his performances depict him as a solid actor who often ably filled secondary roles on stage. In 1932, reviewers commented favourably on his performance in the starring role as an unassuming, middle-class professional 'who carried murder in his heart'. 'He moved with convincing informality', the reviewer continued, 'from the delightful to the dreadful and nothing was finer than the manner in which in the final scene he gradually brought the direction of suspicion on himself.'[86] These reviews and internal SADC documents demonstrate that Ath was well liked and respected.

Upon hearing of her husband's sudden death in the summer of 1937, Mabel called off a performance in Eastbourne, but rather than disappoint her fellow actors, she continued with her scheduled Worthing performance the next day. 'Naturally in a case like this', she told the press, 'one feels that it will be an ordeal, but the possibility of loss of work for others has convinced me that I shall be doing the right thing if I put the profession before my private feelings.'[87] It is difficult to know if Constanduros's 'show must go on' attitude masked genuine grief at her husband's loss or whether it covered up the fractures of a broken marriage.

Marital strain seems to have fully developed by the time Mabel stepped into Savoy Hill for the first time in 1925. In the autobiography, Mabel wrote that 'nobody at home knew I was coming here', meaning that Ath was unaware of Mabel's venture to find employment outside the home. In *Shreds and Patches,* Constanduros noted Ath's horror at her use of a typewriter early in her radio career, as he worried that the neighbours might hear, and 'to his mind, such an occupation was beneath my dignity.'[88] Though 'those in the arts were largely immune from marriage bars', one might imagine that, in an age where married middle-class women with children were expected to remain in the home, a husband as concerned about the neighbours as Ath was would be infuriated by his wife working without his acquiescence.[89] Beyond thwarting societal conventions of feminine propriety, Constanduros also crossed the line from amateur to professional, with its taint of ambition and monetary compensation. Silence within the SADC about Mabel's success is intriguing, and is perhaps at least partially explained by Constanduros's flaunting of these classed and gendered expectations. Beyond the brief comments in *Shreds and Patches* and silences elsewhere in the record, Ath's resistance to her career might be indicated in two 1927 BBC contracts ostensibly witnessed by Ath in which his signature is curiously similar to Mabel's, suggesting perhaps Mabel forged his signature.[90]

Mabel tells her readers that she badly needed the money earned with the BBC in order to send Michael to preparatory school. Of course, Mabel's desire to adhere to societal expectations of femininity in *Shreds and Patches* would also require her to downplay professional ambition and amplify motherly concern in pursuing her career. Throughout her autobiography, Mabel constructs an ambivalent class position that is a hallmark of BBC radio celebrity.[91] In reality, Ath had a healthy income and Mabel's father had signed over nearly £2,000 in stock specifically in her name a year before her debut on radio.[92] Mabel's father made this transaction during the time in which Mabel was actively working with Elsie Fogerty; at the same time, Richard Tilling gave his daughter the stocks in the run up to the Law of Property Act (1925), which came into effect in 1926 and allowed married women to 'hold and dispose of their property, real and personal, on the same terms as a man'.[93] While it is impossible to know for certain why the stocks were given to Mabel, conflict within the home regarding Mabel's budding ambitions might have been a factor. An unpublished extract of *Shreds and Patches* provides a fascinating, if ultimately uncertain, insight into this potential conflict when she writes about her reasons for auditioning at the BBC: 'Even more than money I wanted an outlet for something, some power within me was clamouring to be set free.'[94] This could be interpreted simply as a creative impulse waiting to be unleashed, but it is nonetheless telling that Constanduros decided to leave this detail out of her published memoir. Further deepening the tension that might have existed over Mabel's desires and actions is the possibility that Ath, and those in the SADC and in Sutton more broadly, found it difficult to accept that a middle-aged, middle-class wife and mother chose to forge a career beyond the home, ultimately eclipsing her husband both financially and publicly. Certainly, Ray Strachey's study of women's work in the mid-1930s demonstrates that married women in Mabel's age group were *leaving* the workforce, and not entering it, in middle age.[95]

With Ath safely silenced in the memoir, and readers uncertain of the details of her marriage, Constanduros tells her readers that becoming a BBC star was financially empowering. By 1929, she had earned enough to rent her own flat in Kensington, which was, she confided, 'one of the thrills of my life'.[96] Constanduros argues that her work schedule necessitated living in London, but rather than sojourn to Sutton when not performing with the BBC, she bought a cottage in Bury, West Sussex (and thus more remote from London than Sutton), where she spent time with Michael during his school holidays. 'Greater even than the thrill of renting a flat was the joy of going for the first time into my very own house,' she remembered.[97] The financial independence that came with being a star permitted Mabel more freedom from the marriage and the marital home, and perhaps, with the (possible grudging) acquiescence of Ath who preferred his life in Sutton, where he could pursue his amateur stage acting and his hobby of beagling, avoided the scandal of divorce. Certainly, given the BBC's moral stance on divorce, it is highly likely that Constanduros would have preferred to avoid such a drastic move.

The extant evidence about the Constanduros marriage is intriguing, but ultimately silent as to the true nature of the marriage. Her nephew Denis, who collaborated on numerous projects with Mabel and who lived with his aunt and uncle during the First World War, felt there could not be two more incompatible personalities: she the life of the party and he a 'latter-day Mr. Pooter'.[98] Nonetheless, her daughter-in-law Hilda believed that although the marriage was strained, it was 'not unhappy'.[99] Incompatibility or irreconcilable differences, however, were not acceptable reasons for divorce until the 1969 Divorce Reform Act; indeed, before this act came into force, the courts were clear that divorce on the grounds of incompatibility alone was not allowable.[100] While it is uncertain whether she would have dissolved her own marriage if given the chance, Mabel did assist her sister Norah in securing a divorce from Ath's brother, Stephanos Constanduros, in 1933.[101] According to Denis, Steph, though charming and handsome, was never financially stable – forever chasing after money-making schemes and dreaming of riches, but when ventures failed playing the sympathy card with family and friends. Ath, the exact opposite of Steph, was perhaps too stable, and too dependable to divorce.

In *Shreds and Patches*, Constanduros wrote of the 'blessed shelter of the microphone'. Behind it, she stated, 'you can be whatever character you choose'.[102] In the public performance of her image, Constanduros played the chameleon: acting according to others' expectations. She, like other early BBC celebrities, cultivated an approachability and ordinariness aligned with the domestic medium in which she worked. At the same time, feminine celebrity required her to adhere to prevailing prescriptions regarding femininity and amplify aspects of an acceptable, if genuine, maternal identity, while simultaneously obscuring professional ambitions and the details of a strained marriage.

4

Variety and beyond

Evolving and cultivating career, 1930–9

In her history of BBC women staffers, Kate Murphy observes that the early BBC offered women 'unique opportunities' to find rewarding and challenging work, with possibilities for promotion into influential and well-paying positions.[1] Like many of the original BBC staffers, both male and female, Mabel Constanduros thrived upon the lack of structure in the inchoate BBC of the 1920s and the early 1930s. Constanduros took advantage of the flexibility of these early years, building her radio celebrity by experimenting with and developing an understanding of both the aural medium and her audience. Further, in the creation of the comedic family, Constanduros carved out a niche, which made her recognizable among a field of already-established radio comics. As will be seen, Constanduros was astute at continually evolving over the course of what would become a long career on radio.

The 1930s were particularly instrumental in this evolution of her career, as she learned to negotiate the boundaries of celebrity and also how to exploit it by branching out of radio into other media ventures where she capitalized on name recognition. In contrast to many other artists who became nationally famous on the BBC, she never abandoned radio; indeed, most of her outside endeavours remained intimately tied to her radio work in ways that enhanced her BBC presence. The 1930s were equally critical in the evolution of the BBC, especially in regards to its stance on light entertainment. When Constanduros began her career in the 1920s, the BBC spent little time or money on light entertainment; but increasing competition from Continental commercial stations in the early 1930s demanded the BBC's attention and action, or they risked 'broadcasting into a void'.[2]

The evolution of BBC Variety

Despite Reith's suspicion of popular entertainment, developments in the late 1920s and the early 1930s forced the BBC to evolve its stance on light entertainment. Listeners, radio critics and wireless manufacturers alike pressed the BBC for more variety entertainment. Asa Brigg's analysis of programming in the first two years of the Corporation indicate that on average, the listener was offered light entertainment only three to four hours *a week*, so it is perhaps not surprising that in 1927, the *Daily Mail* published a poll demonstrating that readers preferred variety hours to any other form of broadcast on the BBC.[3] At the same time, the Radio Manufacturer Association demanded that the BBC 'lighten its programme' to make it easier to sell more sets.[4] As LeMathieu has noted, the BBC suffered a great deal from 'the continuing tension within the BBC between giving the public "what it ought to have", and yet not ignoring "what it wanted"'.[5] Further pressures from Continental commercial stations and the British entertainment industry, as well as fears of the increasing Americanization of British entertainment, forced the BBC to pay more attention to the public's programming desires.

The BBC faced its first substantive competition in October 1931 when Radio Normandie, which could reliably reach listeners across the entire south coast of England, began offering a commercial gramophone programme after the BBC ended its Sunday transmissions.[6] But the establishment of Radio Luxembourg constituted a far graver threat to the BBC's grip on the nation's listeners. Luxembourg's potential broadcasting reach far eclipsed that of Radio Normandie, and BBC executives 'fought to contain Radio Luxembourg within national borders or at least force it to stop broadcasting in "foreign" languages'.[7] Despite these efforts, Radio Luxembourg began English-language broadcasting in March 1933.[8] These commercial stations offered popular American-style entertainment that the BBC tried to avoid.

The threat of Americanization was another impetus that forced the BBC to rethink its popular offerings. As early as 1929, Director of Outside Broadcasting Gerald Cock sounded the alarm about increasing American influence in British entertainment. Specifically, Cock worried over what he called the '"trans-Atlantic octopus" … with its tendencies towards merger and acquisition of music publishing, record labels and film studios'.[9] The fear was that American entertainment conglomerates might contract quality British artists and thereby, Cock argued, 'severely limit our programme material', signalling 'the end of the BBC as an independent organization and the advent of competitive and American-influenced broadcasting'.[10] Thus, Martin Dibbs argues, concerns that American artists and programmes might 'eventually swamp Britain's distinctive cultural character if left unchecked' led to the BBC 'assum[ing] the unofficial guardianship of British popular culture and devised strategies to mitigate the situation'.[11]

Against this backdrop of emergent commercial broadcasting from the Continent and fears of Americanization, the BBC's approach to light entertainment became more responsive to the public's wishes for more variety programming. As part of a major restructuring in 1930, a 'Revue and Vaudeville Section' of the Productions department was established, with Val Gielgud as director of productions and John Watt at the head of Revue and Vaudeville. Under the new section, a 'coherent entertainment policy began to emerge'.[12] The section deepened the commitment of the Corporation to provide light entertainment, producing in-house variety programming and initiating new, and wildly popular, variety series such as John Watts's *Songs from the Shows* (1931), *Music Hall* (1932) and *Kentucky Minstrels* (1933).[13] Such efforts further underscored the BBC's concern to safeguard British culture by producing high-quality, popular, home-grown entertainment.[14]

The Corporation went further when it established the Variety department in 1933 under the direction of the 'debonair' Eric Maschwitz.[15] Maschwitz came to the BBC in 1926 after running into Lance Sieveking; within a year, the once penniless Maschwitz catapulted from assistant director of outside broadcasting to managing editor of the *Radio Times* and, finally, replaced the first editor of the publication, Walter Fuller, upon his death in 1927.[16] Maschwitz breathed vivacious life into the Variety department from 1933 to 1937, in what was considered the 'Romantic era' of Variety, according to *These Radio Times*, a 1951 nostalgia programme.[17] During his tenure on the *Radio Times*, Maschwitz strongly advocated the development of light entertainment on the BBC, and as Head of Variety, he introduced numerous innovations to British broadcasting. Under his leadership, the department quickly grew in staff, creative freedom and power.[18]

Maschwitz was under considerable pressure to deliver quality popular entertainment due to an ongoing feud with George Black of the General Theatres Corporation (GTC), who reinstated the age-old artist broadcast ban in 1931.[19] In an effort to increase GTC's influence, Black offered use of its artists if the BBC agreed to pay an annual fee of £30,000. While a similar agreement existed for serious music and opera, which made the BBC a significant 'patron of a minority art', acceptance of Black's proposal would mean commercial control of BBC popular entertainment.[20] As David Cardiff has argued, this constituted a challenge to the BBC to prove that they could compete with commercial interests by providing quality entertainment programming.[21] This dispute thus forced Maschwitz to search out talent elsewhere, telling radio critic Sydney Moseley that he intended to 'comb London and the provinces for talent'.[22] True to his word, the Variety department discovered and promoted a raft of new radio talent in the early in 1930s, with humour that translated well over an aural medium, bringing on such acts as Jeanne De Casalis, Beryl Orde, Gillie Potter and Ronald Frankau.[23] He also tapped concert party artists, who were not only cheaper than variety artists but, since they performed only during holidays at seaside reports, also enthusiastic about broadcasting as it constituted an opportunity for year-round employment.[24] Finally, Maschwitz orchestrated the Variety department's move out of the stuffy confines of Broadcasting House and across the street to gain more studio space and establish the BBC Theatre at St. George's Hall.[25]

Faced with what Maschwitz later called a 'seemingly vast and empty schedule', Variety produced a number of original plays that could compete with contemporary stage successes, and Variety staffers brainstormed and experimented with numerous new programme ideas.[26] From this impetus to fill the schedule, Maschwitz and his team developed the wildly popular *In Town Tonight* and a popular light music programme, *Café Collette*, designed to counter the influence of American jazz by offering Continental alternatives.[27]

For nearly the first fifteen years of the BBC's existence, BBC audiences had to scour the schedules to find their favourite comedic performers and characters: comedic acts, like the Bugginses, were spread out across the broadcasting schedule either in solo spots or intermittently in regularly scheduled Variety programmes. Under Maschwitz's direction, however, the BBC began to develop the concept of serializing comedy. American broadcasting had long relied on the series format to ensure long-term advertiser dollars, but the BBC was reluctant to standardize their schedules through the use of such series, both because of its association with American broadcasting and for fear of encouraging laziness in its listeners. Nonetheless, these series did offer some benefit to the BBC in that they were cheap to produce and provided an efficient means through which writers and performers could develop characters and situations. Serialization was attractive to performers because it meant the promise of a long-term contract (something offered on Continental stations) and the potential increase in popular interest audiences became more familiar with them over time.[28]

The Strange Adventures of Mr. Penny: The copyright saga of the first BBC sitcom

BBC radio's first serialized situation comedy was *The Strange Adventures of Mr. Penny*. The programme initially aired in November 1936 and ran for two seasons before its main writer sold it to Radio Luxembourg, despite much protest by the Variety department. BBC audiences could expect to hear the first season, which consisted of six fifteen-minute episodes, every Saturday night at 8 pm. The second season of twelve episodes ran Mondays at 7.45 pm from April through June 1937, usually directly following the popular variety programme, *Monday Night at Seven*.[29]

Every week, the audience was treated to some misadventure had by the BBC's own Little Man: the most ordinary of low-level civil servants, Mr. Penny (played by Richard Goolden), who lived at 14 Acacia Villas in Tooting Bec with his wife (Doris Gilmore). Action always began in the home, with Mrs. Penny rushing her husband off to work with orders to run errands on his way home or to remember an engagement in the evening. Once out of the house, the fun commenced with Penny bumbling his way into danger with international criminals or misunderstandings with the law. Ultimately, through innocence or misinterpretation of motive or situation, Penny would courageously disarm the situation and win the day, totally oblivious of his heroism. Throughout, Penny, meticulous, proper and pedantic, is the BBC's version of Strube's incorruptible (and loveable) ordinary little man of the 1930s.

Most episodes in both BBC seasons follow a similar plot as the pilot episode. In the pilot, Mr. Penny, a by-the-book accountant for the London Transport Board, was ordered to collect a fare from an errant passenger who turns out to be an international crime boss. Eager to demonstrate the importance of his errand, Penny shows up at the criminal's hideout and declares that he is there 'on behalf of His Majesty's Government'. A mysterious woman lurking in the shadows asks if he's with 'the service'. When he responds that he is, the woman, who is a British secret agent, takes him for the undercover agent she's been expecting, hands him a revolver and vanishes. When the crime boss meets Penny, he tries to tempt him first with a beautiful woman (to whom Penny responds with 'excessive embarrassment', as noted in the stage direction) and then offers him £2,000, then £5,000, and finally £10,000. Each time, Penny steadfastly refuses the bribe and finally names his price: 4 p for the bus fare owed. Special branch shows up at precisely that moment to apprehend the bewildered criminal and congratulate Penny for his bravery. A flustered Penny continues to press for the four pence fare until the inspector finally hands him the fare. When Penny returns home at the end of the show, his wife asks after his day, to which he responds flatly, 'very dull'.[30]

At the end of the first season, a Christmas episode, Mr. Penny is approached in Marble Arch Park by a woman who leaves an infant in his care. The childless Pennys end up adopting the baby (after numerous misunderstandings were cleared up, of course), and though misadventures similar to the pilot continue to occur at work and around London in the second season, several episodes develop of the family side of the Pennys.[31]

In the 1960s, the main writer of the show, Maurice Moiseiwitsch, remembered feeling stunned by the warm audience response to his 'small plays' about Penny, which made him 'a success overnight'.[32] This sentiment, however, shrouds the controversy that swirled around the series as Moiseiwitsch attempted to cash in on his BBC success after its second season ended in 1937. In July, Moiseiwitsch floated the idea of putting Penny on the silver screen, to which the BBC responded that they required 20 per cent of the fee given to Moiseiwitsch by the film company.[33] When, two months later, the BBC learned that Moiseiwitsch had 'supervised and arranged for the recording' of the BBC's pilot episode of *Mr. Penny* at Columbia Studios, a legal battle erupted between the BBC and Moiseiwitsch over copyright and intellectual property, which underscores the fluidity of the creative production of programmes on the early BBC and the potential copyright challenges that such methods presented to the BBC.

Max Kester, the producer of the series, argued that Moiseiwitsch had no right to the Penny name or the series, contending that much of the series was actually envisioned, developed and written by himself and others in the Variety department. According to Kester, Moiseiwitsch presented several plots in the fall of 1936 with a central character named Penny, but the dialogue was unsuitable for broadcasting and the characterization of Penny uninteresting. As such, Kester asserted that the Penny that BBC audiences knew and loved was essentially a creation of BBC Variety Staff. 'Mr. Penny', he wrote to Director of Variety Eric Maschwitz, 'was entirely conceived in this office – his liking for long words and pedantic phrases; his guileless trust; his inability to see a joke or when his leg was being pulled; his paper cuffs; his methodical business methods; his lack of imagination.'³⁴ Further, Kester stated that it was his idea to create a BBC version of Strube's cartoon Little Man and argued that he and other Variety staffers wrote much of the dialogue for the first seven episodes. Hallmark elements of *Mr. Penny*, such as the opening domestic sequence and the audible totting up of figures for fades between office scenes, were also inventions of the Variety department. Finally, it was Kester's idea to develop the domestic side of Penny in the second series. Everyone was in agreement, however, that Moiseiwitsch had penned the final eleven episodes.³⁵

Since the 1920s, Max Kester had been billed as having written and/or produced several variety programmes; however, as has been seen in the case of *Mr. Penny*, the process by which the BBC accepted new authors and new materials was fluid. Pressured to provide more popular entertainment, BBC Variety was constantly on the lookout for new talent and new writers. Indeed, Kester published a manual offering guidance to interested authors on *Writing for the BBC* in 1937. In the book, Kester estimated that only one out of four hundred scripts received by his department were suitable for broadcasting.³⁶ As such, Kester offered numerous tips on how to write broadcast-worthy entertainment. Eager to minimize the flood of unacceptable full-length scripts jamming the Variety department's mailbox, the BBC asked writers to submit ideas only. If producers liked the idea, they would then ask for a full treatment. But, as was seen in the case of Moiseiwitsch, the BBC was also willing to develop a particularly good idea. The manual reassured 'new authors' that they would

> be aided in their efforts by a highly-trained staff of experts at Broadcasting House. For these experts, like the technicians employed by the film companies who turn published short stories and novels into scenarios, can revise and prepare a script which contains the germ of a good radio idea into suitable material for the microphone.³⁷

Despite the creative role BBC staffers played in working ideas into good broadcast entertainment, there seems to have been little guidance on how to protect the intellectual property of the BBC. For instance, Kester felt that as a BBC staffer, he had no right to press for payment or recognition of rights in the case of *Mr. Penny*.³⁸ While Maschwitz and others were convinced of the BBC's rights to the series, they were nonetheless in a difficult position, as Moiseiwitsch had always received billing as the sole writer. The BBC thus felt it necessary to pay Moiseiwitsch for his ideas and then 'sever the inconvenient connection ... with this rather difficult person'. At this point, Maschwitz hoped to continue the series into its third season without Moiseiwitsch's 'aid or interference'.[39] Moiseiwitch was offered 20gn. for his claim to Penny, on the assertion that his role in the series was minimal and that he had already breached contract by offering film rights to British National Films without the permission of the BBC, as well as by broadcasting material developed by and large by BBC staffers.[40]

In response to the claims made by Kester and the BBC, Moiseiwitsch's lawyer laid out a strenuous argument asserting his client's rights to *all* of the broadcast material, as well as the name of Mr. Penny. Though he admitted that evidence submitted by the BBC demonstrated Kester's hand in the writing of much of series one's dialogue, Moiseiwitsch's lawyer leveraged the creative fluidity of the BBC's programming processes to his client's advantage. First, he dismissed the importance of BBC-created character elements as 'superficial', and argued that writing changes were simply Kester's 'interpretation upon the character of Mr Penny in the same way that every producer or actor interprets, in his own style, the character with which an author provides him'. While Moiseiwitsch's lawyer agreed that Kester was entitled to copyright for the original dialogue, he nonetheless argued that Moiseiwitsch still held the 'basic copyright in his original work'. Further, Moiseiwitsch claimed that Kester had threatened to cancel the series if he did not develop the domestic side of Penny in the second series and intimated that Kester was actually trying to cash in on the success of Penny for himself. For extra measure, the lawyer chastised the BBC for writing a contract that took 'unfair advantage' of an individual with no business experience and suggested that the BBC's meddling in affairs between the British National Film Company and Mr. Moiseiwitsch might result in their being named in a potential lawsuit over monies owed his client for film rights.[41]

In the face of a withering and detailed argument, the BBC immediately agreed to every concession put forth by the lawyer, which included a nominal 10 per cent of royalties made on Penny.[42] The BBC was given the opportunity to engage Moiseiwitsch for future episodes, but crucially, was forced to 'withdraw all claims that it has made to any rights in my Client's work or the title thereof'.[43] Given the fraught relationship between Moiseiwitsch and the Variety department, it was decided to jettison the series.[44] Ultimately, Moiseiwitsch took the series to Luxembourg and British National Films rolled out *Meet Mr. Penny* a year later.

The copyright struggles over *The Strange Adventures of Mr. Penny* offer fascinating glimpses into both the internal workings of programme creation from inception to broadcast and the BBC's battle to maintain its monopolistic position vis-à-vis Continental radio stations. After efforts to shut down English-language broadcasts from the Continent failed, the BBC tried to restrict its artists from appearing on Radio Luxembourg or Radio Normandie, and also attempted to block the broadcast of BBC material on other stations. According to Martin Dibbs, however, 'Many artists found that it was financially worthwhile to ignore these threats, and while some were dispensed with, others were considered essential to the BBC and retained, thus creating discrimination and inconsistency in BBC policy.'[45]

When Constanduros informed the BBC that she wished to sell some Buggins material to Continental stations in July 1936, the BBC protested that it had a claim to certain popular broadcast characters, stating:

> It is quite obvious that we cannot prevent artists from accepting these engagements, but we do feel that characters created for and first introduced to broadcasting through our programmes should only be broadcast from our stations. Characters like 'Mrs. Buggins', 'Mrs. Feather', 'The Vagabond Lover' etc. are ones which we claim to have a special interest and their inclusion in commercial programmes would deprive them of any value to us.[46]

This last sentence demonstrates the threat that the BBC made to artists who wished to broadcast elsewhere, intimating that should Constanduros sell Buggins material for broadcast on Continental stations, they would no longer be interested in future material. Incensed by the BBC's threat, Constanduros shot back that she had to constantly produce new material for the BBC that could rarely be recycled:

> That material could be used for a year on the Halls but I have to scrap it once it is broadcast. Only by being this extravagant have I kept my place as one of your best-liked comedians. ... Would you prefer that I write new stuff for commercial broadcasting rather than use up material that you have had and finished with?

She went on to chastise the BBC for threatening her and reminded them of her long-term loyalty to the institution, as well as the fact that she could make more money elsewhere.[47] The BBC did not press the matter further, and the Bugginses remained on the BBC, but were also heard on Radio Normandie.

The claim to popular characters that the BBC made in the case of the Bugginses seems also to have been at the root of the BBC's initial response to Moiseiwitsch's actions regarding *Mr. Penny* a year later. However, when Constanduros pressed her right over the Buggins material, it was clear that the Bugginses were her intellectual property over which the BBC had no real claim. Even though Kester believed that the case of BBC ownership of *Mr. Penny* strong enough to win in a court of law,[48] the BBC nonetheless seemed reluctant to pursue litigation. Certainly, as a public institution, it is possible that the BBC did not wish to be perceived as greedily pursuing profit. An internal memo written by Maschwitz early on in the dispute stresses that the case was not about making money, but rather about protecting the BBC's rights and the strength of its contracts.[49] While the BBC was willing to threaten artists interested in commercial broadcasting, and might even pursue legal recourse, there seemed little will in the face of opposition to fully press their claims to copyright or popular characters.

After the legal row over *Mr. Penny*, the BBC abandoned the series, but they did not give up on serialized situation comedy. In fact, the BBC introduced a new situation comedy series at the very same moment the Variety department was engaged in the battle over Moiseiwitsch's claims to *Penny*. This time, Max Kester was billed as writer and producer of *The Plums*, a domestic sitcom that chronicled the life of a loveable down-at-the-heel Northern family who move south after inheriting an estate from a hitherto unknown family relative. *The Plums* replaced *The Strange Adventures of Mr. Penny* in the 7.45 pm timeslot directly following *Monday at Seven* from October to December 1937, was rested, and then once again revived as a popular wartime series in 1942.[50]

Developing career on the BBC

As the BBC evolved in the 1930s, especially in regards to Variety, so too did Constanduros. Thus, while other early comedy pioneers were shunted aside, she remained a staple of BBC entertainment. In the late 1920s, both John Henry and Helena Millais left broadcasting to pursue fame on the more lucrative music hall circuit. As seen in Chapter 3, the results were disastrous for Henry. For Millais, the decision all but killed her career on the BBC.

Though she returned to radio alongside Constanduros and Henry for the twelfth anniversary variety programme in 1934, and returned once again in the 1937 *Scrapbook 1922* programme, Millais was unable to stage a comeback to broadcasting. Despite press in *Radio Pictorial* in January 1938, which reacquainted radio audiences with Millais, behind the scenes, the BBC ignored efforts by Millais in 1937 and 1938 to reboot her broadcasting career, dismissing her as 'not our type' in an internal memorandum.[51] By this time, Millais's song and monologue act was considered outdated. Though she solicited the

BBC again in 1939, Millais only appeared a handful of times in one-off 1930s nostalgia programmes, and once again in the nostalgic 1950s programme, *These Radio Times*.[52]

While Constanduros performed on the very same programmes as did Millais in the 1930s and the 1950s, and though Constanduros and Millais both did Cockney dialect comedy, Constanduros was not taken off air or relegated to the nostalgia market. The Bugginses continued to make audiences laugh on variety revues and programmes, as well as *Children's Hour* throughout the decade. As will be seen in Chapter 5, the Buggins family became iconic in the wartime *Kitchen Front (KF)* programme. Constanduros's longevity can be attributed to both her loyalty to the BBC and the popularity of her family-oriented and 'radiogenic' sketches; more than this, however, Constanduros capitalized on her radio-made celebrity by diversifying into areas beyond broadcasting. As will be seen in Chapter 6, she also carefully nurtured her BBC presence, building on her Buggins fame to enter into and develop other areas of BBC light entertainment.

Radio celebrity brought Constanduros to the music hall footlights as a headline act at the London Coliseum in October 1929. Though a veteran of the amateur dramatic stage, Constanduros had never performed in a music hall; indeed, according to her autobiography, she had never before been inside one.[53] She admitted feeling terrified by this first performance, and, though *The Stage* noted her apparent stage fright, it seems she satisfied her fans, and perhaps even gained a few more by the end of her performance.[54] Constanduros's performance must have been successful, however, since afterwards she was offered, and agreed to, a twelve-week tour and contract. In a 1954 BBC radio programme about her career, she rehearsed the well-worn maternal priorities that informed her career (and underscored her celebrity) when she told audiences that she only took the contract in order to pay for Michael's schooling.[55] But though she toured several times, and began to feel comfortable at the Coliseum, it was clear to her that she was out of her element. Her radiogenic material had difficulty translating to the big halls, and several times her music hall turns fell flat. In the 1954 programme, she recalled Manchester audiences failing to respond to her humour, and remembers once being demoralized by receiving 'the bird': loud, rhythmic clapping by the audience intended to drown out a poor performance, at the Alhambra.[56] Indeed, radio star and comedian Arthur Askey later recalled witnessing this embarrassing performance.[57] Not long afterwards, Constanduros decided to quit music hall altogether.

While Constanduros herself 'felt secretly that my work was unsuitable for the variety stage', Gilli Bush-Bailey convincingly argues that 'conflict between legitimate and illegitimate entertainment' was at the heart of Constanduros's decision to walk away from the variety stage.[58] Indeed, in a draft chapter of *Shreds and Patches*, Constanduros adamantly dismissed music hall as a possible career option for herself: 'To many people it would have seemed the summit of desire – to top the bill on a variety tour. To me it was just a terror. I had never wanted to be a Variety artist .... I had wanted to act in plays.'[59] Fear of losing respectability was key to understanding her aversion to the halls: Constanduros recalled her mother's bias against music halls as 'haunts of vice', and the family was brought up believing 'that going to a Music Hall was almost on a par with getting drunk or stealing money'.[60]

After her trying experience in the halls, Constanduros used her name to increase her chances of gaining work in 'legitimate' theatre. Throughout the 1930s, Constanduros regularly acted in or wrote stage plays for London theatre or amateur stage. In 1932, she appeared on stage with Tessa Deane in A. P. Herbert's comic opera *Derby Day* and played Anne of Cleves in Nancy Price's 1933 production of *The Rose without a Thorn*. In contrast to the terror Constanduros felt on the Variety stage, being in *Derby Day* was to her 'very exhilarating'.[61] Constanduros later took the stage in *The Shoemaker's Holiday* and played Madame Wang in *Lady Precious Stream*, two more Nancy Price productions.[62] She also made several appearances on film in the 1930s, playing opposite Sydney Howard in *Where's George?* (1935) and later that year with Gordon Harker in the charity film *The Story of Papworth Village*.[63] Constanduros and Michael Hogan collaborated on an animated film short starring Stanley Holloway, entitled *Sam's Medal* (1936). Constanduros also adapted two novels for the London stage in the 1930s: *Three for Luck* (1934) and *Cold Comfort Farm* (1936).[64]

Capitalizing on her knowledge and connections in amateur theatre, Constanduros also wrote extensively for the amateur market, forming a long-standing relationship with Samuel French early on in her career. Having penned a two-act play entitled *The Family Group* soon after her start on the BBC, Constanduros approached Samuel French to publish the play, and thus began the 'successful commercial exploitation of that market in sketches, monologues and duologues'.[65] Constanduros penned over sixty volumes for French over the course of her career, two of which are still on the French list.[66] While she profited financially from her amateur stage material, Constanduros was also a strong advocate of amateur theatre, especially for women, and maintained a close relationship with amateur companies in Bristol and Worthing.[67]

Close friend and radio critic Collie Knox once wrote that Constanduros was 'a born "creative" artist ... her head teems with plots for plays and short stories'.[68] Her grandchildren remembered fondly how Constanduros would spend hours writing in bed.[69] This love of storytelling is seen clearly through the numerous works she penned for the BBC and for the stage, but also in her successful publishing career. Just as BBC celebrity opened up stage opportunities, it also provided access to the printed page. Capitalizing on her *Children's Hour* appearances, she published two collections of poems, plays and monologues for children: *The Sweep and the Daffodil* (1930) and *Come Out to Play* (1936). Additionally, Constanduros wrote the lyrics for stage and radio songs that were published as musical scores.[70]

In 1928, Constanduros and Michael Hogan penned *The Bugginses*, a novel about the famous radio family and their neighbours in Walworth. Constanduros then went on to write three more Buggins-related novels without Hogan in the late 1930s, each of which fleshed out the physical and social landscape of the Bugginses' world and gave further depth to characters heard in her radio sketches, while also creating opportunities to invent new characters for radio. Whereas the radio sketches constructed the working-class world aurally, Constanduros's working-class novels employ the same literary techniques as female social explorers who entered working-class homes and dwelt upon the interior detail of the working-class home and neighbourhood in order to divine the character of its inhabitants.[71] As with the literary works of many middle-class social explorers, the storylines in the novels combine knowledge of and sensitivity towards some aspects of working-class life, but simultaneously adhere to middle-class assumptions and suspicions regarding the working classes.[72] Although deeply problematic in its middle-class positioning, Constanduros's efforts to sketch out the social and physical landscape of the Bugginses chronicle life in the densely packed streets of South London on the eve of government rehousing schemes and slum clearances that forever changed the physical and social fabric of the area. By 1938, 25 per cent of housing in Walworth was considered 'unfit for human habitation', and numerous slum clearances in the area wiped away entire streets by the end of the decade.[73]

The radio-inspired novels written by Constanduros in the 1930s and the 1940s were examples of her desire to develop her career and craft, extending the reach of her radio works and her name beyond the radio in ways that were fairly unique for the period. Such attempts to expand audience interest reach back to tactics employed by Dickens to enhance his career (and pocketbook) through speaking tours, and presage the companion film and television novels of the later twentieth century or the more recent multiplatform transmedia 'tentpole' tactics aimed at increasing audience interest in and engagement with films or television programmes.[74] Few BBC performers or writers developed this cross-fertilization of media in the period; Jeanne De Casalis wrote a diary based on her famous 'Mrs. Feather' monologues in 1936 and Maurice Moiseiwitch penned several novels associated with the *Mr. Penny* series, the first appearing in 1938 with Frederick Muller.

Through detailed literary description and the use of flashbacks, Constanduros's Buggins novels enhanced listeners' experience and expanded reader/listener knowledge of the family, their relationships beyond the family circle and the world in which they lived. In the absence of a programming structure that enabled listeners repeated and regular encounters, and thus deeper connections, with characters, Constanduros's radio-inspired novels provided opportunities similar to serialized situation comedy by increasing exposure to the Buggins family and their neighbourhood. It was a strategy that enabled listeners more access to Constanduros's work than the BBC's scheduling structure allowed, encouraging further familiarity with and appreciation of her radio work. The 'companion' novels of their day, these works acted as 'transmedia extensions' of the Buggins' radio sketches. Such extensions across media platforms represents, as Clarke has argued, serve as examples of the economic theory of 'beneficial addiction', whereby consumption of a particular product 'encourages subsequent usage'.[75] Therefore, the Buggins novels could serve to amplify readers' desire for more interaction, both with the radio family and with Constanduros's other works, thus potentially strengthening Constanduros's celebrity and increasing the popularity of the Bugginses.

The first novel, *Bugginses* (1928), develops the back stories of the popular Buggins family characters, as well as three other Constanduros radio sketch characters familiar to BBC listeners: Aunt Maria, Ag and Bert. Here, Buggins fans learn that the family hails from Halcyon Row in Walworth (Southwark), a fictional street we are told lies just off the Walworth Road.[76] While Constanduros and Hogan imagine life within the working-class homes of Walworth, they demonstrate their credentials as expert observers of the working classes by concentrating much of their narrative on street level. Indeed, their knowledge was generated to a large extent by their 'excursions' through the streets of

Walworth.⁷⁷ As Roberts indicated in her oral history of working-class women during this period, the street, and a circumscribed area surrounding it, was a critical focal point of working-class social life: it 'offered a system of support, and with it a system of control'.⁷⁸ The novel thus traces the connections between the on-air characters and introduces new, mostly female, characters who add to the atmosphere of Halcyon Row by fuelling rumour or commenting on the family's conduct from open windows or doorsteps. Mrs. Molar and Mrs. 'Iggins act as the social control in Halcyon Row, letting nothing escape their attention as they police neighbourhood rules, freely advising all on the proper behaviour expected of residents.

Along with other popular Buggins characters, readers of *Bugginses* are given deeper insight into Grandma Buggins's backstory. The depth of her self-serving mischief is plumbed further here than might have been allowed on the respectable BBC. The novel provides insights into her marriage, the birth of her only son (Harry) and her interactions with daughter-in-law Emily (Mrs. Buggins). Domineering and conniving even as a young woman, Grandma convinced her younger sister Maria's 'weak, but pleasantly mannered' admirer to propose to Grandma, instead of Maria. This sleight of hand was achieved not out of love, we are told, but rather out of Grandma's longing to escape domestic servitude.⁷⁹ Harry, who would become Father Buggins in the sketches, came rather late in the marriage, and readers learn that while Grandma loved him in a 'queer, perverted fashion – because it was her own'; she held her husband Walter responsible for the pregnancy and resented him for 'changing the whole manner of her life'.⁸⁰ Harry's life history and the circumstances that led to his marriage to Emily are also provided in the novel.

With her backstory thus outlined, Grandma's main plotline centres on her ongoing and evolving efforts to scam bus and tram companies into awarding her damages for injuries supposedly sustained while riding or disembarking from their vehicles. The scam began innocently enough when Grandma was slightly injured upon disembarking from a bus; however, the deception was helped along by a corrupt lawyer who helped her gain damages on this occasion. Thereafter, the lawyer provided fake eyewitnesses and offered guidance on which bus or tram companies to target. Never one to be manipulated, Grandma is not the hapless victim of the lawyer's scheme, but rather, seeks him out when in need of money. The novel details Grandma's third incident in which she tries to scam the 'William Willings' bus line – this being an obvious play on Constanduros's Tilling Omnibus connections (and, thus, an inside joke to audiences knowledgeable of

Constanduros's childhood).[81] While Grandma's scheming is central to Buggins radio sketches, they never approached the criminality of the novel's bus scam; one imagines that the upright BBC would balk at such on-air behaviour, but the novel format enables more narrative freedom than did the moral constraints dictated by the Corporation.[82]

The novel was clearly meant to appeal to radio listeners who wished to learn more about their favourite radio family, but some of the chapters were also literary re-runs of her popular radio sketches. The novel starts out, for instance, with Grandma's eightieth birthday party and includes much of the same action and dialogue from a popular radio sketch. The eighth chapter fleshes out the radio sketch 'Baby and the Silkworm'. Many of the same plotlines in the novel derive from previously aired radio sketches, though readers are treated to extra dialogue and description.

Mrs. Buggins Calls (1936), Constanduros's first solo novel, also includes numerous radio sketches such as 'Father Buys a Whale' (originally co-written with Hogan and performed in the 1920s), 'The Family Group', and 'Fur Flies'.[83] While most of the stories were indeed previously broadcast, this book also includes a narrative thread that fleshes out Father's life outside the home: following him to the pubs, describing his return to darts and drink, and finally ending with a moralistic tragedy that inevitably leads to his demise. Never broached in radio sketches, the death of father in this novel helpfully explained to radio audiences the absence of father after Michael Hogan left Britain to pursue a career in Hollywood.[84]

While the earlier Buggins novels include many chapters that act as 're-runs' of popular radio sketches or develop well-known characters, Constanduros created new characters and incidents in *Down Mangel Street* (1938) that appeared on radio as a result of the novel. In chapter-length stories, the book offers vignettes of working-class life as it chronicles the lives of several inhabitants of Mangel Street. The Buggins family does not appear in the novel, but we are told that Mangel Street lies not far from Walworth Road in South London. Those familiar with the Buggins's background would easily recognize the connection. While the novel built upon the Bugginses by proximity, it introduced new characters, new situations and a new environment, and thus reverberated back to radio, expanding Constanduros's radio oeuvre. Just prior to the novel's release in 1937, Constanduros paired up with long-time friend and popular radio actress Gladys Young to perform several radio sketches, which were well received by the public; the book also provided Constanduros with a six-episode series during the war.[85]

The 1937 sketches with Young also provided convenient marketing for the novel. Based on correspondence with the BBC, contractual evidence and *Radio Times* listings from 1937 onwards, it seems that *Down Mangel Street* provided a ready resource for radio work for nearly a decade. The 1939 Buggins novel, *Grandma*, similarly introduced new Buggins sketches, opening up yet further on-air opportunities.[86]

In the mid-1930s, Constanduros seemed aware that her working-class repertoire needed updating and therefore used her novels to deepen audience interest in the Bugginses and to develop new characters and situations.[87] Constanduros's foray into publishing and the stage in the 1930s breathed life into her radio career, thus enabling her to evolve her characters, comedy and career while other pioneer comic acts, like Millais's 'Our Lizzie', remained static and largely disappeared from radio. While her working-class material remained foundational for the entirety of her career, Constanduros decided to expand beyond working-class comedy in the last half of the 1930s – an effort that marked the advent of soap opera in Britain.

5

The *Kitchen Front* and popular entertainment during the People's War

On 1 September 1939, the day that Germany invaded Poland and two days before Britain's declaration of war, Constanduros reached out to the directors of both BBC Drama and Variety offering her services if war broke out. This was also the day that the BBC officially (and secretly) switched over to wartime conditions; preparations were made to merge the National and Regional Programmes into the Home Service, while numerous staffers and entertainers were removed from London: in particular, Variety moved to Bristol, and Drama was sent to Evesham.[1] Constanduros herself was on tour in New Brighton, 'marooned', she wrote, in Merseyside, and desperate to get back to Sussex to see her son, Michael, before he was called up.[2] In her letter to John Watt, the director of Variety, she asked for permanent war work with the BBC and argued that her abilities as a writer and actress would be useful in any department.[3] To Gielgud, director of features and drama, and now close friend, she sent a more personal note, but again reminded him of her broad range of abilities in hopes of securing work. A day later, she sent a letter to Arthur Brown, Booking Manager for Variety, offering to work anywhere in the country and giving contact details in case he needed to employ her.[4]

This correspondence in many ways is indicative of Constanduros's management of her professional relationship with the BBC; throughout her entire career, she regularly sent letters in search of work, pitched programme ideas or nurtured relationships with BBC staffers. The letters penned on the eve of war, however, are unique in their sense of urgency to secure work. Much of this urgency, as might be expected, is couched in a deep sense of obligation towards the war effort and a desire to feel 'useful' – a sentiment shared by many as they contemplated the unknown that stood before them.[5] Indeed, to both Watt and Gielgud, she expressed envy that their jobs (and by extension, they personally) were indispensable. To Watt, she wrote reassuringly, 'My best wishes to you. You'll have a big job, a necessary one, cheering everybody up.'[6] To her friend, Gielgud, she confided a need to remain productive and creative, and a fear of village life in wartime: 'Stuck here with nothing of my own work to do in a village of earnest but quarrelsome women squabbling over their bit of war work will drive me crazy. I'd go back to London, but I can't afford, without work, to keep my flat going.'[7] Further, Constanduros was anxious about her son's eminent deployment. One also suspects that behind her patriotic desire to do something of value for the nation at war and a need to keep busy, there was also great concern that wartime conditions might mean fewer opportunities for artists like herself. In a letter to Arthur Brown, she worried about losing the creative stimulation of writing and performing for radio, stating, 'After 14 years of being so busy, I couldn't turn round – it is awful to have one's brain idle. There's plenty of manual work here but that's all.'[8] In the first month of the BBC's wartime footing, it certainly seemed that such work had been curtailed: Variety took only twenty-two performers to Bristol.[9]

Preparations for wartime broadcasting began as early as July 1935, when Reith set down 'The Position of the BBC in War'.[10] More detailed preparations regarding wartime programming were underway in 1938, and a 17 June *Radio Pictorial* article on 'The BBC's Wartime Plans' reassured listeners that BBC engineers were prepared to both ensure minimal disruption of programming and to safeguard transmissions so that enemy aircraft could not use wireless transmitters to target civilian populations.[11] The Munich Crisis later that year precipitated the revival of the BBC Drama Repertory Company (dubbed the 'Munich Crisis Rep' by its members) 'in anticipation of disruption to casting procedures' during wartime.[12]

In April 1939, premises had been purchased to house administrative offices, emergency studios, and the Features and Drama department at Wood Norton Hall (code-named 'Hogsnorton' after an imaginary town used in comedian Gillie Potter's routines), a stately home that once belonged to an exiled Duc d'Orleans and thus 'sprout[ed] fleurs-de-lis on everything from weather-vanes to bath-plugs'.[13] Preparations were also made to move Variety, Religious Broadcasting, the BBC Orchestra and *Children's Hour* to West Region headquarters in Bristol.[14] In August, arrangements were made to transport staffers to their new accommodations and members of the newly formed Variety Repertory Company (VRC) were given letters dramatically marked 'top secret' to be opened upon hearing a particular coded message over the air. That message, regarding a change in wavelengths, was sent out during the 6 pm news on Friday,

1 September, and gave orders for the members to make their way to Bristol immediately.[15] The bulk of BBC staffers, including Features and Drama, destined for Evesham, had decamped London a few days earlier, on 29 August.[16] As for Broadcasting House, the 'entrance hall sprouted barbed wire and bayonets' at the beginning of the war; after bombs fell, the building, which shone 'like a lighthouse whenever there was a full moon', was painted a 'drab green' and a massive blast wall was built to protect the foundations.[17]

Believing that Britain would immediately suffer massive air raids at the beginning of the war, the BBC was initially prepared to entertain its wartime listening public with a stockpile of music and variety gramophone records. Within two days of the declaration of war, the Variety Repertory Company (VRC) was ready to raise smiles with popular sing-song programmes and concert party entertainment. Its first programme, *For Amusement Only*, featured Tommy Handley poking fun at Hitler with a comic song entitled, 'Who is this man who looks like Charlie Chaplin?' and aired Wednesday, 6 September.[18] In the first few weeks of war, the VRC provided up to nine programmes a day, averaging four shows daily.[19] Comedy aimed at Hitler and the Nazi regime, like Handley's song, once banned by the BBC but now allowed, elicited 'gusts of happy laughter' from anxious audiences.[20] Even though some of the members of the Company were highly popular artists, like Handley and Leonard Henry, the public nonetheless grew weary of hearing the same performers day in and day out. Typical of the VRC players, Maurice Denham, a talented impressionist and an original member of the VRC, had by the end of November performed,

> 225 parts in 100 shows, appearing variously as a French peasant, a child of four, a Cockney bus driver, a dude, a dustman, numerous animals, Alf Perkins in *At the Billet Doux* and, in *It's that Man Again*, the Russian inventor Vodkin, the charlady Lola Tickle and the Radio Fakenburg announcer. He also did a little announcing [and] sang solo with the BBC's Men's Chorus.[21]

'I kid myself that listeners didn't always recognize my voice', Denham later remembered.[22] Indeed, an April 1940 programme fronted by star couple Jessie Matthews and Sonny Hale satirized the BBC's output in the first months of the war with 'pompous news announcements that "there is nothing to report", scratchy and hackneyed gramophone records, the "tinny raucousness" of Variety acts, and the lengthy "cast lists" full of repeated names (yet another jibe at the BBC repertory Company)'.[23] By mid-September 1939, Ministry of Information restrictions that required advance clearance of radio performers had been lifted, and the BBC began to employ more artists. The hugely popular pre-war *Band Waggon*, with Arthur Askey and Richard Murdoch, returned to the air, and negotiations began to engage other artists, like Constanduros, to enrich the wartime listening experience.[24]

Entertainment during the beginning of hostilities was initially 'aimed entirely at the big public, and frankly designed to be largely cheerful "background listening that didn't require much concentration between News Bulletins"'.[25] In this context, well-tried, popular characters like Grandma Buggins were deployed. Most of Constanduros's early wartime performances featured the Bugginses: both on variety programmes like *Sing It Through* (October 1939) and *Children's Hour*. The one early exception to this were roles played in the popular political farce, *Adolf in Blunderland* (October 1939 and February 1940), where she acted the parts of both the Queen of Heartlessness and Guinea Pig.[26]

Written by Max Kester and James Dyrenforth, *Adolf in Blunderland* featured Maurice Denham playing 'a young Hitler in frilly knickerbockers [who] longs to be "the biggest man in the world"' and Jack Train as Goering.[27] Constanduros played contrasting characters set against each other in the same scene: The Queen of Heartlessness was a play on Himmler, wearing 'a dress ... stiff with swastikas',[28] while Guinea pig voiced German dissent at a mock trial. The *Times* reviewer recalled this critical moment in the play:

> 'Off with her Swastika', cried the Queen [of Heartlessness], but before she was finally suppressed the guinea-pig had made an outburst with a note of genuine passion, which voiced the feelings of all the suppressed wives and mothers in Blunderland. For a moment there was wild confusion. Then calm reigned once more, and listeners heard, sung to an old German folk-song, the opening verse of the Jabberwocky (new style) ... . 'Twas Danzig and the Swastikoves / Did heil and hittle in the Reich / All Nazi were Lindengroves / and the Neurath's Julestreich'.[29]

The reviewer praised the play as amusing, original and topical. John Watt argued that *Adolf in Blunderland* was ideal propaganda: the play 'succeeded ... because it was a "piece of satiric entertainment, good or bad according to one's taste, and the propaganda aspect of it was, in its creation, entirely secondary to its topical satire"'.[30]

While many cite the return of *Band Waggon* on 16 September as a pivotal moment in wartime programming, behind the scenes, the BBC was only just beginning to make the changes that would put programming on a solid wartime footing.³¹ The war that the BBC imagined, and planned for, in peacetime did not at first materialize, leaving the Corporation open to scathing criticism that lasted well into the autumn, even after *Band Waggon* and *ITMA* (19 September) returned. When the government closed most entertainment venues at the beginning of the war, the BBC represented one of the few means of wartime entertainment, and their early efforts were felt to be entirely inadequate.³² On 11 October, MP Arthur Greenwood compared British wartime broadcasting with that of the French, and found it woefully lacking. 'We have to remember that in the conditions of war, with the limitations there are in public entertainment outside the homes', Greenwowod argued, 'the BBC becomes the main avenue of public entertainment for millions of our people.'³³ He continued, directing his invective at the government and the BBC: 'In these days of train restrictions, fighting restrictions, restrictions here, there, everywhere, and the determination on the part of the Government to make the life of everybody as miserable as possible, it would be well if we could have some brighter entertainment from the BBC.'³⁴ Though entertainment venues began to steadily reopen in October, the BBC nonetheless was the most accessible and popular outlet of wartime entertainment.³⁵ In his assessment of early wartime Variety programming, Dibbs argues that the government should take at least some of the blame levelled at the BBC during this time as the institution was only following the government's cautious lead on wartime entertainment.³⁶

While many disparaged early wartime radio output, others were anxious that the BBC resume television service, which had been switched off at 12.35 pm on 1 September, for the benefit of the roughly 20,000 London-based pre-war television owners who had become so 'used to television ... [that] ordinary sound programmes are unsatisfying and not worth switching on to hear'.³⁷ Viewers were disappointed to learn that the service would not return during wartime owing to fears that German planes could easily hone in on signals from the huge television transmitter at Alexandra Palace.³⁸ In the absence of television and anxious to improve the listening experience, Home Broadcasting Committees were created in mid-September to reassess the wartime situation and make critical changes to peacetime programming plans (perhaps the most significant decision being the one that reduced the number of gramophone recordings and even did away with the word 'gramophone' in the *Radio Times* listings.)³⁹ In November, heads of programming departments were tasked with assessing their output and proposing future programming plans.⁴⁰ According to

Martin Dibbs, by the end of the year, 'radio programmes were approaching their pre-war quality and were more appealing to the audience'.⁴¹

While not in the VRC vanguard of wartime Variety, Constanduros was part of the second wave of artists called up for service on the BBC, and her contracts shed further light on BBC decision-making during the first phase of the war. For instance, on the same day as *Band Waggon*'s return, Constanduros was sent a weekly contract to work in Bristol for the first week in October. While in Bristol, she was issued another weekly contract for the following week. During her time in Bristol, she acted alongside the members of the VRC on various Variety programmes. By November, however, the uncertainties of wartime planning had settled down, and her BBC artist work returned to the pre-war norm of contracting on an individual programme basis.⁴² The Dunkirk evacuations forced the BBC to once again work out contingency plans: Constanduros was asked to contribute plays to a 'library of recorded programmes which might be used in the event of a possible emergency'.⁴³

Serving on the *Kitchen Front*

Early on in the war, writer Naomi Mitchison despaired, 'The only thing I can do is write. And the only people who can write now are the really successful professionals like Priestley and co.'⁴⁴ As with other female writers and artists who contemplated their futures at the beginning of the war, Constanduros's early wartime BBC correspondence demonstrates more desperation than at any other period in her career that she would be unable to do 'the work I know most about'.⁴⁵ In response to these fears, she actively pursued numerous opportunities throughout the war in order to cultivate her career both on radio and beyond. In addition to her private correspondence with the BBC, Constanduros publicly expressed her commitment to contribute to the current war effort, and to establish her credentials with the public, she stressed her experience in comforting and entertaining wounded soldiers during the First World War. While on tour with Roland Gower's *Ma's Bit o' Brass*, Constanduros gave several press interviews in which she was eager to assert her patriotism as an entertainer. The *Daily Herald* ran an item entitled 'Mrs. Buggins in Camp' which relayed the fact that Constanduros was 'anxious to help entertain the troops' with her Buggins sketches.⁴⁶

Constanduros's campaign to continue writing and performing in aid of the war effort resulted in the publication of four novels, numerous French's acting editions, several speaking tours for government ministries, a handful of stage tours, a successful West End play and over 270 wartime appearances on the BBC. This last statistic exceeds that of other well-known and beloved wartime personalities, such as Robb Wilton, and Elsie and Doris Waters ('Gert and Daisy'). Robb Wilton is listed in 145 appearances; the Waters Sisters in 67. In a *Birmingham Mail* obituary for Wilton on 2 May 1957, Constanduros was remembered with Wilton and Tommy Handley as central to wartime memories. Tommy Handley far outpaces them all with more than 500 wartime appearances, though many of these are reruns of *ITMA*. Regardless of repeat performances, these numbers suggest just how ubiquitous these performers were in wartime broadcasting.[47]

Throughout the war, audiences could expect to regularly hear any number of her plays penned with writing partners Howard Agg and nephew Denis Constanduros or of the Buggins family on numerous variety programmes and one-off programmes. Indeed, the Buggins family was conscripted for official war work on the popular *Kitchen Front* (*KF*) programme – a role that guaranteed her place in the wartime memory of many. 'How well I recall dear Mabel Constanduros every morning with her tips … . Nobody dared breathe aloud when she was on and I scribbled notes down,' one woman from Potters Bar remembered about Constanduros's *KF* role.[48] Constanduros did not appear 'every morning', but this comment is evidence of how Constanduros, along with a handful of other contributors among the scores of broadcasters who presented on the daily programme over five years, became synonymous with the *KF*.[49]

The origins of the *KF* programme lie in the Ministry of Food's (MoF's) efforts to launch a food economy campaign in April 1940. This campaign was part of the 'most intense of all the BBC's collaborations with government ministries' during the war, and 'became the collaboration to which every other ministry aspired'. Over the course of this relationship, historian Siân Nicholas argues, the BBC successfully worked out the challenges of 'division of responsibility, style and tone of presentation, and the balance between entertainment and advice'.[50]

The most successful outcome of the initial food economy drive was *Feed the Brute*, a daily series in mid-April, starring the Cockney comedic duo Gert and Daisy sharing cookery advice and recipes. The two-week tea-time series was a phenomenal success, resulting in over 30,000 requests to the MoF for recipes and 50,000 letters of appreciation to the duo.[51] Yet, it was feared that while Gert and Daisy drew large numbers of listeners, the attraction was purely for entertainment purposes, *not* for rationing advice. The MoF and the BBC, backed up by research from Mass-Observation (MO), felt the programme needed an authoritative, male voice to underscore the value of the advice and compel housewives to action.[52] Further, listener response indicated that the tea-time slot was not desirable.[53] With these considerations in mind, the BBC and MoF launched the *KF* programme in June 1940, airing Monday through Saturday at 8.15 am, presumably to allow the housewife to plan her shopping for the day.

The first presenters on the *KF* were writer and popular broadcaster S. P. B. Mais and cookery expert Ambrose Heath. While Mais offered a popular view of 'what to eat and where to get it', seasoned housewives appreciated Heath's knowledge around the kitchen and his 'sensible' advice.[54] Heath's broadcasting approach was replicated throughout the series by many different presenters, who variously discussed 'how to make the best and most economical use of rationed food, how to best spend the "points" ration, how to make "mock" substitutes for unobtainable foodstuffs, and how to make use of unrationed produce and the new food that was increasingly becoming available through Lend-Lease and other important arrangements'.[55] By October, concern was mounting that audience interest in the programme was waning, and producer Janet Quigley was anxious that 'all our efforts would be defeated were housewives to feel that the morning cookery talks were "official"'.[56] In an effort to lighten the tone of the programme, the BBC recruited Freddie Grisewood, a former tennis announcer and long-time host of the radio magazine *The World Goes By*, in mid-October.[57] Average audience figures that month register an impressive 5.4 million, roughly 15 per cent of the listening audience and four times more than any other daytime talk, figures that held fairly steady for the rest of the war, though some popular presenters could fetch higher audiences.[58]

At the beginning of Grisewood's tenure on the *KF*, he broadcast every weekday once every four or five weeks, alternating with other established *KF* broadcasters such as Ambrose Heath, Bruce Blunt, the Radio Doctor and comedienne Jeanne De Casalis.[59] In mid-April 1941, preparations began to change the format to feature different speakers on a daily basis – a change partly driven by Robert Westerby at the MoF to enable the ministry an official broadcast slot.[60] The new format, which began in the summer, featured ministry talks on Monday, Grisewood on Tuesdays and Thursdays, the Radio Doctor (or a health talk) on Wednesdays, guest speakers on Fridays and housewife views or international-themed talks on Saturdays.[61]

The changes to the programme were not always welcome. MO diarist Nella Last appreciated Ambrose Heath's contributions to the programme, but she lamented in her entry for 5 October that 'my little Aunties know more about food value and economy than any two of the wireless clever ones who blah at 8.15 about things that a school girl should know'.[62] One suspects that Last was particularly put off by Grisewood's clueless man-about-the-kitchen routine, which offered little practical advice to a seasoned cook like herself. Indeed, Grisewood's appointment, while popular and successful, was also problematic as it could not mitigate the middle-class tone that the programme often struck. Grisewood could be 'breathtakingly' middle class, as demonstrated in the episode where he kicked his cook out of the kitchen so that he could try to cook a casserole on his own.[63] Two months after Grisewood's debut on the *KF*, the BBC liaison to the MoF, Lionel Fielden, lamented to Janet Quigley that the programme desperately needed a working-class voice.[64] Gert and Daisy returned a week later for a handful of Christmas *KF*, but the MoF and the BBC continued their search for enthusiastic working-class voices to pitch their recipes and the official line.

Eager to reach working-class audiences, and increase audience figures, the MoF's Robert Westerby approached Constanduros in October 1941 to contribute a handful of talks on the *KF*. This manoeuver was typical of Westerby's micromanagement of the programme, a style which often exasperated BBC staffers, but in this case was welcomed by assistant producer Jean Rowntree and Quigley.[65] Prior to this, Constanduros was known to Quigley, with whom she had kept up a fairly regular correspondence since August 1940, mostly in regards to script ideas and broadcasts for Quigley's Talks programme, *Calling All Women*. Constanduros's BBC correspondence during the first two years of war ranged across the Drama, Variety, and Talks departments in her continued attempt to find work, and Quigley and Rowntree were well aware of Constanduros's work ethic and patriotism, and the popularity of the Buggins family. Upon learning that Constanduros was interested, Rowntree swiftly wrote to the director of talks, George Barnes, for approval, arguing that, 'as a means of lightening the series she is about as good a feature as we could get. For one thing she is not an obviously uninterested person dragged in artificially to be bright.'[66] Rowntree's request was quickly accepted, and Constanduros was invited to give four talks for the programme.[67] Constanduros's performances were an instant success, and she was soon signed on for six more talks. The Bugginses thus settled into their regular Tuesday morning timeslot, which lasted (with occasional guest speakers to rest Constanduros and the Buggins material) until VE Day, when they were shifted to Friday mornings.[68] As will be discussed in the conclusion, the working relationship with Janet Quigley endured long into the post-war period as Constanduros would become a regular contributor to the popular *Woman's Hour* programme.

While the Bugginses were recruited to lighten the tone of the programme, their success on the *KF* was due only in part to their comedic touch. Indeed, the producers often received complaints from housewives when variety acts recruited for the programme simply gave a comedic turn and failed to offer listeners tangible advice.[69] From the beginning, Constanduros seemed acutely aware that the *KF* was first and foremost informational. Upon her initial acceptance of the contract, she wrote to Rowntree,

> I would like to consult with you about the material … . I feel people like to be told something really useful every morning or they feel cheated so I'd like to give them a useful food hint or recipe every time – it can be wrapped up in a comedy dialogue but I would like to give them something worthwhile so that they listen again.[70]

Indeed, Listener Research bore out this hunch that *KF* audiences wanted to be both entertained and informed.[71]

Though she often lamented having to decline other departments' requests for her services because of her work on *KF*, Constanduros nonetheless prided herself on providing her audience with good information and appetizing recipes on the ration. Further, she took time to perfect a microphone technique that eased the task of transcribing the steps and ingredients in those recipes. Initial scripts indicate that Grandma or Mrs. Buggins simply read through a recipe once or twice, but by June 1942, Constanduros had evolved her talks such that Grandma gave out recipes line by line after which Mrs. Buggins repeated them; Mrs. Buggins also anticipated listeners' questions by stopping Grandma now and again to inquire about a particular ingredient's availability or utility or simply to ask for clarification.

Constanduros told readers in *Shreds and Patches* that her housekeeper, Bina, helped her cook each recipe in advance. BBC correspondence corroborates this claim: on several occasions, she slightly modified recipes to improve them or outright rejected unappetizing ones. Although recipes were tested in advance at the MoF, her insistence on personally preparing recipes beforehand stems from a 'revolting bacon pudding' she was given to relay early on in her *KF* career. After

Constanduros complained to the BBC, Westerby agreed to send her recipes well in advance of a broadcast to give her time to try them out.[72]

Grandma Buggins has entered the wartime histories as the classic curmudgeonly grouse, especially known for her complaints about the ubiquitous mock substitutes offered up by the programme.[73] This image, however, is only partially correct; analysis of the scripts over the entirety of the war reveals an important evolution in her character and paints a richer, more nuanced portrait of Grandma that highlights the ways in which entertainment and propaganda intersected in such programmes.

One of the most famous broadcasts of the Bugginses on the *KF*, which confirms the stereotype of the wartime grouse, features Mrs. Buggins (Emily) sharing a recipe for Connaught pie, to which Grandma retorts in her cutting monotone deadpan, 'another disguise for parsnips'. Emily then states that the recipe calls for a pint of water, causing Grandma once again to grumble, 'that's one thing they ain't rationed yet'.[74] The interplay between Mrs. Buggins and Grandma, where Constanduros plays Mrs. Buggins as a cheerful optimist to Grandma's bad-tempered foil was the typical their relationship, established from the beginning of the Buggins family sketches, but it was also an effective comedic propaganda tool. While Gert and Daisy's kitchen front comedy usually featured light-hearted silliness in the kitchen, laughing in the face of adversity, Constanduros's *KF* sketches nearly always contained at least one character moaning about austerity conditions or the war.

In the beginning of the Buggins's tenure on the programme, the complaints were filed by Grandma. This comedic device enabled Grandma to voice the frustrations of a nation safely: audiences had grown to expect Grandma's grousing, and therefore laughter at what might be considered critical or defeatist comments was masked by the expected comedic characterization. Constanduros's technique also softened the comedic barb by having Mrs. Buggins offer a patriotic counterargument. Constanduros was careful to include official views of the MoF, working into her sketches current official memos and prevailing ministry or government concerns or campaigns; for instance, in 1942, Constanduros tackled the perennial wartime problem of mothers failing to collect the cod liver oil and orange juice rations entitled to their children.[75]

Initially, it was Mrs. Buggins who voiced the government line, but increasingly Grandma took over this role, eventually trading places with Emily to become the ideal soldier in the People's War. This patriotic transformation of Grandma began to take place in mid-1942. In February, Grandma could still be heard heartily hurling her complaints at the MoF and the government, while Mrs. Buggins shouldered the burden of the ministry line. Typical of these sketches is the broadcast on 10 February 1942, where Grandma complains about beans on the ration:

> **Grandma:** Well, I never. Got to have Lord Woolton's permission before you can go out and buy a measly bean! 'Ow many points are they, then?
> **Mrs. Buggins:** 2 points a pound.
> **Grandma:** Two of my good points for a pound of silly beans?
> **Mrs. Buggins:** You wouldn't want more than that – beans are heavy.
> **Grandma:** Well, I dunno, I'm sure. We shall be rationed for breath next. You know the Government ought to do somethink about this Wore. It's getting' a nonsense.
> **Mrs. Buggins:** They 'ave done somethink, Gran'ma. That's why we're rationed; so everyone can get their fair share.
> **Grandma:** I'll see I get my fair share, don't you worry. I shall count 'em. I'm partial to a nice 'aricot bean. They go down very tasty. Warmin' too.[76]

True to character, here Grandma is greedy about her food and self-absorbed, concerned only with her 'fair share'. Grandma's obsession over food never abates, and it often leads to humorous jokes and storylines throughout the series. For instance, in one 1943 episode, Grandma, who usually spurned male advances, begins cooking for 'Mr. Next Door'. Mrs. Buggins teases Grandma by suggesting she was after his old age pension, but Grandma gets the last laugh. 'Not me', she replies. ' 'E's got a green 'ouse. I'm after 'is tormaters!'[77]

Grandma's classic one-liners continue to pepper the episodes for the remainder of the war, but she gradually casts off her selfishness and begins to do her part for the war effort. In May 1942, Grandma announces she has war work. Mrs. Buggins laughs, 'at close to eighty? You ain't puttin' on trousers and bein' a fireman, by any chance?' 'No, nor a land girl,' Grandma deadpans, 'I'm goin' round to all the 'ouses in our street to sell savin' stamps.' Pleasantly surprised at Grandma's change in attitude, Mrs. Buggins encourages her to go out at once. 'I shall,' replies Grandma,

> I shall arst everybody 'ow they'd like to 'ave their rights took away from them like the mutts in Germany. D'you think the Germans are allowed to pile up a nice little nest-egg like we can with our stamps, I shall say. I got one o' them Slocombes, too. Made it up meself: Sixpence a day Keeps 'Itler away.[78]

Grandma's patriotic rehabilitation coincided with Constanduros's own recruitment to the National Savings campaign and underscores a critical component of the

People's War rhetoric that everyone, regardless of age or gender, had a role to play in winning the war.[79] Grandma's savings campaign was representative of the 'small, ordinary, even mundane, feats compounded by the millions into incredible tides of action', and significantly modelled appropriate patriotic behaviour.[80]

Upon becoming a patriot, Grandma did not lose her irascibility; instead she began to aim her sharpened barbs at shirkers and at people who had grown apathetic about the war effort. In 1943, with cod liver oil and orange juice rations for children still left untouched, Grandma criticized and shamed young mothers who were 'too shy' to assert their rights for their children.

> Shy indeed! When them Merchant Navy fellers risks their lives to bring 'er vitermines in fish-liver oil and orange juice, and the Government's provided 'er with milk the least she can do is stir 'er stumps and go and get 'em ... . If that woman don't take what the Government pervides, she's starvin' 'er child, just as sure as if she left it in its cot without food.[81]

In addition to her intensifying patriotism, Grandma also increasingly commented upon and upheld traditional gender roles and values – a position that Constanduros supported in public appearances for the MoF. Both in public speaking events and on the programme, Constanduros regularly argued that good cooking was the way to a man's heart, and was not only an important wartime skill to acquire in service to the nation but also as useful in one's quest for marital bliss. A newspaper article from 1943 reporting on a guest appearance in Leatherhead for the MoF summarized Constanduros's final appeal to the audience,

> It was not only a war between fighting forces, but one between people, and the most worthy ones would be the ones to survive, and she took leave to say that, in her opinion, Britain was a worthy nation. British women set the tone of that nation. She would quote to them Mrs. Buggins's remark, 'Many a plain girl has cooked her way into a man's heart', and concluded 'So cook your ways into your men's hearts, and don't be pushed out by bad cooking.'[82]

Constanduros's appearances and her *KF* performances supported People's War rhetoric that praised the efforts of the individual on behalf of the nation, but also endeavoured to minimize the potentially revolutionary implications of mobilizing women for wartime by stressing socially acceptable benefits of that war work (i.e. marriage for a 'plain girl').

Whereas Grandma's peacetime demeanour tended to upend gender norms, in wartime, she came to support and even rhapsodize over them. In a November 1942 broadcast, Grandma offered her take on the 'cook your way into a man's heart' platitude, telling teenage Emma, 'if you want to be happy when you're married, you got to learn to cook. A man don't think of 'is wife's face when 'e comes 'ome you know. 'E thinks of 'is dinner.'[83] This reflection on married life does not diverge drastically from Grandma's usual peacetime attitude towards men, but does mark a significant transition in her wartime evolution, as the comment presents multivalent interpretations which seem both supportive of traditional gender roles and critical of marital life. A year later, Grandma had come not only to support societal gender norms, but to reflect them herself. Mrs. Buggins announces this change in a November 1943 *KF* sketch in which she says 'even at your age', Grandma, the once self-centred harpy, would 'be a comfort to a man if we could find one old enough'. Grandma then lectures Mrs. Buggins, and the audience,

> It's a womans dooty to be a comfort – don't forget that. If she ain't got a man she can set to and comfort someone else. Comfort 'ad ought to flow from a woman's presence like 'oney from an 'ive. We shouldn't hear so much about divorce if women did a bit more comfortin'.[84]

By the end of the war, Grandma's transformation was complete. The exigencies of war had not revolutionized her view of life, but had rather reformed it. She was now the optimistic patriot in the Buggins family, chastising Emily for becoming disconsolate over the length of the war or finding the silver lining in recent events: 'since the Germans 'as blew 'Itler's trousers orf 'im, I got more 'opes of 'em. And there's good to be got even out of an evil like Wore, if anybody tries. Look at the people that's comin' out o' this Wore better cooks than ever they went into it.'[85] For those familiar with peacetime Grandma, this change in her character and this particular sentiment would have been striking. While there are no extant records that speak to Constanduros's decision to evolve Grandma's character in this way, it is possible that she felt it necessary to drive home the People's War message after the devastating fall of Singapore in the spring of 1942 – the darkest moment in the war when the British Empire seemed most in peril. Additionally, it is reminiscent of Constanduros's own struggle with gendered stereotypes both in her writing and in her personal life, as will be discussed in Chapter 6. At the same time, it is entirely in keeping with her chameleonic performative abilities and further indicates an incisive understanding of audience (both the listening audience *and* her BBC and governmental patrons). Most certainly, correspondence suggests that Constanduros was fully aware that her work was necessarily both entertaining and propagandistic.

Over the course of a nearly four-year tenure on the programme, only once did Constanduros miss the mark, resulting in a fury of memos regarding a 'suggestive' or 'blue' line in a script submitted in May 1944. In the offending line, Grandma responds to Emily's query regarding her popularity as a young woman: 'Pop'lar? Why, my girl, I've known meself to be nudged black and blue on a bus-ride. There was one feller 'ad a most lovely nudge, I remember – but that's a long time ago.'[86] When associate producer Dorothy Bridgeman struck the line and replaced it with, 'Why men were round me like flies round a rubbish heap', Constanduros took her complaint directly to the new director general, William Haley, dismayed that the taint of 'suggestive material' might be detrimental to her career and argued that Bridgeman's use of 'blue' and 'suggestive' be struck from the record.[87]

Only once before, in 1935, had Constanduros's work been considered too vulgar for broadcast. In that case, 'Ogboddy's Outing' was initially refused by Max Kester because of its numerous references to bodily functions.[88] Here, as in the case of Bridgeman's rewrite, producers were expected to censor potentially doubtful material, guided by the prevailing BBC rule, 'when in doubt, take it out'.[89] Given the lack of official guidance and policy in regards to broadcast vulgarity, censorship of material was uneven.[90]

Constanduros protested that she had used the offending *KF* line in a previous evening Variety broadcast without objection. Finally, Constanduros stressed that there was no remunerative value in doing this work, but rather it was her 'war-work' and concluded that the line was not intended to be blue, but rather a means to make mundane recipes interesting: 'you will appreciate the difficulty of making the constant reading of recipes amusing enough to render it a popular feature. This, I concede, I have done since I am told my listening figures are around 22[%]'. Though the director general considered her complaint a 'storm in a teacup', Constanduros was too important a broadcaster on the *KF*, and on the BBC in general, to risk alienating and George Barnes, director of talks, met with Constanduros in person to hear her grievances. The meeting notes reflect a cordial visit, in which Constanduros 'accepted [his] view, as the person responsible, that the deleted words were undesirable in a Kitchen Front script, but naturally disagreed with it'. Finally, Constanduros again made clear that 'the series prevented her from being offered more important engagements by the BBC. She didn't complain of this, but she wished to show me the importance which she attached to the series.'[91] Like many artists, Constanduros was keen that others recognized her willingness to produce art in aid of the war effort.[92]

Aware that 'conscious propaganda' or heavy-handed methods rarely moved audiences,[93] the government must have appreciated the propaganda value of the entertaining transformation of Grandma from the difficult, self-centred schemer beloved by and known to all as a curmudgeon into a sharp-witted domestic soldier on the home front. Such a transformation of a notoriously difficult and disruptive character into a cheerleader for the national war effort *and* for the maintenance of societal norms was significant, especially in its potential influence on the working-class audiences the government worried most over.

Similar to Gert and Daisy's working-class comedy, the Buggins's *KF* appearances provided an important connection with the working-class audiences who tuned in. The programme attracted a broad cross-class audience, but the 'disproportionately high numbers' of working-class housewives is suggestive of its success in drawing an audience that usually stayed away from cookery programmes in peacetime.[94] In a field made up overwhelmingly of middle-class presenters, touting their cooks and sometimes peddling high-priced recipes on the *KF*, Maggie Andrews has argued that the 'accent, dialogue and familiar cultural reference points', of the Bugginses and Gert and Daisy 'achieve[d] a sense of identification with the [working-class] listeners'.[95] The informational content and pragmatism of the advice given was crucial in securing the programme's success, and Constanduros's commitment to delivering affordable and palatable recipes must have been appreciated by working-class audiences. Yet the 'identification, recognition and celebration for working class audiences' found in the *KF*'s working-class comedy acts also underscores the potential appeal for working-class listeners.[96] At the same time, the London-based humour and accents of these acts might not carry the same impact in regions outside the metropolis.[97] Nonetheless, in allowing her characters to voice complaints about the war and rationing, Constanduros's comedy acknowledged the inconveniences of rationing and reflected the very real experiences of many.

Furthermore, in highlighting working-class grievances and criticizing the inequities of the system, non-*KF* performances of the Buggins family might have further strengthened working-class identification with the family and deepened appreciation of the messaging found in their *KF* appearances. In the half-hour Forces programme, 'The Bugginses Go Gay', the Bugginses tackled one of the most common grievances of working-class and lower-middle-class Britons regarding the rationing system. While many supported rationing as a way to ensure 'fair shares', resentment grew over loopholes that enabled wealthy people access to luxury foods or extended their rations by eating out at restaurants.[98]

In response to popular dissatisfaction over restaurant 'gourmandising', the MoF decided to enact a 5 shilling ceiling on all restaurant meals.[99] This restriction did not, however, solve the problem. Instead, restaurants circumvented the order by charging a premium on items such as wine or by instituting cover charges; high-end establishments where the most egregious inequities could be found (and, incidentally, where many government ministers frequented) were exempt from the order.[100]

In 'The Bugginses Go Gay', Grandma proposes using Aunt Maria's 30 shilling football pool winnings for a nice meal at a 'posh place' in the West End. When Mrs. Buggins questions Grandma's math, Grandma cites 'the papers' that reported the 5 shilling maximum: 'Nobody can charge yer more than five bob for a meal now. Not even if you 'ad roast peacock with sauce.' Thus, she figured with five family members at 5s. each, they still had 5s. left over for transportation. At the restaurant, the comedy turns on misunderstandings and confusions of working-class outsiders entering the alien domain of the upper classes: Grandma balks at the slow service and the measly portions, and Mrs. Buggins is mortified by her family's ignorance and improper behaviour. The family order their meal, which includes extras like coffee and alcohol, while the BBC orchestra provides cabaret entertainment. When the bill arrives, the family are shocked to learn that they owed more than twice what they expected. Indignant, Grandma protests to the waiter, 'But it said in the papers you couldn't charge more than five bob a 'ead' and is told that while this was true, the cabaret cost 'seven-and-six', the orchestra five shillings, and service constituted 10 per cent of the bill. Upon hearing the cost of cabaret entertainment, Grandma responds, 'If I'd known that I wouldn't 'ave listened to it' and Mrs. Buggins exclaims, 'jest as though we couldn't 'ave ate our dinner jest as well without music.' After the waiter explains all of the charges, Grandma feigns illness, loudly proclaiming, 'I've ate somethink! Somethink dretful! It's tyin' itself in knots inside. O-o-h! Send for a doctor! I'm dyin'.' Embarrassed, the waiter hurries the family out of the restaurant and presses them to leave quickly: 'It is causing a disturbance', he asserts, 'people are going away.' While Emma and Mrs. Buggins make a scene about Grandma dying, Grandma plays up the illness until the waiter agrees to waive the bill and sends them home in a taxi. As the family leave, Grandma deadpans, 'Well, that's that and we've still got the thirty bob. Let's go and get something to eat – I'm that hungry.'[101]

In its liberal use of superior laughter, 'The Bugginses Go Gay' sketch demonstrates the cross-class appeal of Buggins family comedy. Educated or cultured audiences might laugh at the uninitiated, crude language and behaviour of the working-class outsiders, while the excess and decadence of the 'posh place' with its French menus, foreign-sounding staff, and unpatriotic actions might elicit xenophobic, pro-British feelings and sneering laughter. Many, regardless of class, might also feel inclined to laugh at the naiveté of the Bugginses in being ignorant of loopholes others employed to take advantage of the system (or wonder whether this was yet another instance of Grandma's ability to fake ignorance in order to outfox others).

More significantly, however, in dramatizing the protests of many over the inequity of the 5 shilling MoF restriction, 'The Bugginses Go Gay' further deepened the possibilities for working-class and lower-middle-class identifications with the Buggins family. Grandma's assertion of her right to enjoy a 5 shilling meal in the West End demonstrates the supposed wartime class levelling inherent in such governmental orders (and People's War rhetoric); indeed dialogue between the waiter and the family suggested that such levelling had occurred, since the Bugginses were neither categorically dismissed from the establishment nor treated with disdain – until Grandma's feigned illness threatens to scare off potential customers. At the same time, the arrival of the bill and the explanation of upcharges exposed the classed rifts that still existed in wartime, demonstrating the massive gulf that existed between those who could afford to pay for luxuries and those for whom 30 shillings represented a windfall. Once the hollowness of the regulation was exposed, Grandma's classic machinations to outmanoeuvre the system by gaining a free meal for the entire family are not aberrant or abhorrent, but rather heroic and patriotic. Instead, the restaurants and the upper classes who gained more than their 'fair share' become the villains of the home front. This People's War heroism, while most likely appealing to lower-middle-class and working-class audiences, might also appeal to those who could afford such luxuries, but who were equally angered over the inequities of the situation.[102]

Thus, by taking up the grievances of the working classes (and segments of the middle class) and validating their wartime experiences and grouses, the Buggins family could act as valuable agents of propaganda. Due to its communal and intimate domestic nature, as well as its ubiquity, radio was uniquely placed to disseminate propaganda through formal and informal means, outwardly through official pronouncements and more subtly couched behind laughter or 'infiltrated' throughout programming.[103] Entertainment propaganda was a form of '"white" propaganda: the necessary fostering and maintenance of the

British people's innate will to win".[104] The transformation of Grandma from curmudgeonly grouse into People's War patriot acted as excellent entertainment propaganda, recruiting audiences to commit to the war effort and become part of the People's War. At the same time, it represented important war work that both demonstrated Constanduros's commitment to the war effort and simultaneously ensured her continued relevance on radio and strengthened her celebrity.

6

Mother of the BBC

Portraying the 'ordinary', family and femininity, 1936–45

As was seen in Chapter 4, Constanduros expanded the world of her working-class characters by novelizing her radio sketches in the 1930s, but she also recognized a growing need to diversify her repertoire beyond working-class comedy. In 1935, Constanduros wrote two scripts for regular BBC features – *Conversation in the Train* and *Decision* – that led away from her comedic origins. *Conversation in the Train* put the listener in the position to eavesdrop on a 'conversation' about topical issues written by different personalities and complete with all the atmospherics and sound effects of a commuter train; the *Decision* programme consisted of 'soliloquies on the theme of making a decision', also written by different authors.[1] Her contributions to these programmes represented what she thought were insights into 'ordinary human life', mildly humorous in their observations and considerations of day-to-day middle-class experience – middle-class being considered 'ordinary' to both Constanduros and to the BBC. Both sketches were popular, and perhaps this success convinced her to expand beyond working-class comedy.[2]

In March 1936, Constanduros began a correspondence with Val Gielgud that resulted in her dramatizing 'ordinary' middle-class life – efforts that led to the forerunner of British soap opera. Some of her earliest radio monologues, such as 'Mrs. Smythe-Brown Buys a Book', poked fun at middle-class women, but the popularity of the Buggins family typecast her as a writer and actress of working-class comedy. Desperate to break free from this confinement, but unsure how to do so, Constanduros suggested that she use a pseudonym for her middle-class dramatic works. Gielgud, however, encouraged her to write under her own name, commenting, 'I don't see why [Constanduros's name] should be indefinitely sealed to the Family Buggins.'[3] This decision to branch out beyond comedy broadened broadcast opportunities and deepened Constanduros's relationship with the BBC. While Constanduros continued to write working-class comedy for the rest of her career, this expansion of her repertoire resulted in *The English Family Robinson (EFR)* – a series that, according to Constanduros, could have been entitled 'Anybody's Family' and became the template for British soap opera in the 1940s.[4] Though embarrassed of his role in bringing soap opera to Britain and dismissive of the 'aesthetically contemptible and sociologically corrupting' *Mrs. Dale's Diary* (and countless other popular soaps that followed in its train) Val Gielgud reminded readers in 1965 that Constanduros's Mrs. Robinson was in fact the 'lineal predecessor to Mrs. Dale'.[5]

When Constanduros proposed broadening her oeuvre beyond comedy in 1936, she imagined herself writing about 'ordinary' family life.[6] Her first play in this vein, 'One Saturday Afternoon', according to *Radio Times*, demonstrated Constanduros's 'gift for putting Everyman on the map'. Her exposition of a 'typical Saturday afternoon' in the life of an 'ordinary' family was clearly a middle-class suburban one: the plot followed father to the golf course, son to Brooklands motor racetrack, daughter in her exploits with a 'highbrow young author', and Mother as she whiled away the afternoon at home in eager anticipation of the moment the family returned once again to the domestic fold.[7]

Constanduros's foray into narrating 'ordinary' family life was part of a larger shift in the 1930s towards an expanding interest in the everyday and, in particular, in the private sphere. Constanduros's work on the family, both in comedic working-class tones and 'ordinary' middle-class prosaism, was representative of the efforts of a number of women writers, such as Marjory Spring-Rice and Margaret Llewellyn Davies, who lifted the veil on the inner sanctum of working-class homes, and similar to Jan Struther, 'who began to perceive the fabric of everyday life as a fit subject for writing' in the interwar period.[8] The establishment of the social research organization MO in 1937 is also indicative of the growing interest in everyday life in the period.[9]

Constanduros's Buggins family comedy is arguably an early example of the growing entertainment value of the family and the everyday, which predate these efforts. The popularity of such entertainment on radio, consumed by a larger, more diverse audience than were reading interwar novels or Struthers's *Mrs. Miniver* column in the *Times*, serves to strengthen Alison's Light's arguments regarding 'how far the domestication of the British had been popularly elevated to the status of national character' by the late-1930s.[10]

By this time, BBC listenership was roughly representative of the nation's class composition.[11] Though Listener Research and the pressures outlined in Chapter 3 forced the BBC to become somewhat more responsive to listener needs, especially as regards Variety entertainment, programming decisions in the 1930s nonetheless still reflected the staunchly middle-class, suburban outlook of BBC staff and writers demonstrated in the 'typical' weekend day dramatized by Constanduros in 'One Saturday Afternoon'.[12] Constanduros's second venture into the 'typical' household was a serialized light drama entitled *The English Family Robinson* and was written in collaboration with Constanduros's nephew, Denis. The template that the Constanduroses created in *EFR* proved remarkably enduring, serving as the model for later radio and television British soap operas, and further underscored the middle-class suburban mind-set of the interwar BBC.

Mabel and Denis collaborated on several projects before *EFR*, and through Mabel's influence at the BBC, Denis secured a handful of solo broadcasting contracts previous to the series. His first full-length solo play, *The Fox's Mask*, was broadcast in November 1937; prior to that, he wrote an episode for the 1936 BBC series *Decision*, and co-wrote a handful of musical comedies and fantasies with his aunt. As opposed to Mabel's popular fare, Denis's solo endeavours were acclaimed as avant-garde: *The Fox's Mask* was considered similar 'in its satirical intent' to Tyrone Guthrie's cutting-edge radio plays *Squirrel's Cage* (1929) and *The Flowers Are Not for You to Pick* (1930).[13] Denis was not, however, trained as a writer, but was instead an artist, and is best known in this vein for his contributions to the 1930s Shell marketing campaigns alongside Paul Nash and Graham Sutherland; he also collaborated with his aunt to illustrate several of her working-class novels, including *Down Mangel Street* (1938).[14] Never able to make a full-time career of his art, Denis's radio work was largely a means to provide for his family, and he eventually became 'a highly respected radio and television writer in his own right'.[15]

Mabel Constanduros came up with the idea for the *EFR* series after learning of the successful NBC prime-time serial radio soap opera *One Man's Family* while in America in 1937.[16] Her pitch to the BBC suggested they elevate the class register represented by previous radio families such as the lower-middle-class Pennys or the working-class Bugginses and Plums. Constanduros imagined the new family to be

> a couple living perhaps at Sutton or Wimbledon, with three children – a few steps higher on the social scale … . I should suggest the sketches last about eight minutes and concern themselves with the everyday happenings which

are familiar to us all. The Father, Mother, and three Children should be well characterized but not at all exaggerated. I suggest it be called 'Anybody's Family' or some such name.[17]

Constanduros conflated 'Anybody's Family' with her own: proposing to situate her ordinary family in the same Metroland suburb where she had experienced middle-class domesticity herself (and from which she subsequently escaped). Gielgud further supported this conflation between the ordinary and middle-class suburbia when he suggested a possible name for the series as 'The Thames Ditton Family Robinson', referencing a middle-class London suburb similar to Sutton.[18] Though not discussed in the correspondence, the title seems a playful reference to Johann David Wyss's *The Swiss Family Robinson* novel. The correspondence regarding the development of the serial *EFR* thus reveals how Metroland suburban middle-class experience was central to the portrayal of the national norm on the BBC in the interwar period. Indeed, the *Radio Times* declared that the Robinsons were 'as near to real people as you can expect on the radio' and announced the series as 'everyday happenings in an everyday household'.[19] While talks on everyday life, everyday problems and conversations with everyday people were commonplace on the BBC since the 1920s, *EFR* was one of the first attempts to dramatize the everyday on the BBC.

Ultimately, Constanduros decided to settle the Robinsons in the fictional 'Strutham', a rather thinly veiled reference to Streatham in South London. This was a significant choice, which problematizes the suburban Metroland image of the nation initially imagined by both Constanduros and Gielgud. Streatham was an area familiar to Constanduros: situated midway between Constanduros's childhood home in Peckham and her married home in Sutton. She once acted for the Streatham Anomalies, an amateur theatrical group in the area.[20]

In the first half of the twentieth century, Streatham was struggling with an identity crisis as it evolved from a rural retreat for wealthy Londoners into an inner London suburb.[21] According to one local historian of the area in 1936, Streatham was 'fast losing its identity – one might even say its soul – in a Greater London'.[22] Streatham had become, by the 1930s, a vibrant 'entertainment centre' of South London, marked by its impressive Pratt's department store, theatres, cinemas and ice rink.[23] The Streatham/Strutham of the Robinsons, then, was representative of the pressures numerous Britons – regardless of class or region – faced in the period: the ribbon development derided by intellectuals such as

JB Priestly, the rapid transformation of rural and semi-rural areas into suburban spaces, and the suburban areas gradually engulfed into larger urban spaces.[24]

Significantly, however, Strutham was not Streatham: it was imaginary and could thus be elastically employed as representative of any number of environments in listeners' mental landscapes. Strutham's unabashed suburban identity might speak to the roughly 25 per cent of the population who lived in suburban areas at the end of the 1930s.[25] Indeed, while some critics might disdain the suburbs (and by extension, the programmes that portrayed life in them) as 'full of "mean and perky little houses that surely none but mean and perky little souls should inhabit with satisfaction"', those 'mean and perky little souls' might appreciate a positive mirror of their lives depicted on air.[26] Further, while the tone of the 'ordinary' in the Robinsons was distinctly middle class, lower middle- and working-class listeners might aspire to the lifestyle of the family, and still others, regardless of class, might aspire to the warmth and relational cosiness enjoyed by the Robinsons.

EFR was the epitome of an 'ordinary family' as conceptualized by the BBC in the late-1930s: 'not too chic, urbane or radical, not too vulgar, rowdy and fractious, but respectable, nice and inoffensive'.[27] As the voice of the nation, the BBC had the power to represent the people, and in portraying the middle-class, suburban Robinsons as unproblematically 'typical', *EFR* did the work of constructing a national character in which the middle-class family was elided into an imagined national unit which represented 'the unifying thread' linking all classes in the nation together.[28] *EFR* can therefore be seen as part of the interwar conservative reworking of Englishness identified in Alison Light's seminal work, *Forever England*.[29] The interwar BBC's conception of the ordinary family, 'with its quiet pleasures was', as Paddy Scannell has argued, 'a judicious solution to the problem of establishing a social norm – a set of aspirations, tastes and habits which might be assumed as widely shared and acceptable throughout society.'[30]

In an article introducing *EFR* to *Radio Times* readers, it was argued that

> the chief appeal [of the series] for most listeners is that though dramatic it is not theatrical … . Their weekly adventures will be those that may have happened to thousands of listeners and their families during the week … though nothing sensational is likely to happen to them, you will probably soon feel that you know them as well as you know anybody you meet in the shops, at the golf club, or in the morning on the 8.45.[31]

The characters were intended to be eminently ordinary and recognizable to listeners, and the writers sympathetic to the plights of 'ordinary' existence:

> Charles Robinson is just like any number of suburban householders. He works in an office though he doesn't talk much about it when he gets home. His job is one of those that mean hurrying breakfast, catching the train in the morning, and – with luck – putting it all behind you when you get home at night. He has been with the firm long enough to be in the running for a manager's job if there is a vacancy. On the other hand, he is old enough to have every reason for apprehension if there is any prospect of getting the sack.[32]

Mr. Robinson, therefore, was an 'ordinary' middle-class, middle-aged work-a-day man never fully secure in his employment, seeking refuge in his home and family. Meanwhile, the article explained, Clara Robinson 'is just as normal. There are myriads of wives like her, not clever but very sensible, doing the difficult job of running a family without getting any particular credit for it.'[33] Much of the action of the series occurred in the home and focused on Clara Robinson's relations with the family and their domestic servant; yet this article takes pains to sketch out Charles' backstory, ascribing to him, and his work, central importance. While Clara is the true main character of the series, she *and the women she is meant to represent* are given no backstory in the *Radio Times*; they, and the home they keep, are hardly worth notice or description. Thus the BBC's own advertising for the series minimizes the dramatization of women's lives in ways that continue to plague discussions of soap opera.[34]

The first instalment of *EFR* was set at home on a Saturday morning, with the family jockeying for use of the family's car, nicknamed 'Ella', as they planned their day around the breakfast table. Teenage Joan (played by Elizabeth Gilbert) wished to have the car so that she could go to field hockey practice and return home in time to change for a date later in the afternoon; older brother Peter (Harold Reese) hoped to take 'the girl all boys in Strutham were crazy on' to Brooklands; Mother (Constanduros) wished to take John (Clive Baxter), the youngest, to the dentist; father (Ralph Truman) had an important golf game to attend to; and John wished only to back the car out of the 'garidge'. (Father immediately correcting him 'Garage, my boy … . Don't they teach you to speak at school?')[35] Shirley (Megs Jenkins), the maid, provided caricatured working-class comic relief to most of the sketches.

In the third sketch, 'Mrs. Robinson Copes with a Situation', which aired on 21 October 1938, Mrs. Robinson confronted Shirley about items that had gone missing. In the novelized version of this sketch in Constanduros's *A Nice Fire in the Drawing Room: A Story about Ordinary People* (1939), readers are given a deeper sense of how agonizing this exchange was for Mrs. Robinson than might have been relatable in the radio version. While the dialogue gives one a sense of the difficulty Mrs. Robinson felt in having to confront Shirley, the novel enables more insight into the mental anguish caused by the prospect of such a confrontation. The family, having encouraged her to question Shirley, left Mrs. Robinson to tackle the situation alone:

> She answered everyone as sensibly and coherently as she could, waved good-bye to them all as they disappeared, hurrying down the road to the station, and came into the house again feeling as though she had just been through a minor kind of earthquake. Now she was left alone to cope with the most awkward situation she had experienced in all her married life .... She must say the unpleasant things she had to say now, before the business of the day began, before Shirley began to chatter in her confiding way, before they had begun the daily tasks they shared with such a comfortable understanding.[36]

After some gentle questioning about the missing items, Shirley tearfully confessed that her family had fallen on hard times and that her boyfriend also expected 'gifts'. Mrs. Robinson benevolently suggests to Shirley that a boyfriend who led her to steal, an act which 'risked prison – because you know some employers might even have gone as far as that', was hardly worth keeping.[37] Once the contrite Shirley promises to leave the boyfriend and to never steal from the family again, Mrs. Robinson allows her to stay on and generously offers a 10s pay rise.[38] At this, Shirley quickly shifts interests to another boy, chatting away in her usual bright banter. Constanduros's treatment here of the servant and master relationship echoes the kind-hearted paternalism of Constanduros's own personal experiences with family servants, discussed in Chapter 2. It further exposes middle-class prejudices towards the working classes and highlights middle-class expectations of classed femininity: the gravity with which Mrs. Robinson approaches the situation is striking in comparison to Shirley's initial dramatic tears and quick emotional recovery. Finally, the exchange underscores the emotional intimacy of servant and employer that existed in smaller middle-class homes of the interwar period.[39]

Though the series aired in the wake of the Munich crisis, nothing outside the family circle of servants, neighbours and love interests for the teenage children touched the Robinson's semi-detached. Struther's Mrs. Miniver, on the other hand, had been appearing in the *Times* since 1937, and weathered the crisis throughout September with the newspaper's reading public: airing worries over the future and trying on gas masks in preparation for war. On 6 October, the day before the first *EFR* aired, a Miniver column appeared entitled 'Back to Normal', in which Mrs. Miniver reflected upon the changes that the crisis had wrought on her family and on her own outlook. While Miniver remained largely above the fray of day-to-day domesticity, never, for instance, 'ordering a mutton', the Robinsons were instead insulated from the national and international, immersed in their everyday private domesticity.[40] Listeners may have appreciated the domestic escape *EFR* offered after the crisis that broke over Europe in September as they revelled in a brief moment of 'peace in our time'.

The Robinson family returned for a one-off playlet entitled *Cruising Family Robinson* in June 1939, and once again, domestic drama insulated the family from the world beyond their middle-class suburban comfort zone. Through a series of events which included their daughter's engagement, the cruise which would have taken Mr. and Mrs. Robinson and their daughter abroad for over two weeks ('As far as Athens') ended as a secret getaway for the parents, *sans* daughter, to their usual (comfortable) holiday spot at Bognor. Instead of disappointment, Mr. and Mrs. Robinson express relief at not having to go abroad, and avoiding the possibility of foreign intrusion into their safely moored private lives. When the series returned in 1940, however, the outside world had invaded the Robinson household.

At the beginning of the war, Gielgud suggested that Mabel and Denis submit Robinson features 'describing their wartime activities'.[41] Her first attempt at writing in this vein, a piece about evacuees, was rejected due to the touchy nature of the cross-class conflict presented by the evacuation process and expressed in the play.[42] In January 1940, Howard Rose (the producer of the 1938 The *EFR* series and the 1939 playlet *Cruising Family Robinson*), having received a number of requests for the Robinsons' return, attempted to reboot the series on a recurrent basis, hoping to follow the family as they coped with the day-to-day challenges of wartime life.[43]

When the Robinsons finally returned on 30 April 1940, Howard Rose stepped up efforts to establish the series as a regular feature and pressed Constanduros to recruit Denis to write a number of topical plays centred on the family. Constanduros eagerly agreed, but worried about Denis's availability, given that petrol restrictions made it difficult for the two to collaborate as she was in West Sussex and he in Wiltshire. Further, she explained to Rose, Denis had joined up, though he was Grade III and she thought him 'unlikely to be called up'. Still, he was reluctant to commit to ongoing BBC as he felt it his duty to carry on working in a war factory.[44] In the event, the Constanduroses did manage to write three twenty-minute wartime *EFR* plays that ran in the summer of 1940, culminating in the last of the series on 7 August, 'Red Warning at the Robinsons'.

The three wartime *EFR* episodes continued the concept of 'everyday happenings in an everyday household', inflected by wartime realities, stresses and drama. The Robinson characterizations remain the same: they are still the ordinary family listeners had grown to know as they knew their fellow commuters on the 8.45. In wartime, the Robinsons are once again meant to be representative of 'anybody's family' and very easily transition from their comfortable day-to-day peacetime existence into the 'ordinary' heroes of the People's War: Father joins the Home Guard, the family digs up the lawn and tennis court to dig for Victory, Shirley's boyfriend joins the army, newlywed Joan's husband Michael is in the RAF, Peter is desperate to be in uniform, young John keeps an eye out for spies and Mother manages to hold the family together without tears.

The final episode of the wartime Robinsons, 'Red Alert at the Robinsons', demonstrates how the Robinsons simultaneously dramatized the ordinary in wartime and supported People's War propaganda. The episode begins with the relational drama of Joan and Michael, who are experiencing their first marital argument. John informs the family that he thought he heard an air raid siren, and the family scramble to the shelter in the cellar. But when an aunt who is living with the family refuses to come to the shelter, Mrs. Robinson feels it her duty to remain with the aunt; meanwhile Joan wishes to drive to Michael's airbase so that she can apologize to him. Mr. Robinson cuts through the chaos and demands that everyone seek shelter (leaving the stubborn aunt to her own devices above stairs). John gathers up the neighbours, the Wilsons, and with Shirley and her boyfriend in tow, they all scurry below stairs.

The Wilsons are insufferable shelter companions, and much of the episode centres on their annoyances: Mrs. Wilson ('Pussy') worries over a skittish, barking lap dog, while a slightly tipsy Mr. Wilson ('Tommykins') brightly offers rum to the shelterers. Shirley's boyfriend, 'Orty', begins card tricks to ease the tension in the shelter. But Orty's card trick banter edges on the blue side, which no one but Shirley thinks are funny. Finally, Mr. Wilson recognizes Orty as a convicted housebreaker. When Orty confesses that peacetime economic circumstances led him to steal, the Robinsons support him as he is now in uniform. The Wilsons are exposed as the true wartime shirkers in their selfish concerns over their wartime 'sacrifices', such as the loss of the tennis club's courts to make room for victory gardens, Mrs. Wilson's weekly hair appointments cut to a fortnightly basis, and the loss of two maids and an omelette pan. When the couple attempts to leave, they find the door jammed. Mrs. Wilson panics while Mr. Robinson and Orty try to break open the door. Finally, Orty saves the day by crawling out the coal chute and picking the lock to get inside the house. Michael returns to help open the jammed shelter door and then informs them that the real air raid warning just sounded and they all have to shelter again.

The relational dynamics of 'Red Alert at the Robinsons' are believable and recognizable: newlywed arguments and annoying neighbours who impinge on family shelters. Further, as heroes of the People's War, the Robinsons recognize character and duty above class. While Orty is clearly cast as the working-class outsider by telling blue jokes, quoting popular BBC Variety show catchphrases, he is embraced by the group (and by extension, the nation) by virtue of his uniform. Orty further redeems his criminal past by breaking into the house to save the family. At the same time, the Robinsons eschew class loyalties and are critical of the middle-class Wilsons.

This last episode in the wartime lives of the Robinsons was considered the best of the three by producer Howard Rose, who approached Assistant Director of Drama and Features Moray Maclaren to make the Robinsons a long-term serial; however, Maclaren would only agree to continue them on an intermittent basis. While the Home Service's Drama and Features department proved resistant to any Americanization of programmes, particularly that of a long-term, regular series, the Overseas Service had few reservations about such methods.[45] Not long after 'Red Alert' aired, Ernie Bushnell, North American programme organizer for BBC Overseas Service, outlined a series to the director of the Overseas Service very much along the lines of the Constanduros model, 'dealing with the daily doings of the average British family, particularly in wartime'. In order to win over the Americans, however, Bushnell proposed a format with which Americans were comfortable: a serial 'to be run American-style, five or six days a week at the same time daily for 15 minutes'.[46]

Bushnell employed Alan Melville to write the series for the North American Service, which debuted in April 1941. *Front Line Family* (*FLF*) was stunningly similar to *EFR*. The given names of all the principal characters had changed, but the Robinson family name remained, as did the structure of the family: *FLF* was complete with one teenage daughter and two sons, each about the same age as in the Constanduros version. *FLF* proved popular, and remained on air throughout the war and well into the post-war period as *The Robinsons*, becoming the direct predecessor to the popular long-running soap opera, *Mrs. Dale's Diary* (1948–69).

In January 1942, Constanduros was approached to take up the *FLF* series after writer Alan Melville's hasty departure, and attempts to employ a new writer, American expatriate Mrs. Ronnie Colley, fell through.[47] *FLF* had been shifted to Drama and Features in the summer of 1941, and upon the crisis that broke over Melville's departure, the assistant director of the department, Laurence Gilliam, reasoned that *FLF* needed a 'woman writer' who could write 'the inter-play of individuals within the family'; at the same time, Gilliam imagined that the series required a writer who could depict 'the "real" story of Britain at war', and therefore needed to be male.[48] In effort to resolve these tensions, Gilliam's first choice was to tap the established writing partnership of Constanduros and Howard Agg.

Howard Agg, a dramatist who had published a few plays both individually and in collaboration with Phillip Johnson in the mid-1930s, initiated a partnership with Constanduros in 1937 when he contacted her to write women-centred amateur stage plays. After an inauspicious beginning in which Constanduros, exasperated at the loggerheads to which they came in their initial writing sessions nearly abandoned the partnership, the two eventually settled into a working relationship that resulted in a prolific and decade-long collaboration.[49] By the time Gilliam approached Agg and Constanduros to write for *FLF*, they were an established writing team, having penned thirteen plays, four novel adaptations, and two six-episode series for broadcasting.[50]

Given the long-term commitment and strain of writing a regular series, Agg who, by then had become a BBC staffer and also handled contract negotiations for collaborative work with Constanduros, pressed for a long-term contract amounting to £1,800 for each. The BBC initially balked at the price, stating that staff script writers were grade B1, and therefore not entitled to more than £640 a year.[51] However, the Empire Service felt the popular *FLF* 'a most important programme – as it provides our principal opportunity for carrying propaganda in an entertainment vehicle', and therefore seriously considered paying a premium to secure quality writing talent. A handwritten note on the memorandum agreed, stating that *FLF* was originally developed 'on the cheap' and the risks of losing the popular programme necessitated that the BBC pay market price for the 'best available' writers.[52] Considering the import of the programme, Gilliam asked Agg and Constanduros to write several trial scripts in competition with another writer, Basil Woon, in order to secure the future of *FLF*.

By mid-March 1942, negotiations with Agg had broken down, BBC staff finding him to be quite 'unreasonable' about the matter, and Woon was thus engaged as the sole writer for the series.[53] This exchange was indicative of Agg's dealings with BBC staffers, who felt him an imperious negotiator who pompously leveraged a special arrangement that allowed him to negotiate higher fees above the usual BBC staff rate when collaborating with Constanduros.[54] Agg's handling of their contract relationship with the BBC on this matter and numerous others, exposed fault lines in Constanduros and Agg's relationship that eventually led to the dissolution of the partnership in the 1950s, and will be discussed in the next chapter.

Writing femininity

The Constanduros/Agg collaboration resulted in numerous and varied wartime programming, including several adaptations of Somerset Maugham's work and a particularly well-received, and well-compensated, version of Dickens's *Bleak House*[55]; nearly twenty original plays; and two multi-episode serials. The two serials were radically different, one a thriller and the other a middle-class situation comedy, and give insight into the range of the pair's collaborative work. Constanduros and Agg's BBC wartime collaborations purposely avoided reference to war in their writing, because, Agg maintained, 'we ought to be able to think up quite as amusing situations without resorting to this subject'.[56]

Both wartime serials ran during the summer of 1941 on the Home Service and the Forces. In an October 1940 letter to Gielgud, that included a draft episode of *On the Run*, an eight-part serial, Agg briefly described the action of the piece:

> It is the story of a murder; the kidnapping of the principal witness for the defence; and the subsequent chase of the kidnappers by two young – and we hope amusing – journalists of opposite sexes, who are always just a lap behind. The chase ends in a lonely cottage on the Cornish coast, with a shooting affray. The distant sound of wedding bells brings down the curtain.[57]

The synopsis lays out some hallmark features of the writing partnership, regardless of genre: the inclusion of what one internal BBC reviewer in 1945 derisively termed the 'usual Constanduros/Agg would-be funny bright dialogue', romantic tension and the promise of a happy ending.[58] The series proved popular, and was later made into a novel.

The other series that ran in the summer of 1941 featured Richard Goolden (famous for his bumbling Mr. Penny act) and Constanduros in *Mr. and Mrs. Sparkes*, a situation comedy that traded on the popularity of its two stars and its 'toe-curlingly painful representation of the "quiet, domesticated couple living in a small suburban house near London"', similar to the popular 1980s television situation comedy, *Ever Decreasing Circles*.[59] The series veered away from any wartime references as it followed 'Ducksie' (Mr. Sparkes) and 'Mummie' (Mrs. Sparkes) through humorous domestic misunderstandings and intrigue, ranging from Mummie's accidentally bidding on a rather destructive goat to a close scrape with a burglar and a faintly serio-comedic episode in which the two question the suspicious actions of a husband in the disappearance of his wife.[60]

The introduction to the Samuel French version of *Mr. and Mrs. Sparkes* (1941) participates in the usual cultural disdain of suburbia, noting the couple's 'soul-less' suburban home with its fumed oak and knick-knacks, 'like hundreds of its kind, entirely without character'.[61] As Bush-Bailey has argued, this bleak description of suburbia may provide some insight into Constanduros's own experiences in a similar suburban environment.[62] The character sketches also suggest echoes of Constanduros's Sutton life: Ducksie is strikingly reminiscent of Ath, which is described as an uninspiring portrait of the 'little man'. Ducksie is a cheese salesman who was 'kind, meek and tolerant – except, occasionally with his wife, when he can be quite surprisingly terse and dominating'.[63] The introduction further presents a picture of Ducksie suggestive of family memories of Ath:

> He speaks very precisely and lends to every topic of conversation – be it the weather, gardening, or the morning train – a serious consideration that is most impressive, though in anyone else it would seem a little comic ... he has no sense of humour, but in spite of it manages to be likeable.[64]

Denis Constanduros remembered Ath at Sunday dinner during the First World War in similar strains:

> Uncle Ath, tilting back his head to see below his glasses, would begin a long story while carefully carving the minute wartime joint, describing at extreme length how, while processing down the aisle with the rest of the choir, he happened to notice that one of the tiles on the floor was slightly out of position and how he very nearly – but not quite – tripped over it; breaking off occasionally to say to my brother and myself, 'I won't give you too much, old fellow, because I know you aren't hungry.'[65]

Ath was admired in his family for his honesty and his work ethic, but Denis confided, he was 'always something of a bore' who 'was, in our more raffish family, looked upon as something of a figure of fun'.[66] Ducksie's exacting manner, detailed memory for train tables and fear of change may be further echoes of the suburban domesticity Constanduros escaped when she bought her London flat in the 1920s.

If Ducksie was patterned somewhat after Ath, it would be difficult to find Constanduros in Mummie. According to the introductory character sketches, Mummie was 'quiet, gentle and unobtrusive, and always very conscious of her husband's superiority, which one doesn't suppose she has ever thought of questioning'.[67] Mummie's mishaps were often the result of incompetence and an inability to confront others, like her neighbour, Mrs. Bocking, 'a gaunt, sharp-featured lady with an acid tongue and a genius for gossip. Beside her Mummie presents the spectacle of a chirping little wren against a swooping hawk'.[68] One suspects Mabel encountered Mummie in Sutton, either in one person or as a composite of suburban housewives. Possibly she imagined this to be the role she was supposed to play in real life, but could not bring herself to do.

Bush-Bailey has observed, 'Constanduros's writing uses many voices to work out her own place in the positions that women were negotiating in both private and public spheres'.[69] Given Constanduros's own experiences and the prevailing discourses in interwar popular British culture, it is not surprising that her most critical caricatures of femininity were found in the suburban housewives she created and performed. Much of her ambivalence regarding domestic femininity was infused with 'debates about home and the "wifely life"' found in other popular forms of writing during the 1930s.[70] Much of her work includes an embedded critique of female domesticity that Alison Light has argued is indicative of middle-class feminism, an 'assumption that there is something essentially stultifying and degrading in domesticity'.[71] Constanduros's portrayals of suburban housewives were often non-confrontational, 'not clever' housewives bound to home and family like Mummie or Mrs. Robinson, whom Constanduros seemed to personally loathe and yet, her caricatures stopped short of outright contempt. Mummie's meekness is humorous and likeable, her incompetence acts as the comedic motor behind the sketches; Mrs. Robinson's fear of confrontation (as seen in the episode where she confronted Shirley about theft) was not paralysing, but ultimately showed an admirable (if patronizing) kind-heartedness, making her the unassuming, self-sacrificing hero of *EFR*. While not nearly as withering as the critiques other female interwar writers levelled at suburban housewives, there still existed a veiled 'scorn' for a 'breed of woman who merely enjoyed her "labour-saving" home, who got respectability on a mortgage, social status and its rewards on the never-never'.[72]

At the same time, Constanduros seems to have recognized that working-class domesticity might be altogether something different, even desired, in her working-class housewives. While her middle-class housewives were always tinged with negative attributes such as described Mrs. Robinson and Mummie, Constanduros was publicly very clear that she intended Mrs. Buggins to be the 'hero' of the Buggins family. She once told *Radio Pictorial* that she created Grandma, 'one of the tiresomest and cussedest creatures I could imagine – to show off Mrs. Buggins' sweetness of character'.[73] Such contrast, of course, also makes for excellent comedic opportunity. But while Mrs. Buggins may have been sweet in contrast to the curmudgeonly Grandma, she was also more confident, confrontational and commanding than any of the middle-class suburban housewives Constanduros created. The Bugginses, significantly, were others: they were the cheeky Cockneys 'amongst whom I have always lived' whom she admired for their 'cheerfulness, their imperturbability, and their particular brand of humour'. 'Mrs. Buggins', she told *Radio Pictorial* readers, 'is drawn from the people I admire most – the typical British working man's wife – cheerful under incredible difficulties, good humoured, capable, industrious and, above all, a good sort'.[74] Constanduros's versions of working-class femininity, which she could admire from afar, contrasted starkly with the middle-class femininity with which she was intimately familiar.

As an actress, Constanduros played various versions of femininity across classes, from the sweet and meek to the sharp-tongued and strong-willed. The latter, it seems she enjoyed the most, as evidenced in rave reviews of an amateur stage performance of 'The Choice' in 1925. The local *Advertiser* wrote of her performance, 'Sarcastic, outspoken, and clever in repartee, [Constanduros] made the most of her opportunities and introduced the chief element of laughter into the story. Her acting was perfect and she added another success to her list'.[75] The Sutton *Herald* lauded, 'As Lady Jemima Ballardaile, Clarissa's aunt, she was entrusted with a character such as she loves to depict. Sharp-tongued and cynical, with a love for biting epigrams, she was one of the outstanding successes of the evening'.[76]

On air, Constanduros's voice talent enabled her to embody many different versions of femininity simultaneously. 'Behind the blessed shelter of a microphone, you can be whatever character you choose', she wrote, 'since your appearance can neither help nor hinder. You can play anything, from a child of six to an old woman of eighty.'[77] Further, the microphone enabled one to cross-class boundaries and play with gendered performance. In her Buggins sketches, she often played the 'sweet' Mrs. Buggins and the 'cussed' Grandma together, mixing in the voices of aunts and neighbours who constituted varying shades of femininity between the two. The tension between 'cussed creatures' and 'sweet' matriarchs makes for good comedy in the Buggins family sketches, but also represents a preoccupation with the battle between prevailing models of femininity that Constanduros continually confronted and navigated throughout her career. At the same time, all of Constanduros's writing placed a central emphasis on women's spaces and women's experiences, presenting a range of diverse voices and possibilities, thus opening up spaces for female listeners to negotiate their own meanings of the representations of femininity drawn in her work.[78]

Mother of the BBC

Constanduros's BBC correspondence is indicative of her negotiation of competing models of femininity, and it demonstrates the 'blurring identities of wife, mother and worker within the home and within the workplace' that Claire Langhamer has identified in women's working experiences in the post-war period.[79] At the same time, Constanduros fought to establish her credentials as a professional writer and artist both in public narrative and behind the scenes in correspondence with the BBC. While some have argued that theoretically, professionalism can create a gender and class neutral space of inclusion, in reality this is rarely the case.[80]

While professionalism is a mantle easily bestowed upon men, women must tirelessly labour to convince both the public and themselves that they are deserving of the designation. This was certainly the case in interwar Britain, as more and more women sought professional work. As Ray Strachey counselled in her 1934 manual for career-minded young women, beyond professions in defence, the Catholic Church and the Stock Exchange, 'there is practically no theoretical exclusion of females at all. Theoretical admission is not, of course, the same thing as real opportunity ... nevertheless, the removal of legal barriers had definitely opened the doors.'[81] While women in this period had to consider the marriage bar, Strachey noted that these restrictions did not apply to 'women musicians, painters, actresses and writers'.[82]

Nonetheless, Constanduros and other artists battled against a process of 'pseudo-inclusion', which allows for the presence of women, while simultaneously rendering us invisible through assumptions that underscore the normative as male.[83] This process can be seen through language employed by those who worked closely with Constanduros at the BBC. When Maschwitz wrote an article in the 1933 *BBC Yearbook* about the need to recruit new talent for Variety, his list of essential attributes of worthy candidates was decidedly male:

1. He is thoroughly trained in microphone work. He can work with or without an audience.
2. He takes the trouble to prepare special material, and renew his material.
3. He is instinctively aware of BBC standards and gives us the type of material suited to our mixed audience.
4. Eventually, he appears on the stage or screen as a BBC 'Star' and, if he is a good artist, does indirect propaganda for us.[84]

Labouring under such assumptions, it is not surprising that Constanduros felt compelled to strenuously defend her position as a *professional* both in her correspondence with the BBC and with the public. In *Shreds and Patches*, she was at pains to demonstrate that her elevation to star pay in 1925 meant that she had crossed the threshold between amateur and professional. She explained to her readers what this meant:

> A professional writer or performer may never fall below a certain level of achievement, though her work may be above that level often. I had to learn to write to order and to turn out respectable material whether I felt in the mood for it or not. I had to discipline my mind, for engagements came thick and fast, and more and more material had to be found.[85]

Constanduros's use of 'her' in this passage is a significant counterbalance to Maschwitz's employment of the male pronoun. Confronted with the normative he, Constanduros asserted her right to be seen as a professional. Barbara Thiele has argued that '"he" is assumed to be the all-inclusive pronoun, even though a close examination of the text makes it all too apparent that the author literally means "he"'.[86] Also important in this passage is Constanduros's distinction between amateur and professional, which was a particular concern of female artists asserting their professionalism. In her work on female architects and designers in interwar Britain, Jill Seddon has argued that it was crucial for female professional artists to distance themselves from the assumed position of woman as amateurs by creating a 'recognisable body of work, identifiable with a single individual … . The achievement of such a goal is of particular significance in these fields where the presence and output of amateurs has been, and still is, problematic, particularly for women.'[87] Given the importance of amateurs, such as herself, to the development of the early BBC, it was even more important for Constanduros to prove that she was no longer an amateur, but had become a bona fide professional.

Careful always to assert her professionalism and confident in her abilities, Constanduros also had to navigate the treacherous waters of a woman in the workplace, the dangers of which were outlined in a 1954 study on educated wives:

> She must avoid both the rocks of aggressive insistence on her status and also the mud-flats of self deprecation. She must be both feminine and masculine, but not lean too far one way or the other. She must try to combine in herself some at least of the attitudes which were once believed to be found only in men, with a liberal allowance of the qualities that marriage and motherhood engender. In a predominantly masculine world she must restate feminine values and she must insist on the importance of human relationships.[88]

Constanduros's communication with the BBC adheres to the maxims found in this passage: a continual balancing act of masculinity and femininity.

Constanduros could be confident and assertive in her correspondence with the BBC, as when she questioned inequities in the payments received for her work. When, for instance, she was offered 12 gn. for a contribution to *Conversation in the Train*, she wrote to remind the Copyright department that she had been paid 15 gn. in the past, while Denis had received 12 gn. for the same work. The clear message was that *she* was the well-heeled professional and should be paid more than her nephew, who had only just begun his writing career. She finished the letter with a terse, 'I am quite willing to accept the same fee as I had before for this one.' The BBC responded by apologizing and bumping her fee up to 15 gn.[89] On another occasion, Constanduros learned that her solo writing was not compensated as much as when she partnered with men, and complained:

> I still think I am being paid too little. A musical show is much more trouble to write than a straight one and I don't see why, when Denis and I separately get 1 gn an hour for what we write and Howard Agg and I get sometimes more why I alone should be paid less. I am the most experienced writer of the three with 18 years of writing for the air – as much, possibly, as any author writing. And nobody has kept up this standard, I believe, for so long.[90]

This passage is indicative of much of Constanduros's negotiating style, schooling staffers on the distinctions between various types of writing, and stressing her experience, longevity and popularity when negotiating fees. Here, she demonstrates the professional knowledge of writing in different registers; later in her career, she often underscored the difficulties of writing adaptations versus original work, explaining the necessity of multiple readings of the work and the challenges of rewriting action and dialogue to fit the radio format and yet remain as true as possible to the text. Additionally, Constanduros asserted her right to control her works, arguing that no one but herself was allowed to perform Buggins material on the BBC or anywhere else in the world.[91] As mentioned earlier, it was critical for professionals to maintain a recognizable body of work.

But while Constanduros confidently asserted her professional position in negotiations, she always ended in a conciliatory manner. In the letter mentioned earlier regarding unequal pay for her solo writing, she closed with the following sentiment: 'As it is, I could insist on being paid the just price, but I won't because the BBC as a whole has always treated me so very fairly. This is the exception.'[92] This balancing act was usually successful: the BBC often capitulated and either gave Constanduros her asking fee or compromised, as happened in this particular instance.[93]

Constanduros was also very careful to nurture close professional relationships with BBC staffers, especially producers and top decision makers. Initial contacts with staffers were professional in tone, using titles and full names in salutations, carefully explaining her positions and demonstrating her knowledge of the trade in the body of the letters. After several contacts, however, Constanduros invariably invited the staffer to lunch, because, as she told the script editor in the Drama department, Barbara Bray in 1954, 'I always like to meet personally anyone with whom I do business.'[94] In most cases, salutations both to the staffer and to Constanduros become friendlier after the lunch date. For instance, initial correspondence with Charles Lefeaux, acting script editor for Drama after Sieveking left due to illness in 1951, was addressed to 'Mr. Charles Lefeaux'; after lunching together, Constanduros switched to 'My dear Charles' and Lefeaux reciprocated.[95] Often, the correspondence increasingly became more personal and informal, using given names, asking after children and spouses, offering health advice or referencing other personal information. BBC staffers often reciprocated Constanduros's overtures, responding with increasing informality; few, such as Barbara Bray, chose to continue the relationship on a strictly professional level, despite Constanduros's best efforts.[96] This style of correspondence is contrasted by the letters of Constanduros's close associate, Barbara Euphan Todd (Bower), who was famous for her Worzel Gummidge books and children's radio and television series. In over eleven years of correspondence with staff at *Children's Hour*, Bower never used the familiar and always steered clear of informal, personal communication.[97]

Much of Constanduros's networking and nurturing of relationships took place beyond correspondence or the halls of Savoy Hill or Broadcasting House. She often lunched with staffers at the Ivy Restaurant in London, and enjoyed entertaining BBC colleagues and friends both in London and at her Sussex cottages. BBC correspondence to individuals like producer Howard Rose, Val Gielgud, and Assistant Director of Variety Charles Brewer, referred to cocktail parties given in London and weekend outings to her cottage in the country.[98] *Daily Mail* radio critic Collie Knox referred to such sojourns in the country in a brief biographical sketch of Constanduros in 1947, telling readers:

> Some of my happiest moments have been spent with Mabel at her home [in Sussex] when, with four or five mutual souls, we have spent hilarious evenings playing word games ... I recall the hours I have spent with Mabel, Monckton Hoffe, the playwright, Grizelda Harvey and Michael – all wizards at versifying and inconsequent imaginings.[99]

Though part of the BBC artist culture, these social events were important networking opportunities that eased relations between herself and the BBC, and ensured her continued success on radio.

In her professional and personal life, Constanduros was hardly 'unobtrusive', like Mummie in the Sparkes series; and while she was always clearly confident in her abilities, she was also very careful not to be seen as too grasping or assertive in her professional dealings. Further, as in her self-representation in *Shreds and Patches*, she seemed more comfortable employing a maternal femininity in her professional relationships, cultivating her career through nurturance and the performance of emotional labour. With Howard Rose, for instance, she was alternatively admiring and encouraging of his work. In letters with close male associates, like Gielgud and Rose, she was also interested in and supportive of personal relationships with other women, approving warmly of their decisions to marry (as she did with her son Michael).[100]

Constanduros often assumed the mantle of motherhood in her relationships with male BBC staffers. In addition to taking keen interest in their love lives, she worried over their health, offering advice on health matters or sending vitamins or medicine when they were ill.[101] She sent presents to colleagues' children for Christmas and expressed concern and condolences to female staffers whose sons were missing, injured or killed during the war. As in the case of Denis Constanduros and Howard Agg, as well as numerous others like John Rorke, Gladys Young and David Kossuf, Constanduros was an unstinting supporter of actors and writers trying to carve out a career on the BBC. Ursula Bloom specifically credited Constanduros with helping her break into writing for radio, remembering that 'Mabel was extremely helpful; she talked to me and showed me some of the outstanding points that, left to myself, I doubt if I should have learnt for years. I mentioned ideas for plots, and she put her finger on a couple of possibles'.[102]

Having come to radio in her mid-forties, many of the BBC staffers and actors with whom she worked were closer to her son's age, and in her interactions with colleagues, she chose to perform the role of Mother of the BBC. In *Shreds and Patches*, she might eschew middle-class domesticity in order to cultivate her inner creative muse, but she very carefully cultivated a maternal image in the narrative representation of her relationship with her son, Michael. In writing the family into radio, she demonstrated the viability of domesticity and family as successful and popular entertainment, paving the way for later radio and television programmes that focus on the portrayal of the recognizable and identifiable 'ordinary' family. In dramatizing the day-to-day domestic life and relationships that have become the foundation of both soaps and sitcoms, Constanduros was a path-breaker in the development of two genres that have often shaped how the nation imagines itself at home.

7

Reimagining family and managing career in the post-war world

In February 1944, Mabel and Denis Constanduros sold Sydney Box the film rights to their successful wartime West End play, *Acacia Avenue*. The stage play enjoyed a respectable run of over 200 shows at the Vaudeville from October 1943 to April 1944, and was considered one of three 'ace' plays bought by Box and his wife Muriel as vehicles to jumpstart their independent production company.[1] The film adaptation of the play, *29 Acacia Avenue* (1945), marked the beginning of a four-year relationship with the Boxes that yielded five movies written or co-written by the Constanduroses. These films are representative of broader social and cultural efforts at reimagining the ordinary family and retrenching peacetime femininity in the immediate post-war period. Due to a lack of primary sources that shed light on the creative process behind the writing of the Box films, it is difficult to be certain of the precise level of Constanduros's contribution; nonetheless, these films underscore her efforts to manage a career in the last decade of her life and demonstrate the various intersections that existed between media at the time. For a while, the collaboration with the Boxes fuelled Mabel's hopes for cinematic stardom. Ultimately, she would remain a BBC radio writer and performer, leveraging film experience in aid of her radio career and working tirelessly to further develop opportunities within a BBC that was itself both maturing and diversifying.

Acacia Avenue revived the Robinson family from *The English Family Robinson* (*EFR*) series, and picked up the storyline of the pre-war BBC sketch, *Cruising Family Robinson*. The theatre production imagined the drama that ensued in the Robinson household while the parents vacationed clandestinely in Bognor Regis (see Chapter 6). In the radio play, action and dialogue focused on the parents; the children acted only as devices to set up their plotline. The first act of the theatre production, *Acacia Avenue*, however, slightly reworks the BBC sketch in order to develop the children's characters and storylines, while also introducing new characters as love interests for the younger Robinsons. The play then follows the two generations in their various intrigues: the parents (played by Gordon Harker and Dorothy Hamilton) providing light humour against the coming-of-age moral dilemmas with which their children wrestle while they are away.

In the original pre-war BBC play, Peter's motive for staying home was to attend races at Brooklands with a friend. Wartime changes in youth culture and fears about increased sexual freedom for women, however, underscore a reworked plotline that amplified the sexual tension in the stage play: a young and naïve Peter (Rhoderick Walker) is seduced by a racy and profligate girlfriend Estelle (Miki Hood), while Joan (Yvonne Owen) and fiancé Michael (Hubert Gregg) embark on a trial marriage. As the parents prepare to leave on holiday, Estelle deploys both seduction and verbal insults to pressure Peter to go away for a weekend tryst instead of joining the elder Robinsons. Meanwhile, Michael and Joan settle down to a romantic picnic in the Robinson's living room where Michael suggests that their squabbles over class differences are in fact the result of the pent-up sexual frustration of engagement. Tensions dissolve once Michael convinces Joan to throw caution (and middle-class respectability) to the wind. The Robinsons, back early from their holiday, return home just in time to save their daughter from certain moral ruination, shocked to find Joan alone with Michael, who scandalously emerges on the scene in a dressing gown. Before Mrs. Robinson swoons over the horror of what 'people may say', Peter (who had had enough of Estelle's manipulative ways and cancelled the weekend getaway) helpfully shows up and covers for his sister in the nick of time.

While the heightened sexuality of the play can be attributed to the shift from radio to stage and loosening wartime morality, it is also likely that these storylines were largely the work of Denis Constanduros. Though no documentation exists on Mabel's reflections regarding the re-writing of the Robinsons' adventures, Denis's diary provides some clue. Much of the diary makes clear that Denis felt that his aunt's writing was too popular, and he felt conflicted by the prospect of making good money to support his family and selling out to popular taste. Thus, generally disparaging of *Acacia Avenue*, he felt his contribution to the play was to lend it some authenticity. The play, he wrote, 'is much more Pix's than mine in spirit. I think if she had written it by herself it would have been much more false and not nearly as good, but on the other hand I couldn't have written it myself at all.'[2] Denis's own youth must have entered into the narrative and, certainly, his pre-war diary echoes some of the sexual angst and intrigue

Figure 3 Mabel and Denis Constanduros pose with Gordon Harker, the star of their successful wartime theatre production, *Acacia Avenue*. Photo Credit: Kind thanks to Denis Constanduros's daughters, Stephanie Down and Celia Martin.

of the Robinson youth. Indeed, the generational conflicts played out on stage may well underscore the generational push and pull of the writing process: the Robinson youth being more indicative of Denis's experiences and insights, while the parents' dialogue seems much more demonstrative of Mabel's entrenched and very successful comedic writing style.

The parallel intrigues of the different generations also enabled audiences to contemplate the extent to which changing wartime attitudes towards sex and marriage posed dangers to society; the parents' storyline set out traditional values and expectations, while using humour to lighten the touch of their children's possible moral transgressions. Since the consequences of the children's actions are never fully articulated or probed, audiences were left to decide for themselves the possible stakes involved. The sexual adventures of Peter and Joan, and the presumed consequences of their actions, could therefore be viewed as cautionary tales for audiences fearful of the extent to which the war had eroded respectable society and prompted the increasing autonomy of youth; on the other hand, audiences who embraced the changes brought on by war might find the storyline outmoded by societal prescriptions, which necessitated conservative denouement in favour of traditional values. For cosmopolitan, forward-thinking or youthful audiences, the elder Robinsons are figures of fun: their little Englandism, mundane domestic existence and unromantic relationship reminiscent of the humour of the Pooters in *Diary of a Nobody* – indeed, one reviewer likened the play to the novel.[3] In the film version and most likely in the stage play, Gordon Harker who was known for his Cockney acting roles, overstated the pretentious middle-class enunciation of 'proper' English for humorous effect. Yet, in the aggregate, the humour is not overly contemptuous of the Robinsons – they may be old-fashioned and fussy, but are loveable and even capable of their own amusing, if non-threatening, intrigues. The play ends in a compromise between the traditional and the new: everyone's respectability (and virginity) remains intact and the young couple enjoy a quick, three-week engagement instead of the three years the Robinsons waited before their marriage.[4]

Sydney and Muriel Box retained much the same plot as *Acacia Avenue* in their film adaptation, with the exception that Peter's role was once again re-written, this time as more sexually risqué than in his stage incarnation. In *29 Acacia Avenue*, Peter (Jimmy Hanley) ditches his 'nice' girlfriend for an older, more experienced woman, Faye (Carla Lehmann), and the two embark on what is clearly meant to be read as a sexual relationship: Peter becomes a regular visitor at Faye's mansion, and in one scene, the two kiss and recline in an embrace as the camera dissolves to the next scene. The affair comes to an abrupt halt when Faye's husband catches the two together on one of their rendezvous. The extent of Peter's naiveté is then revealed when we learn that the world-wise Faye was using him to establish evidence of adultery and thus secure a divorce. Mr.

Robinson steps in to resolve the conflict between his son and the cuckolded husband, ensuring that Peter's reputation is unscathed by the possibility of being named in a divorce case.

The sexual misadventures of the Robinson youth nearly bankrupted the Boxes' independent film company before it got off the ground. The finished film languished in financing purgatory for nearly five months at the end of 1944 as the major theatre circuits balked at what they considered immorality. After watching a sneak preview of the film with an enthusiastic working-class audience in a notoriously rough house, Arthur Rank turned the film down flat. The Boxes' diary recorded that Rank

> said the film would have a serious effect on the morals of the youth of this country, and practically encouraged the sexes to live together before marriage. No argument could move him on this point and he felt so strongly about it that he offered to pay £45,000 for the picture if we would allow him to shelve it and so save the young people from its wicked influence![5]

The Boxes seemed genuinely surprised by Rank's moral outrage, and felt Mabel Constanduros would be 'shocked ... to hear that someone thinks her story dirty!'[6] Indeed, the Boxes believed that resistance was less about morality and more about industry control, feeling 'suspiciously like a film "ring" designed to "squeeze" them'.[7] But Rank's concerns underscored the conservatism of the British film industry and its reflection of broader societal anxieties brought on by the perceived loosening of morals as well as fears over the damage done to the sanctity of marriage as a result of the Second World War.[8] Others in the British film industry reacted similarly to Rank: Warner Brothers rejected the film out of hand, and while Columbia's representative thought the film 'naughty but not dirty', some at Columbia feared that the film was too risqué for certain audiences.[9] Indeed, concern over the immoral message of the film likely rested on the lack of sexual restraint displayed by its middle-class characters: the Robinson children do not demonstrate the restraint expected of them, an attribute played so brilliantly by Celia Johnson in the highly acclaimed *Brief Encounter*, released seven months later. Further, the favourable reaction of the house may also have pricked Rank's middle-class conscience: the working-class 'hand' at the end of the film could not have assuaged fears of the film's reckless sexuality and immoral message. As will be seen, film reviewers more fully articulated some of these anxieties. Ultimately Rank's attempt to shelve *29 Acacia Avenue* represents an unsuccessful moment in a period in which UK film industry leaders sought to contain the potentially revolutionary effect of the war in a 'rhetoric of transience, a sense of "only for the duration"'.[10] Rank lost the battle to control the post-war narrative in this particular case: Columbia bought the film in April 1945, which did well in both UK and US markets.[11]

While the sexually charged escapades of the youth in the film ultimately resolved in favour of traditional middle-class values, numerous movie critics were concerned by the dangers of simply showing these middle-class 'young suburbanites [as] a pretty avid lot'.[12] *Kinematograph Weekly* was more playful in its assessment that 'the gist of the picture is that exuberant youth will not be denied and that tender pulses beat as fast in seemingly respectable suburbia as in the East End and sophisticated Belgravia', but all reviewers registered unease with the younger generation's indiscretions, particularly in the heart of 'ordinary' middle-class suburbia.[13] Indeed, the reviewer for *Today's Cinema* felt a better title for the film was, 'Sex comes to Suburbia'.[14] As hinted at in *Kinematograph Weekly*'s review, the implication of sexual (mis)adventure among middle-class youth was most striking in the film: the middle-class backbone of British society, moral paragons against the threats posed by both the working and upper classes since the nineteenth century, were now in danger of witnessing their children undermine their prised moral superiority. Indeed, while some critics appreciated the realism of the movie's suburban atmosphere, the recognizable characterizations and interplay of the parents, they recoiled at the youth in the film, who were felt to be 'extraordinarily self-centered' and 'whose animal yearnings are denied the saving grace of genuine comedy'.[15] *Kinematograph*'s reviewer summed up the film as, 'Although of the family, not for the family'; it was primarily for the 'stout-hearted and broad-minded "populars"'.[16]

Moral outrage on the part of critics did not stop British or American audiences from flocking to the film. Audience reaction cards handed out at a sneak peek of the film in January 1945 at the Astoria Odeon in Tooting gave an average approval rating of 90 per cent, and every respondent hoped for another film along the same lines.[17] Once in general release, the Boxes made at least double on their investment, and the film ran for a year on Times Square as *The Facts of Love*.[18] While these audience figures may be evidence of the 'box-office insurance' of salacious films,[19] ultimately the film supported traditional values and prescriptions: the sexual double standard was upheld in that Joan remained virginal while Peter gained a valuable education in relationships with the other sex. Next, divorce is repudiated: Faye's attempt to escape her marriage is thwarted and her husband regains control over his wayward wife. Finally, while the younger generation could be somewhat assuaged by winning the right to a short engagement, sex was to be safely contained within marriage.

The controversy over *29 Acacia Avenue* cannot (and should not) be mistaken as being evidence that the film was radically sexual for the period; rather, it was the perceived degradation of the ordinary middle-class British family by selfish and unrestrained youth that provoked criticism and unease: the whisper of youthful sex in middle-class suburbia was most disturbing to the critics. The transgressions of the Robinson youth are mild in comparison to 'social problem' films of the period that depicted juvenile delinquency and criminality,[20] but their (contained) sexual adventurousness does demonstrate what Claire Langhamer has called 'a gentle subversion of established norms' during the period.[21]

Szreter and Fisher's oral history of sexual attitudes among both working-class and middle-class individuals born between 1905 and 1924 reveals that sexual intimacy prior to marriage was common, and that while both classes were concerned about the consequences of premarital sex (pregnancy, venereal disease, desire and damage to respectability/marriageability), the 'resolve to preserve virginity' among middle-class respondents was paramount.[22] Thus, the criticisms over the 'avid' Robinson youth may well underscore the success of the film's intended call to ordinariness: middle-class audiences (and reviewers) were encouraged to see themselves in the Robinsons, but the realism may have cut too close to the fragility of middle-class respectability.

Much as the BBC touted the ordinariness of *EFR* in the 1930s, advertisements for the film adaptation of *Acacia Avenue* capitalized on this sense of the ordinary and recognizable to draw in audiences, proclaiming, 'Meet the Robinsons! You know them – they live next door to you – in fact – they are you!'[23] The opening prologue of the film, set against a tree-lined street shot of middle-class suburbia, furthers this attempt to foster audience identification with the family, unashamedly eliding ordinary with middle class and encouraging the national audience to imagine the action, the place and the characters of the film as their own:

> If you take the first on the left and the second on the right when you leave home, you will find yourself in Acacia Avenue, even though your local Council has been careless enough to give it a different name. To all the residents in all the Acacia Avenues, this film is affectionately dedicated. None of the characters in this film is entirely imaginary and some resemblance to people you know is quite reasonable.

Film reviews repeated the theme of a 'comedy of the lives of a typically English family who live in "Acacia Avenue" – a truthful story about the Robinsons, Wilsons and Joneses – the kind of people who are 'The Andy Hardys' of Britain'.[24] To audiences familiar with the 'Hardys', a popular American film franchise which began in 1937 and starred a young Mickey Rooney, connection to the all-American family would have signalled a light-hearted comedy oriented around the youthful dramas of likeable teenage characters.[25] Indeed, Jimmy Hanley, who played Peter in the Box adaptation, sported the same boy-next-door charisma as Mickey Rooney's popular portrayal of Andy Hardy, though rather less exaggerated, and therefore more believable than Rooney's acting. In line with trends in the 1940s British film, *29 Acacia Avenue* depicted the supposedly ordinary British family with more realism than its American counterpart, but nonetheless offered an idyllic picture of family life.

The next Box-Constanduros film collaborations returned once again to the construction of the ordinary family in the post-war world. The first of these films, *Holiday Camp* (1947), made allowances for more flexible understandings of the post-war family brought on by the experiences and realities of wartime; however, the last three films very forcefully resolve in favour of a return to a peacetime 'normalcy' deeply entrenched in the traditional patriarchal nuclear family. In class terms, the progression of the films also underscores a narrowing of classed definitions of 'ordinary': while the central family begins as very clearly working-class in *Holiday Camp*, the latter films tighten the frame of the ordinary, reorienting the family as upwardly mobile working class enthusiastically embracing middle-class conventions and sensibilities. With the exception of the last of the films, all of the films include deep criticisms of – and in some cases, grave warnings against – assertive or sexually suggestive femininity.[26] Finally, the films actively participate in a broader cultural initiative to reimagine post-war national identity.

'Warm-hearted, work-a-day people, full of high spirits'[27]: The Huggetts

In July 1946, Denis and Mabel Constanduros embarked on a long-term contract writing for the Boxes (now at Gainsborough), which launched a new 'ordinary' family for the post-war peace.[28] The Huggett family was first introduced as the primary focus in the 'quasi-portmanteau' Box production *Holiday Camp*

(1947).²⁹ The film was based on a story from Godfrey Winn and written by a scriptwriting team that included the Boxes, Peter Rogers, Ted Willis and the Constanduroses. Though not clear from the production notes, it is most likely that the Constanduroses contributed much of the Huggett dialogue, especially between Joe (Jack Warner) and Ethel (Kathleen Harrison), in a film that featured 'six deftly interwoven fictional stories'.³⁰ Later correspondence with the BBC makes clear that the Huggett family was indeed Mabel Constanduros's creation.

Set in a Butlins-esque holiday camp, the Huggett family formed the centre of *Holiday Camp*'s narrative: bus driver Joe and char Ethel bring their two children, a grandchild and their daughter's friend on holiday with some 5,000 other Britons eager to get back to normal and enjoy some leisure after the war. Daughter Joan (Hazel Court) is a war widow with an infant, for whom Ethel cares in order to free Joan to enjoy her holiday. Teenage son Henry (Peter Hammond) shows his youthful naiveté when he falls prey to spivs who con him out of his money. Joan's friend, Angela (Yvonne Owen), is on the lookout for a good time (even though she has a fiancé at home) and spinster Elsie (Esma Cannon), who manages to show up in most scenes, is also keen to find a man. The two women become targets for a sexual predator evading police on his trail for the murder of a young woman. The film also follows the fortunes of another spinster, Esther (Flora Robson), in her search for both physical rest and existential meaning after years of caring for her recently deceased mother. Esther's story becomes intertwined with that of a young couple unable to convince the young woman's guardian to consent to her marrying a jobbing pianist.

Holiday Camp was a box-office hit and the most successful Gainsborough film during Sydney Box's tenure as managing director of the firm.³¹ Part of *Holiday Camp*'s success can be attributed to the fact that it did not have to compete with Hollywood: the film hit the silver screen at the beginning of the American film embargo, which came into force after the Labour government levied a 75 per cent tax on Hollywood films.³² The embargo also served to accentuate the Britishness of the film. Reviewers embraced the nationalism of the film and its characters; one critic stated, 'We talk like this. In the first place, it is extremely English and paints a holiday as it is lived by many thousands of citizens at the moment.' The critic then went on to snub the Americans by saying, 'Whether it will gate-crash the cinemas in America, I neither know nor care.'³³ Elspeth Grant of the *Daily Graphic* applauded the film for its 'completely British air of good humour and grousing'.³⁴ Further, the realism of the camp's *mise en scéne* would have been recognized by many who took advantage of increased leisure time and higher disposable income to enjoy an 'all-in' holiday experience at camps like Butlins after the war. Camp life depicted in the film was closely patterned after the Butlin's experience: the ubiquitous 'Radio Butlin' announcements over loudspeaker, the daily round of entertainments ranging from talent shows to beauty competitions, communal dining, dancing, swimming baths and plenty of opportunities for social mixing.[35] This was a British film that held up a mirror to the nation at that particular moment in time.

According to the critics, the one fault of the film was the storyline of 'Binkie' (Dennis Price), the sexual predator, which was patterned off the headline-grabbing murders of Neville Heath in 1946. Yet, as Robert Murphy has stated, this storyline (and, I would add, that of the spivs who cheat Henry out of his money) articulates very real post-war anxieties and thus is equally part of the *zeitgeist* embodied by the film.[36] While Murphy does not detail these anxieties, Binkie's storyline underscores the potential dangers of assertive female sexuality. Joan's friend Angela unabashedly flirts with and pursues Binkie, whose cover story leads campers to believe he was an RAF pilot (thus implying his integrity and trustworthiness). Their affair is explosive and destructive: though he is often rough and violent with her, she is nonetheless drawn to him and agrees to marriage (even though we know she is already engaged). In the end, she finally becomes disconcerted by his violent behaviour and dumps him. Desperate for a victim, Binkie now eyes Elsie, who has flirted with him throughout the film to no avail. Excited that she's finally 'captured' her man, Elsie innocently agrees to a romantic walk on the cliffs, never to return. Whereas the punishment for an overly assertive (innocent or otherwise) female sexuality is violence or death, Joan is rewarded for rebuffing Binkie's initial advances by meeting an attentive and wholesome mate, Jimmy (Jimmy Hanley).

Binkie also points up the potential dangers of communality, whereby individuals unknown to others easily disguise their true character and intentions. Yet the film has also been read as a celebration of 'the people' and the successful mixing of the classes.[37] This positive reading of communality is evident in the storyline featuring upper-middle-class Esther and the young couple, Valerie (Jeanette Tregarthen) and Michael (Emrys Jones), who hope to marry. When Esther learns that Valerie is pregnant, she first attempts to convince Valerie's guardian to allow the marriage. When this predictably founders on the guardian's middle-class respectability, Esther offers to house the couple and help them get on their feet. Esther, who has sacrificed for others and been denied a family of her own, now has a chance at familial happiness. Chance encounters in this case are positive: the three (and eventually four) erstwhile strangers will be bound together as a family. The film thus embraces alternative visions of family: a reality for many in the wake of a war that had severely disrupted family life.

While communality has its benefits, *Holiday Camp* elevates family above wartime communality.[38] Joan's chance meeting with Jimmy will lead to marriage, and (it is assumed) a stable family life for her daughter. When spivs cheat Harry out of money, Joe shows himself world-wise by rescuing his son (and thus his family) from the burden of an overwhelming debt by playing the spivs at their own game. Joe, who throughout the film was 'ineffective or ignored' thus restores order within his family and re-establishes patriarchal power.[39] Furthermore, while Joe demonstrates that he is clearly capable of running a racket, he does not do so for monetary gain, but rather to protect his family from those who seek to destroy it. Thus, Joe and his family are representative of what one reviewer celebrated as 'the great majority – honest people who despite inflation and changing values, hang on to fundamental decencies in our traditional way of life'.[40]

The Huggetts returned a year later as 'Britain's very own family'[41] in *Here Come the Huggetts* (1948), written by the Constanduroses, the Boxes and Peter Rogers. The film focuses on the everyday lives of the Huggetts at home and at work, and it further invites audiences to imagine the family's values as representative of the nation. Moving the family from the holiday camp to the home firmly reorients post-war society away from the communal to the individual family. Moreover, the centrality of the Huggetts' home in the film and its depiction of a caring and loving family demonstrates Langhamer's assertion that the home was '*the* blueprint for reconstruction in postwar Britain'.[42] Within the context of the post-war housing crunch, the family's home must also have been an object of desire for many cinema-goers: though modest, the Huggetts' home and its mod-cons would have seemed luxurious to many in 1948.

Remarkable (and unexplained) changes have taken place since *Holiday Camp*: bus driver Joe, reprised by Warner, is now a works foreman with more than twenty years' experience with the company, and char Ethel, played once again by Harrison, is a full-time housewife. They are now the proud parents of three daughters: Harry has inexplicably disappeared from the family, yet the same actor (Peter Hammond) who played son Harry in *Holiday Camp* now appears, rather awkwardly, as a hopeful suitor to a newly introduced daughter, Susan Huggett (Susan Shaw, who played Harry's love interest in *Holiday Camp*!). Hazel Court, who played Joan Huggett, is now replaced by Jane Hylton, who takes on the role of eldest daughter *Jane*, no longer a war widow with an infant in arms but rather long-time fiancé to airman Jimmy Gardner (Jimmy Hanley, *Joan's* love interest in *Holiday Camp*!)[43] who is about to be demobbed. Amy Vaness plays Grandma and a young Petula Clark rounds out the family as 'Pet' Huggett. Seventeen-year-old sex symbol in the making Diana Dors appears in one of her first significant film roles as Mrs. Huggett's sexually precocious niece.

Reverberations of wartime are evident in both Diana Dors's performance and in Jane's storyline. Picking up on the wartime 'moral alarm' caused by reckless feminine sexuality,[44] Diana Dors plays Di, a selfish and lazy good-time girl who disrupts and threatens Huggett family life. Di's overt sexuality and laziness unsettle the Huggett daughters, as well as Joe, but Ethel has agreed to help her cousin Edie's (Dandy Nichols) daughter while she convalesces and so the family suffer Di's presence. Joe is pressured by Ethel to help her secure a job at the works, but when Joe covers for Di's continued negligence at work, he is demoted. Di shows no remorse and offers no appreciation of her uncle's sacrifice, but instead continues to enjoy nights out with Peter's free-spending boss, Gowan (John Blythe). On one of their outings, she persuades Peter to borrow the Huggett's car without their permission. Gowan and Di get Peter drunk and crash the car, nearly ruining Joan Huggett's wedding. As in *Holiday Camp*, assertive female sexuality is presented as problematic and destructive.

Couched as it is within ordinary family life, Di's threat to the fabric of the Huggett family is perhaps more dangerous than the sensational melodramatic sexuality portrayed in Diana Dors's other 1948 Box production, *Good Time Girl*.[45] In the family's eventual triumph against this threat – Joe proves himself worthy to his boss by responding to a fire alarm that threatens the works and is given back his old job, while Joan's wedding is narrowly saved – we see the post-war continuation of wartime rhetoric that elevated British values of 'self-restraint, moral fortitude, and cheerful altruism' embodied by the Huggetts against the selfish moral laxity of spivs and good-time girls who undermined family and, thus, the nation.[46]

The enduring challenges of wartime are also presented in Jane's fears regarding marriage to a fiancé about to be demobilized. Jane's concerns echoed the very real challenges couples faced upon the return of a husband or fiancé after years of wartime service. Resettlement was often difficult for returning veterans: re-establishing peacetime work was frequently challenging, and wartime experiences often created distance between couples. Demobbed soldiers might return home to find their partners transformed by increased wartime independence and women might find that the trauma of war had irrevocably altered her husband, fiancé or boyfriend. As social historian David Kynaston notes, 'the possibilities for tension and strife, even when both were emotionally committed to each other, were endless'.[47]

In the film, Jane is thrown into despair at the prospect of marrying a man she feels she no longer knows after a four-year absence. At the same time, she is distracted by bohemian intellectual, Harold Hinchley (David Tomlinson), who confesses his love to her. Hinchley offers Jane the prospect of a union of equals, based on shared intellectual interests, and promises not to 'bind you hand and foot' by marriage, which he views as uncivilized and an 'archaic survival of a past age'. In the end, the fears plaguing Jane about Jimmy are shown to be unfounded: Jimmy hasn't changed, and the two marry, with hopes of emigrating to South Africa. Despite trends that saw increased divorce after the war, the film offers a hopeful future for marriage and the family. Indeed, Harold's rather woolly headed characterization and pretentious manner of imagining a future as equal companions outside marriage renders the prospect of such a relationship laughable, further underscoring the primacy of traditional marriage as a social institution. Finally, the rewrite of the elder Huggett daughter's storyline from war widow with child to young fiancé without child suggests that the flexibility that envisioned alternative forms of family in the immediate post-war period has narrowed, harkening the triumph of marriage and the traditional nuclear family as the 1950s draw near. In contrast to *Holiday Camp*, alternate constructions of family and marriage are no longer allowed.

Presented alongside the 1947 Royal Wedding, Jane and Jimmy's wedding further serves to link the Huggetts to the nation. While Jane and Jimmy prepare for their wedding, the rest of the family camp out to get a glimpse of the royal couple on their procession to Westminster Abbey. Due to the antics of Grandma, however, the family miss their opportunity to see the procession, but they are nonetheless confirmed as patriotic in their endeavour, 'underlining the Huggetts' status as the national family'.[48]

The family returned once again as the British silver screen's representative of the nation a few months later in *Vote for Huggett* (1948). This time, Joe Huggett's solid British values of decency, honesty and 'cheerful altruism' are employed to protect his community against political corruption and businessmen's scheming. In the film, Joe is persuaded by calculating businessman Maurice Lever (played by Hubert Gregg) into running as a 'Progressive' for local council on the basis of Joe's idea to build a lido as the community's war memorial. Both Lever and

'Moderate' alderman Hall attempt to profit handsomely from their respective war memorial schemes, while Di and Gowan hope to capitalize on their own land deal, all of which puts an unwitting Huggett at the centre of a corruption scandal that nearly ruins his campaign and his family's respectability.

Huggett plays the man of the people in his campaign, decidedly above the fray of politics, but willing to work hard for his community (which he considers a family). In his stump speech, he states, 'I'm not much of a speechifier. It's not in my line. I believe in getting things done, not talking about them. So I'm not gonna give you a lot of 'ot air ... we'll leave all the 'ot air to the House of Commons'. In the end, Huggett foils the various intrigues of Lever, Hal, and Di when he convinces eccentric elderly sisters to cede some of their riverside property for the lido, free of charge, to the council.

The film depicts both moderates (code for Conservatives) and progressives (Labour) as corrupt and self-serving. The narrative of the film 'celebrates local democracy, public service and government by decent men',[49] especially in its resolution. *Vote for Huggett* was expressive of a popular post-war suspicion of and disenchantment with party politics that stemmed from discomfort with the politicking of the first post-war election in the summer of 1945, particularly Churchill's famous 'Gestapo' speech.[50] At the heart of the film is a pervasive 'cynicism with bureaucracy and the political process'.[51] Huggett, the common or 'decent man', is pitted against scheming politicians who threaten the community, and by extension the nation; and while Huggett stands as a progressive against the moderates, his solution upsets the moderates as equally as it does 'his' party. Placing community before party, Huggett's actions echo the wartime elevation of the people over party, expressed so eloquently in J. B. Priestley's popular 1940 BBC *Postscripts*: indeed, Huggett perfectly embodied Priestley's avowal that one should not think 'in terms of a political party', but rather of 'social justice and decency'.[52] Huggett's 'amateurish' politicking is also indicative of a core theme in Britishness that elevates amateurism over efficiency.[53]

In the final Huggett film, *The Huggetts Abroad* (1949), the strains of four years of post-war austerity have worn down the family's effervescent cheerfulness and stress fractures have emerged among the 'people'. The gloom of austerity and community conflict prevails over the beginning of the film, accentuated by a carping neighbour and the incessant pouring rain that dominates every shot. Fed up, the entire family decides to emigrate with Jimmy and Jane, and embark on an overland journey to South Africa. To cover the costs of the trip, the Huggetts welcome an unknown Canadian, Bob (Hugh McDermott), who is secretly a diamond thief. After much intrigue in the sands of northern Africa, the family happily give up the overland adventure to return home, leaving Jimmy and Jane to find their way to a new life in South Africa.

Despite the Boxes' feeling that the film was by far the best of the three solo Huggett offerings, *The Huggetts Abroad* was the least successful of the series and was scorned by the critics.[54] Film historians have skewered the film for its 'little Englandism'[55], expressed not only in the denouement, but also in several insular comments by Ethel, who confuses South Africa with South America and waves off the family's laughter with, 'It's the same thing – natives and all that.' Later, Ethel compares Algiers to Bournemouth. While little Englandism most certainly defines this film, its lukewarm reception among contemporary audiences was less about narrow-minded nationalism and more to do with its departure from everyday life in favour of fantastical intrigue in the African desert. As one reviewer noted, the draw of the films 'resides in the humour and observation with which their family life is drawn and the natural background is ... the suburban street ... [which is] the proper scene of their activities, not the African desert'.[56] The poor reception of the cinema-going public might also be attributed to the overwhelming gloom that had overtaken the cheerful family. As director Ken Annakin later observed, the appeal of the Huggett films was largely in their positive portrayal of 'ordinary' British life.[57] While it is impossible to know the exact extent, or intent, of Constanduros's contributions to the film projects discussed in this chapter, efforts in all of the films to engage audience identification demonstrates that she continued to participate in wider conversations about ordinariness in the post-war period.

Revisiting the ordinary: Class and desire in the post-war period

Film historian Jeffrey Richards has argued that the Huggetts (and BBC television's *Grove Family*) are direct descendants of the Buggins family, stating that all three families 'endors[ed] the same basic values'.[58] Elements of the Buggins family do in fact infiltrate the Huggett films. Grandma Huggett is not nearly as mischievous as Grandma Buggins, but many of the same comedic malapropisms ('my feet are in perjury') are sprinkled throughout her dialogue, and staple Constanduros characters from the 1930s Buggins radio sketches and books are continually referenced in the film.[59] However, as has been seen in the previous interwar and wartime discussions of Buggins comedy, it would be problematic to consider the Bugginses as 'endorsing the same basic values' as do the Huggetts. Even during their wartime makeover, Buggins family members are often incredibly self-serving, wasteful and outré. The Bugginses were never intended to be 'ordinary' or representative of the nation. When considering the 'set of traditional values and solid dependability' that the Huggetts embody,[60] it is more appropriate to connect the Huggetts (and the Groves) to the lesser-known, though influential, *EFR*.

The Constanduroses did not settle the Huggetts in the Bugginses' Wandsworth, but rather chose to situate them in the same fictional town as the Robinsons: Strutham. This is an interesting choice, for it suggests that a subtle reworking of the imagined national family has taken place in the post-war peace. As was seen with *EFR*, middle-class (London) suburbia was at the core of the BBC's interwar presentation of ordinariness. Suburban London still rests at the centre of the nation with the Huggetts, and the use of a fictional setting once again assists in audience identification. Indeed, the press book for *Vote for Huggett* indicates that the fictional location and scenes in the film were

> calculated to make local audiences all over the country recognize typical features of their own lives include[ing] school-room meetings, an election result declaration, a local newspaper office, factory activities, youth club work and even back-fence gossip. *Vote for Huggett* is the sort of film that has something for everybody.[61]

As with *EFR*, the films traded on both the fictional setting of Strutham and the recognizable day-to-day happenings to encourage engagement with diverse audiences.

While characterizations and the family's values are important features for engaging the sense of ordinary, the Huggetts' home is a focal point of desire in all the films (with the exception of *Holiday Camp*). The semi-detached home featured a garden in the front, a work shed in the back with a small garden, a garage (and car), a fixed bath and a water closet, and, in *Here Come the Huggetts* (1947), the installation of a telephone creates the central drama for Mrs. Huggett. Since many at the time endured poorly maintained rental units, the communal living of council flats or the unpalatable 'fungus-like outcroppings of those tin huts called "pre-fabs"',[62] the owner-occupied home on a quiet suburban street must have been a dream for many, like the MO who stated that 'four walls and a roof is the height of my ambition'.[63] Many in the audience would have been without the luxury of a fixed bath and water closet, which was considered 'a major social dividing line' in the period.[64] Further, very few would have had a telephone at this time; indeed, a full ten years later, only 16.5 per cent of British households had a telephone, and most were owned by the upper classes and the upper bands of the middle class.[65] Though the Huggett children are excited by the prospect of the telephone, Mrs. Huggett fears the negative impact it might have on her home and family. The film explains the installation of the phone as a necessary part of Joe's recent promotion, but the chaos created by its presence is suggestive of the pull of modernization and the concerns had by many regarding the intrusion of modernization into home life.[66]

In the Huggett films, the classed frame of ordinariness has expanded from the solidly middle-class Robinsons to embrace those within the fuzzy boundaries that encompass the affluent working class and the lower middle class. While the Huggetts of *Holiday Camp* are easily identified as respectable working class, the Huggetts at home are more difficult to situate. Many film historians and contemporary commentators alike have variously identified the Huggetts as upper-working, respectable working, lower middle or middle class. Yet, the Huggetts do not comfortably fit any of these categories. Joe and Ethel's accents and professions in *Holiday Camp* are firmly working class, and backstory clues in *Here Come the Huggetts* suggest working-class origins. Ethel's suspicion of the telephone in *HCH* is also considered indicative of what film historian Phillip Gillett calls 'working-class conservatism'.[67]

One significant scene in *Vote* shows Ethel busily doing the front step, prompting the upper-class alderman's wife to mistake her for the 'help'. Certainly, this scene could speak to the post-war shortage of domestic help, but Ethel does not use this excuse, as might be expected of a solidly middle-class housewife used to some help in the home; instead, she avoids discussing the issue as if it is merely part of her usual routine. Later, when the alderman's wife deploys class difference to unsettle her, Ethel hides her anxiety by rushing off to make a 'nice cup of tea', an action Richards has pointed out is emblematic of working-class culture in Orwell's writing.[68] Further, the downstairs floor plan of the Huggett home is suggestive of a traditional working-class plan: the back room serves as the all-purpose living and dining area, while the front room is set aside for special occasions and visitors with its piano, china cabinet and unwieldy decorative table centrepiece.[69]

The house has the feeling of having been lived in for a while, and thus suggests that the Huggetts have been established in the area since the interwar period. Their car, a British-made Ford Prefect E93a Tourer, was made in 1938.[70] The economical and comfortable four-seated Prefect, priced at £155, with ample space in the boot was perfect for the 'cost-conscious family man'.[71] Some working- and lower-middle-class families owned cars before their socioeconomic betters, and hire-purchase made that prospect somewhat easier in the interwar period.[72] Yet, British consumers were suspect of hire-purchase well into the 1960s, and creditors, swayed by classed prejudice, were unlikely to extend such an option to those in the working class.[73] Further, the cost of car ownership went beyond the price tag: running costs have been estimated at one-third the initial cost of the car.[74] Therefore, in 1949, only 3 per cent of the working classes owned a car, 11.5 per cent of the lower middle classes and 26.5 per cent of those in higher classes.[75]

While the parents' accents and idioms are clearly of the working class, the children's accents are solidly middle. Gillett argues that middle-class accents in a working-class household would have felt like a 'jarring intrusion', but since he feels the family is 'transitional', an example of 'the working classes making good', they do not seem so out of place.[76] Instead, the Huggetts seem to fit more securely into what Jon Lawrence has identified as longer-term economic and social trends of the affluent worker, which he sees developing in the interwar period rather than in the commonly assumed post-war period.[77]

Alternatively, Andrew Spicer contends that the middle-class elements of the family's life are not meant to be representative of social mobility or pretensions at all, but rather emphasize the family's claim to ordinariness; their character and values indicative of an 'all-purpose stratum of ordinary decency and "respectability"'.[78] This 'all-purpose stratum' speaks to an attempt to continue into the post-war period the wartime rhetoric that blurred the lines of class and region in order to construct a national unity steeped in supposed common values. As Jeffrey Richards has argued, the values embodied by the Huggett family are part of 'a continuing cultural strand' in which 'the multiple identities – London suburbs, British nation and British Empire – interlock and are centred on permanent values [of] work, thrift, patriotism, family, loyalty, marriage'.[79]

More importantly, the fuzziness of class and the overarching value system celebrated in these texts may be highly effective ways to further activate audience identification. As mid-century sociologists like Elizabeth Bott noted, subjective class identities can be 'flexible, inconsistent and elusive'.[80] Revisiting mid-century studies of the affluent worker 'problem', Lawrence has shown that many interviewees spoke of their class in 'vague, catch-all formulations' and exhibited what he calls 'deliberate evasion of class placement'.[81] Therefore, the ambiguity of the Huggetts' class status discussed here can engage these vaguely defined class subjectivities.

In at least a few working-class markets in the North, the film series underperformed, suggesting that at least some British working-class audiences may have been uncomfortable with the uncertain class status presented in the films, but regionalism or accent may have played as much, if not more, of a factor than the fuzziness of class depicted in the films.[82] At the very least, the films painted a picture of a warm home and a happy family that many in the post-war period desired, and while the Huggetts' comfortable lifestyle may have been unattainable for many in 1948 and 1949, audiences could luxuriate in it for a blissful ninety minutes of escapism.

Evolving and adapting on the post-war BBC

Constanduros imagined that the Huggetts film franchise might help her launch a successful film career, such as her one-time writing partner Michael Hogan now enjoyed in Hollywood. These hopes are reflected in Denis's observations of the opening night of *Holiday Camp* in August 1947:

> Pix [Mabel] had ordered an enormous Rolls Royce to take us to the cinema (the Gaumont, in the Haymarket) … . There was an expensive and fashionable crowd. We were sitting in good seats, but not among the cream of the elite; the air was blue with the smoke of flashlights, but they did not flash for us. This, naturally, did not surprise or worry me, but I could feel Pix seething with thwarted stardom at my side.

Denis thought his aunt's hopes outsized, summing up the experience at the Gaumont in his diary with his assessment of their film work: 'I fancy the films will not being us immortal fame, but at least they brought me a cheque for £675 last week which is something of a solace.'[83] The Huggett films turned out to be a sideline for the Constanduroses and, 'thwarted stardom' aside, Mabel never walked away from her radio career. Indeed, even as the two Constanduroses were writing the film series, Mabel wrote to Val Gielgud hoping for more BBC work because she felt that the film writing 'does not anything like fill my time'.[84] Post-war correspondence with the BBC demonstrates that Constanduros maintained a vigorous drumbeat of proposals to various departments – suggesting original ideas and reworked versions of her earlier radio plays, while also leveraging her cinematic and stage experience in order to gain commissions.

In 1948, Constanduros hoped to initiate a radio series that focused on the day-to-day life of the Huggett family and in late-September, just before the film debut of *Here Come the Huggetts*, the BBC commissioned Mabel and Denis to write twelve episodes for a Huggett series.[85] However, by mid-October, the series air dates were postponed and the project was put on hold. Even though the Constanduroses had already written six of the requisite episodes, the series stalled due to difficult negotiations with Arthur Rank, the Boxes and the principal actors.[86] A few weeks later, with negotiations still unsettled, Constanduros suggested that she jettison the Huggett (and Rank) association altogether in the delivered scripts and create a new family, but the BBC wanted to wait out the situation.[87] When the series was postponed indefinitely in December, Director of Variety, Michael Standing explained to Constanduros that the primary reason was due to cast negotiations; though not communicated to Constanduros, BBC memoranda confirms this: Jack Warner wanted more money and more lines, Petula Clark's father insisted she sing and dance in every episode, and Kathleen Harrison was not at all keen on the series.[88]

Over the next few years, Constanduros tried to plump for a working-class family radio series commission, but to no avail. While she and Denis managed to secure a commission for a six-episode middle-class family series in 1950 entitled *Father Knows Best*, starring Eric Portman, efforts to create a Cockney family series in 1949 that Constanduros hoped would be a vehicle to boost David Kossoff's acting profile also failed to materialize. Long-term negotiations in 1952 to bring about a working-class domestic sitcom starring Richard Goolden and herself entitled *The Smalls at Home* were similarly unsuccessful.[89] Given these examples, it might be tempting to believe that the BBC was not interested in broadcasting working-class family entertainment; however, a BBC assessment of the series plot summaries for *The Smalls at Home* suggests that the BBC did in fact feel the working-class angle attractive, but rejected the series because they felt the writing thin and recognized the plots from a series proposal Mabel had previously floated, entitled *The Browns of Brixton*, which never made it on air.[90] A year after the BBC rejected *The Smalls*, the Huggetts made it to radio in *Meet the Huggetts*. This time, Warner and Harrison were on board, but Eddie Maguire – not Constanduros – was brought on as the writer. No explanations regarding the decision to engage Maguire, co-writer of the popular radio comedy *Ray's a Laugh* – or mention of the Constanduros connection – exist in the *Meet the*

Huggetts series files, nor in either Mabel Constanduros's or Eddie Maguire's BBC files.[91] The new series continued the class ambiguities of the films and proved successful, enjoying a long run from 1953 to 1961.[92]

Constanduros's desire to adapt the Huggett family for radio is representative of the ways in which she often exploited various media in hopes of furthering her radio career. As has already been discussed, she turned to novelization of the Buggins family and neighbourhood in the interwar period to deepen ties with the radio audience and to expand opportunities for further radio work. Similarly, as discussed earlier, *Acacia Avenue* had roots in both *EFR* radio sketches and in a novelization of the Robinsons written by Constanduros and Howard Agg in 1940. After *29 Acacia Avenue* hit the silver screen in Britain, the Constanduroses adapted the stage version for radio, which aired on *Saturday Night Theatre* in August 1945 and again in January 1948; in September 1948, Mabel and Denis took television audiences to a theatre production of *Acacia Avenue* at the Intimate Theatre in Palmers Green.[93] Further, the main plotline of the film *Vote for Huggett* (1948) was recycled from a sixty-minute 1947 BBC Home Service Saturday matinee play, *Lido Ladd*.

While these cross-media adaptations proved successful, Constanduros had less luck recycling earlier non-Buggins radio material on the post-war BBC. Attempts to bring back a 1937 musical 'fantasy of the Catcham Green Flower Show' entitled *Horti-Mania* in September 1945 were dismissed out of hand by producer Tom Ronald who thought 'the line dialogue very dull and her lyrics most amateurish. The plot ... cannot, I feel, interest an awful lot of people.'[94] With the exception of the Buggins material, which continued to be popular for the entirety of her career, Mabel rarely attempted to recycle previous radio works out of hand after this rejection. Instead, Constanduros sometimes tried to float plotlines and dialogue from earlier works under new guises as she had done with *The Smalls at Home*. As stand-alone series or plays for the Home Service or Light Programme, these efforts largely failed; Constanduros did, however, read several of her earlier radio works or extracts from the 1930s novels on the Light Programme's *Mid-Morning Story* from 1947 to 1949. She also tried, unsuccessfully, to exploit the post-war changes to the BBC by offering new material for the Third Programme.

The Second World War constituted a watershed moment in British light entertainment, significantly reshaping Constanduros's prospects on the post-war BBC. Wartime changes in programming, especially the introduction of the Forces Programme, offered listeners far more entertainment and choice than had the interwar BBC. Conversations about post-war broadcasting began in 1943, with the concept of three major channels or programmes beginning to take shape over the next two years.[95] It was left to Director General Sir William Haley to make these ideas a reality. Haley realized that the BBC had to acknowledge the changes war had wrought and, while respecting the principle of Reithian programming, adapted it to the post-war world with the introduction of a tripartite system of programming. This system acted as a 'pyramid of culture' and consisted of the new Light Programme and the Home Service, which were introduced to peacetime audiences in July 1945, and finally, the Third Programme which came on line in September 1946.[96]

The Light Programme took over from the General Forces Programme (GFP), broadcasting much the same content and following the same broadcasting schedule from 9 am to midnight; indeed, some listeners discerned 'precious little difference in the type of fare provided' between the two channels.[97] Meanwhile, the GFP was relegated to short wave transmission, while many popular wartime programmes eventually shifted to peacetime by updating their titles: *Mediterranean Merry Go Round*, for instance, became the popular *Much Binding in the Marsh*.[98] Meanwhile, the Home Service remained the 'staple service' of the BBC,

> appealing to all classes, paying attention to culture at a level at which the ordinary listener can appreciate it; giving talks that will inform the whole democracy rather than an already informed section; and generally so designed that it will steadily but imperceptibly raise the standard of taste, entertainment, outlook and citizenship.[99]

The 'pyramid of culture' that Haley envisioned was meant to sample the best of culture, information and entertainment in accessible chunks, and thus eventually raise the standards of the audience without their noticing it. Haley hoped audiences would be led from popular content on the Light up through slightly more serious treatments on the Home, all the way to the apex of British cultural offerings on the Third. Some in the BBC, however, worried that listeners would remain content with 'background listening' on Light and never move up the pyramid.[100] While audience figures suggest that few listeners were enticed to move beyond the Home Service and were indeed quite content with the Light, implementation of this new system of programming was a recognition of the significant changes brought on by the war: audiences would hardly accept an attenuation of BBC offerings by a return to the interwar model.[101]

The post-war BBC enjoyed a high degree of popularity, trust and prestige, but pressures loomed that forced the BBC to become more competitive.[102] While not a significant threat in the immediate post-war period, the reboot of BBC television in June 1946 and the resumption of *Radio Luxembourg*'s English programmes in December 1946 increasingly worried BBC administrators as audience figures for radio declined in the 1950s.[103] The BBC estimated that in 1948–9, *Luxembourg* captured 3 per cent of the total listening audience (roughly one million listeners), though the percentages must have been higher in areas where the Continental station's signal was stronger, such as the South of England.[104]

Television was also on the rise at the end of the 1940s: between June 1948 and March 1949, the number of television licences doubled from 50,000 to 100,000 and, according to a BBC report into television, there were 'unmistakeable signs of TV becoming less and less a "rich man's toy"'.[105] These numbers would soon increase, as the opening of Sutton Coldfield transmitter in 1949 extended the reach of television into the Midlands.[106] At the same time, internal pressures also changed the landscape of post-war BBC: studio equipment was out of date, producers were overworked and competition between the three new Programmes left departments, such as Variety, in what Martin Dibbs calls a state of 'exhaustion'.[107] The BBC also put in place mechanisms to ensure quality output, inaugurating, for instance, a Variety Script Section in 1947 to 'assess, advise and improve existing material and encourage emerging writers'.[108] Since the mid-1930s, *Children's Hour* and Drama scripts had been reviewed by readers who assessed the quality and suitability of the writing for radio, and provided running time estimates of scripts; but this process became more standardized and formal, as evidenced by the pre-printed Drama Script Readers' Reports found in Constanduros's files from 1950. Further, attempts by the BBC to balance the continued commitment to the Reithian mission with an increasing willingness to consider audience demand must also be factored into the environment within which Constanduros attempted to secure commissions in the post-war period.

The difficulties that Constanduros faced in getting her work on air in the post-war period might suggest that her work was no longer popular. Yet, extant Listener Research surveys on those programmes that did make it on radio suggest that audiences found Constanduros's works entertaining; for example, her 1948 adaptation of Helen Simpson's *Saraband for Dead Lovers* was rated in the top three Home Service programmes for the night of 14 August 1948.[109] It is thus possible that the light fare Constanduros had built her career upon was still potentially popular with audiences, but that the BBC's standards had shifted away from her style of writing. As Dibbs has demonstrated, the Light Programme became more serious in the post-war period.[110] In 1947, Norman Collins, Controller of Light, introduced several programmes intended to add weight to the Programme including *Radio Newsreel* and *Curtain Up!*[111] Two Constanduros/Agg adaptations of Somerset Maugham's works featured on *Curtain Up!*, but internal BBC readers increasingly dismissed Constanduros's original work as naïve or out of date.

Criticism of an original radio play about divorce, sent to the BBC in 1949, is representative of the criticism BBC script readers levelled at her writing during this period: 'An appallingly banal and magaziney treatment of a complex, serious subject, the play strikes me as both immature and amateurish.'[112] Others skewered her for trying to pass off works on the BBC that they felt fit only for the amateur stage.[113] While it is possible that this criticism indicates that Constanduros's writing was becoming outmoded, however, it is more likely suggestive of both the increase in seriousness on the Light and a new generation of staffers than in a broader shift in audience attitudes towards Constanduros's works. Since the BBC was the final arbiter of what they *felt* the listening audiences wanted or needed, it is impossible to know for sure whether listeners had tired of her material.

Certainly there is a palpable sense of frustration in Constanduros's letters with new staff in both Drama and Variety in the post-war period; new relationships had to be cultivated as she had done in the interwar period. When she felt unduly dismissed or ignored, however, she often circumvented new post-war staffers by tapping long-time relationships. In 1949, when staff failed to respond to her ideas about creating a serial centred on actor David Kossoff, Constanduros sent a note to Val Gielgud, who was at the time shuttling back and forth across the Atlantic while juggling dual roles as Head of both Television Drama and Sound Drama[114]; she complained about the delay and wished him 'back in the harness again'.[115] In this particular case, the serial did not come to fruition, but staff became more responsive to her subsequent letters.[116]

Several years later, when Constanduros proposed *The Smalls at Home*, the working-class sitcom vehicle for herself and Richard Goolden, she tapped long-time staffer Gale Pedrick (then Head of the Script Section in Variety) to make it happen. Pedrick spent nearly fifteen months trying to convince various BBC departments to accept it. Even though *The Smalls at Home* was ultimately rejected, it is significant that Pedrick exhausted all possible avenues, seeking out the Head of Variety (Standing) and the soon-to-be Head of Variety

(Hillyard), as well as the regions and Drama.[117] When he queried Head of the Drama Script Unit, Charles Lefeaux, Pedrick explained his persistence writing: 'as Mabel Constanduros is such a very old hand I feel it is only fair to be able to say truthfully that I have done my best to interest everybody possible.'[118] Some felt that the series might be 'attractive' based on the acting ability of Goolden and Constanduros, but Lefeaux felt the scripts too 'pre-war' and finally nixed the idea.[119]

While staffers could be ambivalent about her writing, Pedrick's machinations and positive comments about both Constanduros's writing and acting in reader's reports and other internal memoranda suggest that she still commanded respect at the BBC and enjoyed popularity among listeners. Further, as Dibbs has noted in his history of the Variety department, even with the elevation of scriptwriting to a 'recognised profession' and a new crop of promising scriptwriters emerging in the post-war period, the BBC still suffered from a shortage of good radio writers.[120] Constanduros was at least a proven and popular writer; it would have been foolish for the BBC to ignore her wish to continue writing. Further, she consistently demonstrated a strong work ethic and sense of professionalism. When scripts were rejected, Constanduros engaged in correspondence and dialogue (often over lunch) with staffers and producers to rework her material into a more acceptable form. When, for instance, Val Gielgud rejected her original play *Feathers in the Wind*, based on the 1935 Rattenbury murder, Constanduros revised the play several times with Gielgud until she gained a contract later that year. When the play finally made it to the desk of BBC reader Cynthia Pughe, ordinarily a harsh critic of Constanduros's writing, Pughe praised it as 'One of the best things Miss C. has done', noting that the dialogue was 'extremely competent' and the character development strong.[121] *Feathers in the Wind* was eventually rejected in December 1951 on 'policy grounds'; though the specifics were never enumerated, one would imagine that the sexual impropriety at the heart of the Rattenbury murder case must have influenced the decision.[122] On another occasion, the BBC commissioned Constanduros to adapt Charles Reade's novel *Hard Cash*, but Assistant Head of Drama E. A. Harding voiced concerns over the length of the adaptation, worrying the treatment was not long enough. Constanduros asked Harding for more direction and time to edit the adaptation, reminding him of her credentials, stating, 'I have arranged two of Dickens' books as serials, several of Somerset Maugham's as Radio plays, had two plays produced on the London Stage, written (and published) six or seven books and been writing for Radio for twenty-three years. I think I can be trusted to turn out something workmanlike.'[123] Harding let her complete the adaptation, but eventually rejected it on the grounds that in retrospect, the novel seemed too difficult to adapt.[124]

Constanduros increasingly turned to adaptations in the post-war period. During the war, Constanduros and Howard Agg collaborated on a number of successful adaptations, some of which – such as Somerset Maugham's *The Painted Veil* – were recycled after the war. This decision was partly a response to the changing landscape of light entertainment on the BBC, but Constanduros also found the work appealing. As she confided to Val Gielgud in 1946, 'Adapting makes a relaxation when one doesn't feel quite energetic enough for original stuff, or is too busy for a long spell of work'.[125] Busy cultivating her film career, Constanduros turned to her love of classic British literature – especially Dickens, Scott and Gaskell – for BBC commissions.

Giddings and Selby assert that the 'BBC early established almost a proprietary right over the adaptation, production and broadcasting of the British literary classics', with the first recognized adaptations of *Westward Ho!* in 1925 and Conrad's *Lord Jim* in 1927.[126] While *Westward Ho!* and *Lord Jim* are firmly established as the earliest BBC adaptations, it seems that the regions were experimenting with the genre long beforehand. 5SC (Glasgow) aired the first radio adaptations, written and produced by R.E. Jeffrey, the first being a 1923 adaptation of *Rob Roy* scheduled at the end of the evening's programming, which suggests the production might have lasted as long as 195 minutes. This adaptation featured a cast of fifteen, with Jeffrey playing Rob Roy MacGregor and Jeffrey's wife in the role of Rob Roy's wife, Helen MacGregor; the wireless station orchestra and the First Royal Scots Fusiliers Military Band provided music.[127] Two other adaptations written specifically for the microphone appeared that fall on 5SC, written and produced by Jeffrey, but after he left to take up a position as productions director in London the following year, few adaptations aired on 5SC.[128] Other regions also aired novel adaptations in 1924 and 1925, but nothing quite as ambitious as Jeffrey's work. Indeed, once in London, Jeffrey was involved in bringing novel adaptations to 2LO, as producer of *Westward Ho!*

2LO and the Home Service produced other adaptations and novel readings in the 1930s as stand-alone programmes; as with the serialization of other genres mentioned already, serialization of novel adaptations appeared in the late-1930s, the first being a twelve-episode adaptation of *The Count of Monte Cristo* in 1938. A year later, the nine-episode *The Prisoner of Zenda* established what would become the popular Sunday tea-time slot for classic serial adaptations; thus,

Giddings and Selby date the beginnings of the genre 'as an ongoing feature of broadcast drama' to *Zenda*.¹²⁹ Adaptations also featured on the popular wartime *Saturday Night Theatre*, beginning in 1943; Peter Black remembered that the 'classic serials emptied the public libraries of any book they chose'.¹³⁰ As many of these adaptations featured nineteenth- and twentieth-century British authors, they were an important feature of the larger wartime BBC enterprise to protect British culture and project national identity.¹³¹ The war firmly established the genre, ushering in a golden age of classic radio serials.

Throughout the early post-war period, Constanduros repeatedly sent requests to Gielgud for commissions to adapt Dickens in particular. Following a successful 1944 adaptation of *Bleak House* with Agg, in which Dickensians responded favourably, Constanduros plumped for nearly two years for the pair to gain the right to adapt *Great Expectations*, which aired in fall 1948.¹³² Once again, this broadcast adaptation was a success, even with Dickensians: the reviewer for the quarterly *Dickensian* found the acting and production superb, and appreciated dialogue that 'reproduce[ed] the full effect of the unspoken text'.¹³³ The pair followed this up with the BBC's first adaptation of *Our Mutual Friend*, starring a young Richard Attenborough, in 1950. The series was not well received and the Agg/Constanduros writing partnership, already frayed, disintegrated over this, one of Dickens's most complex novels.

Constanduros understood from the beginning that *Our Mutual Friend* would be a difficult adaptation, given the number of characters in the text and the complicated plot, but once the pair managed to win the commission, she and Agg embarked upon the writing in August 1949. Constanduros's solo and collaborative adaptations had often been praised for fidelity to the original text, but Gielgud suggested that the pair might offer a more 'radical' adaptation this time, as BBC policy was becoming more favourable towards adaptations that fit the medium rather than adhered too much to the original work: 'I am not for a moment suggesting that violence should be done to the spirit of the original – that spirit which you have so admirably succeeded in retaining in your adaptations', he wrote, 'but from the point of view of radio mechanism I think it is sometimes the case that the adaptor has felt too sternly confined by the architectural blue print of the original writer'.¹³⁴

Nonetheless, once the script was in hand, the Assistant Head of Drama E. A. Harding worried that Dickensians would skewer the BBC over the minimization or elimination of the several of the novel's characters, especially the Veneerings and the Podsnaps.¹³⁵ Gielgud, however, stood on his original assertion that the medium was as important as the original text, arguing that writers were free to use 'their creative license'.[136] Nonetheless, producer Hugh Stewart was hesitant about the writers' decision to remove the novel's 'social conscience' characters from the adaptation though, he told Constanduros privately, he understood the choice, given the complicated nature of the novel.[137] Harding and Stewart were right to worry: the *Dickensian* reviewer was positively distraught by this new Constanduros/Agg adaptation, particularly the loss of the aforementioned characters. While the reviewer appreciated the 'extremely difficult and complex' plot of the novel, he questioned 'leaving out half of the characterisation which distinguishes the book. There was ... no Podsnap, no Veneering, no Twemlow, no Lammle, no Fledgeby, no Tippins'.[138] Similar critiques regarding adaptors' decisions to dispense with the 'social chorus' have since plagued subsequent adaptations of the *Our Mutual Friend*. In his assessment of the 1976 (dir. Peter Hammond) and 1998 (dir. Julian Farino) BBC television adaptations of the text, Sean Grass has argued that while the loss of these characters makes sense in terms of 'streamlining an enormous plot ... it also has the effect of stripping away some essential part of the novel's broader critique'.[139]

The aforementioned exchange over *Our Mutual Friend* draws early BBC radio drama into debates over 'fidelity' to the original text that have long been central to critical and popular receptions of cinematic and televisual literary adaptations, especially of beloved nineteenth-century canonical texts.[140] Certainly, it demonstrates that the BBC, and Gielgud in particular, was alive to the ways in which the constraints and possibilities of the particular media used in an adaptation cut across the concern of fidelity, and by necessity violated the literary original.[141]

The Constanduros/Agg adaptation of *Our Mutual Friend* suffered from other concerns beyond the removal of the 'social chorus'. The *Dickensian* reviewer was willing to concede the difficulties of plot and character streamlining, but felt that the 'dramatisers seemed to come off worst in their tussle with the story', mixing up character lines and giving Attenborough's John Harmon the unenviable task of narrating the whole story – even the storylines his character could have known little to nothing about.[142] Given their reputation as skilled adaptors of literature, it is hard to imagine how – despite the inherent challenges thrown up by the novel – the pair managed to so thoroughly miss the mark on this adaptation. One clue to this mystery is correspondence between Constanduros and the BBC in which Constanduros insists that the work go out under the pseudonym, H.M. Sussex. Gielgud, however, believed that the writers' 'prestige would inevitably go some way in counterbalancing the criticism' that staffers anticipated, and the BBC decided ultimately not to allow the pair to broadcast as Sussex.[143] Gielgud explained Constanduros's request to Harding by mentioning a falling out between the writers: Constanduros apparently believed Agg failed to pull his weight on the writing, and thus wanted to disassociate both herself and Agg from the project.

Agg seems to have moved to Sicily around the time that the pair won the commission to write *Our Mutual Friend*, and became increasingly difficult to contact. Several times in Constanduros's correspondence with the BBC, staffers asked after Agg, suggesting that the BBC was unable to contact him. Constanduros's responses to these queries struck a tone of exasperation, as she was also unable to get a response from him. On one occasion, Constanduros contacted the copyright section seeking a fee that they told her had been sent to Agg, suggesting that he might not have always passed on fees due her. At around the same time, Constanduros had to apologize to a producer for the poor quality of a script the pair sent to the BBC; in this, she claimed Agg typed the script. Though nothing exists to suggest the exact damage caused to the adaptation as a result of this personal and professional conflict, it might explain the failure of the adaptation overall. Certainly, the two would never again collaborate together on new material. Indeed, henceforth, they directly competed for commissions. At one point, both Agg and Constanduros independently asked for a commission to adapt the novel *No Name*. Constanduros was furious when she learned that Agg had been given the commission instead of herself, claiming that she had asked for the commission long before Agg requested it.[144] Indeed, the affair became so heated that Gielgud – a friend of both – pressed Agg to write her in an effort to defuse the situation.[145]

Adaptations had become so popular by this time that the Drama department was now overwhelmed with suggestions for suitable novels to adapt from writers keen on gaining commissions. From the late 1940s until her death, Constanduros regularly sent short notes to Drama staffers, floating between two and six novels at any given time. In 1952, just after the dust up over *No Name*, Lefeaux wrote to Constanduros complaining that he received so many requests, some simply lists of upwards of thirty titles, that it 'is impossible ... to say which of a number of suggesters got in first'. Therefore, Lefeaux suggested, it would be better, 'both from your point of view and ours, if you can send each of your suggestions in the form of a short plot outline, together with some selling reasons of why the suggestion would make good radio'.[146] While she still continued to send brief notes hoping for commissions of suggested novels afterwards, Constanduros increasingly bent to BBC demands by sending plot summaries, though she (and the BBC) admitted that short summaries were not her strength. Nonetheless, BBC staffers were often patient with her on this point, coaching her on how to improve them and giving her the benefit of the doubt.[147]

Increasing demand from writers to adapt novels for radio resulted in more competition for commissions. When both Constanduros and novelist Olivia Manning asked for a commission to adapt Elizabeth Gaskell's *Wives and Daughters*, the BBC decided to ask both writers for a fifteen-page dialogue treatment for which they were paid 20gn.[148] According to Manning's biographer, BBC readers disliked her proposals because they thought the scripts were too packed with dialogue and the characterizations lacked depth.[149] Constanduros's version was thus preferred and she was given the commission. Nonetheless, Lefeaux insisted Constanduros significantly rework some of her ideas, especially the use of narration, arguing, 'Mrs Gaskell is one of the authors with whom narration is largely unnecessary, and that the information can, with a little ingenuity, be worked into dialogue form.'[150] Even though she worked diligently for several months to produce an acceptable adaptation of *Wives and Daughters* and, in 1954, reworked the original to fit the new six-episode Sunday night Home Service programming slot, more than two years later, the serial had not yet been aired.[151] Somewhat exasperated, Constanduros wrote to Barbara Bray asking if she might have the original scripts back, so that she could adapt her version of *Wives and Daughters*, and another radio adaptation that had previously been accepted but had also not made it on air, for television. Bray returned the scripts, but also stated that the BBC still planned to run both on radio, and thus had made copies.[152] In the event, *Wives and Daughters* aired on radio after Constanduros's death and, though the other script that Constanduros requested was reviewed for production in 1962, it failed the reader's assessment and never aired.[153]

Conclusion

Mabel Constanduros continued to entertain audiences right up until a heart attack put her in hospital in December 1956. Directly after her death in February 1957, friends and staffers at the BBC considered commemorating her life on radio but, ultimately, the BBC decided against it. After the huge outpouring of grief and official commemoration in the wake of Tommy Handley's untimely death in 1949, some worried that henceforth the BBC would be obligated to memorialize the death of every radio celebrity.[1] In the event, *Woman's Hour* warmly remembered her in its December review of 1957.

In the months leading up to her heart attack, Constanduros was as active as ever. She wrote and performed in a regular Buggins series spot on *Woman's Hour*, offered comfort on *Children's Hour* in a talk entitled 'On Being Frightened', and appeared in a twelve-episode adaptation of *David Copperfield* as Mrs. Gummidge for children's television. The broad sweep and variety of Constanduros's radio career is shown in the *Radio Times* listings of her appearances and productions in 1956–7: a light comedic play with nephew Denis, a new production of *The Laughing Mirror* written with Howard Agg in the 1940s, readings on *Morning Story*, an acting role in a serious (Third Programme) DG Bridson radio play, appearances on *Children's Hour* and numerous Buggins family sketches.[2]

Buggins family comedy remained popular with radio audiences in the 1950s. The Bugginses featured in a number of nostalgia programmes and on talks about early radio in the post-war period. Constanduros remembered her BBC radio days in popular productions like *These Radio Times*, a scrapbook programme that featured anecdotes and reminiscences of early wireless personalities and staffers, interspersed with recordings of old performances. She also gave a number of talks about her early days as a celebrity and recounted the origins of the Buggins family in various programmes, such as *Through the Stage Door* and on *Woman's Hour*.

Constanduros developed a close relationship with *Woman's Hour*, broadcasting regularly with the programme from 1947 until her death. The popular and enduring programme initially had a rough start when it was introduced on the Light in October 1946, but caught its stride within the year. By August 1948,

Woman's Hour moved to the Home and became a castle programme, attracting a wide range of listeners to radio during its timeslot.³ The magazine format was aimed at 'intelligent women', and featured topics on home, children, health and beauty, and items designed to provide women with new interests, as well as a recipes and short serials.⁴ The Bugginses continued their popular wartime recipe segments on *Woman's Hour* through the darkest austerity years at the end of the 1940s, and in the early 1950s, Constanduros was asked back to perform new Buggins material. In 1953, she began a new Buggins family serial, which quickly became a *Woman's Hour* favourite, and ran until just weeks before she was hospitalized at the end of 1956.⁵

The new *Woman's Hour* series kicked off with the Bugginses preparing for, and then attending the Coronation celebrations. After this successful venture, Constanduros was asked to write monthly episodes to begin in October that year.⁶ The eight-minute episodes featured Mrs. Buggins recounting events in her life with Grandma inserting her caustic asides, rather like a humorous working-class version of *Mrs. Dales Diary* without the supporting cast. These 'episode[s] in the life of the Buggins family' picked up where the 1930s novels left off, with a widowed Mrs. Buggins caring for her children and suffering Grandma's usual antics.⁷ The series quickly introduced a love interest – Mr Podd – and a storyline which Constanduros developed over a number of episodes until audiences and staffers alike clamoured to hear wedding bells.⁸ Once the couple finally married, the series was devoted to winning Grandma over to the likeable Mr. Podd. In one such episode, Mr. Podd tried to win Grandma over with a 'tele-set'. Podd's gesture was eventually accepted by the curmudgeonly Grandma, but the newlyweds found they now had to share the television with the entire neighbourhood: children offered sweets to Alfie and Emma for admission, housewives stopped in conveniently to visit and husbands fetching their wives stayed over to watch a comic, and all remained until the last television transmission of the evening.⁹

Aired just ten days before ITV's first transmission on 22 September 1955, the 'tele-set' episode captures the excitement of television, just as the new media began to take off in Britain. The neighbourhood response is humorously reminiscent of the arrangements made by friends, family, and all and sundry to watch the Coronation festivities in 1953 or to catch FA Cup Finals on the television.¹⁰ Though radio was still the 'dominant output' at the time, the number of radio-only licences were declining, while the number of combined radio and television licences began to soar.¹¹ Under the direction of pro-television Director General Sir Ian Jacob, funding for television was also on the rise from 1952.¹²

Meanwhile, working-class television ownership was on the rise as hire-purchase was made easier in 1954.[13] With working-class audience numbers reaching nearly 60 per cent of the viewing audience, television was no longer a 'luxury of the rich'.[14]

Nonetheless, radio was thriving. *Mrs. Dale's Diary*, *the Archers* and *The Goon Show* captured loyal listening audiences and, technologically, radio was the better medium in the mid-1950s.[15] One popular music producer remembered, 'Television was terribly expensive, the pictures weren't very good and the programmes were rather awful.'[16] Radio was also considered the more professional medium, and many believed that the public would prefer listening in to looking in. In 1948, Superintendent Engineer for Television D. J. Birkinshaw believed that television would displace 'a portion only of Sound', reasoning, 'There is such a vast range of material broadcast on Sound alone which the public appears to want as a permanent feature of radio entertainment, but which would be intolerably dull if transmitted visually as well as orally.'[17] Still, concerns about the power of television to supplant radio were percolating throughout the BBC.

When, in 1950, Constanduros wrote to EA Harding offering more radio plays, she sounded a note of alarm about the power of television: 'Radio has been my life for twenty-five years. I admit fear to think we may have to go down before television.' Yet she remained committed to radio, and felt it could weather the competition, finishing the letter, 'I don't believe myself that we shall. But at least, if we do, let us go down with flying colours. And I would like to help to keep our colours flying.'[18] Harding's confident reply echoes Birkinshaw's sentiments:

> I don't for a moment think that sound radio is going down before what is so disgustingly described in America I believe as Video, though if and when – and it is a big if and I think it will be a long when – there is something like national coverage by television, I am pretty sure that most of the audience for popular drama will want to look as well as listen in.[19]

Harding's disdain for the American-ness of television here echoes long-held BBC suspicions of commercial broadcasting in general, and American influence in particular, and underscores the tone of the conversation regarding the new medium in the post-war period.

Val Gielgud, who was for a short period Head of Drama for both Sound and Television, argued that British television had little to learn from the American example. For him, broadcasting in America was more about the end goal of marketing and selling goods – little thought went into the art of broadcasting in America. There, he wrote, 'The tradition of sound-radio has been to lower the standing of the professional broadcaster *as such* to that of the proverbial bottle-washer. Emphasis has been laid on the selling angle of programme items as opposed to their intrinsic quality.'[20] If anything were to be learned from the Americans, it was what *not* to do. After studying television in America, Gielgud felt that American actors were not schooled in proper television technique, producers had no power over broadcasts and material was not thoughtfully chosen for the new medium. Further, the Americans were too dazzled by television: 'Actors, directors, executives, even sponsors, varied between almost lyric optimism and quasi-neurotic excitement. Television was the Works. Television was the Future. Television after all was going to Pay Off.'[21] Gielgud worried that British television might similarly succumb to the excitement of the new technology. 'It is a mistake to be so fascinated by the means at one's disposal', he argued, 'that the end becomes in comparison unimportant.'[22] He further lamented the 'makeshift' nature of post-war British television, dominated by improvisation and insufficient resources.[23]

Constanduros agreed. Though reluctant, Constanduros did perform on, and write for, television from time to time. Constanduros told an original short story on a 1949 *Designed for Women* television programme, though she complained that the compensation for the story hardly made her effort worth it.[24] Three years later, *Portugal Lady*, her historical drama about Charles II, which was rejected for radio in 1950 on the grounds that 'costume "pieces"' were not appealing to radio audiences, was picked up for television. In 1953, she reprised her radio role as Earthy Mangold on television in the four-part children's series, *Worzel Turns Detective*. Just after the shooting of this series, Constanduros complained to Gielgud about television:

> What a bastard art it is. I do hope it will never oust sound. I don't see how it can as it is all in the hands of chimney sweeps and the like. I don't wonder you shook the dust off your feet with joy. How can anybody get results from TV as it is now? Never the same makeup girls or cameramen for rehearsal as for transmission. I think, though, that powerful duologue plays might do well, don't you?[25]

Gielgud responded,

> I confess I share most of your apprehensions about TV. It is exasperating because if only people would give rather more thought to the problems instead of trying to do too much too quickly and too elaborately, a genuine medium might well

emerge. Unfortunately, the TV audience is both voracious and stupid and we have no-one of Reith's caliber at this end to resist adequately the more moronic type of public demand.[26]

Both radio professionals, who had cut their teeth in similar improvised circumstances in radio's early days, were now impatient with the enthusiasm and experimentation that swirled around the new medium. Written at the same time that the BBC was preparing to televise the upcoming Coronation and consumers were scrambling for their own television sets, correspondence between Gielgud and Constanduros seems now to concede, though with great anxiety, that television would eventually eclipse radio. Indeed, while both protested the new medium, they nonetheless debated ways in which the BBC might improve the experience, both of acting and viewing.

Gielgud's concern over the degradation of the Reithian mission underscores an emergent relaxation of attitudes towards the provision of popular entertainment at the BBC, especially after the introduction of commercial television. These changes spilled over into radio in 1957 with the BBC's policy statement on *The Future of Sound Broadcasting*, which spelled the end of Haley's post-war 'pyramid of culture' scheme and argued that the Light Programme must compete not only against both Continental radio and domestic television but also against increased leisure opportunities beyond these media.[27] Thus, from September 1957, the Light would exist only to entertain, while the Home would carry news and current events, talks, features and drama (both serious and light), with some variety sprinkled in. As Martin Dibbs has observed, 'The reorganisation was not designed as an audacious move to retain the radio audience but instead one which reflected the momentous changes which were taking place in both broadcasting and society.'[28]

The Mother of the BBC: Invisibility and influence

Mabel Constanduros's death coincided with the fundamental re-imagining of the BBC heralded by *The Future of Sound Broadcasting* and the rapid overtaking of the now well-established and respected sound broadcasting by the new and exciting 'tele-set'. Had she lived, it is possible that she may have made the jump to television, expanding and adapting her career as she had done successfully for thirty-two years. Indeed, as was seen earlier, there were already signs that she was willing to work on television.

But Mabel Constanduros belongs firmly to the radio age, helping to evolve radio from an amateur adventure into a professional, respected and popular medium. Early pioneers and radio stars like Constanduros and John Henry experimented with the technology and pointed the way to proven techniques, genres and characterizations that others built upon. In the process, a new generation of entertainers further pushed the boundaries of the possible – both in terms of genres and technology, but also in regards to propriety – marking a significant shift in the history of BBC entertainment. This new generation of entertainers and writers, such as Jack Warner, Dick Bentley, Ted Ray, Jimmy Edwards, Tony Hancock, Frank Muir and Denis Norden, became iconic names, leaving early pioneers behind as barely perceptible, illusive shadows in the history of the BBC and British entertainment.

The history of entertainment is often read backwards: starting with developed genres and known writers and artists before working back through the decades. Television has had such an enormous presence since the middle part of the twentieth century that the drive to chart the past in this way has inevitably been defined by the exigencies of television production, which themselves have evolved over decades of experimentation and remediation. Indeed, the traditional definition of sitcom has been inextricably connected to television, assuming a thirty-minute, serial format.[29] The emphasis on television in these histories misses the ways in which entertainment grew out of radio and the needs of the medium and its audience. Certainly, links have long been made between music hall, radio and television comedy. Yet entertainment on the early BBC depended on, and was influenced by, amateurs who cut their teeth in amateur dramatic societies, in family drawing rooms and front rooms, and in workplace canteens. Their efforts were steeped in the domesticity and intimacy of the medium, and while some forms of broadcast entertainment were closely aligned with music-hall traditions, others grew out of the needs of an audience listening at home. These new strategies for entertaining an audience at home heavily influenced the development of entertainment on later radio and television, especially the creations of situation comedy and soap opera.

Historians of both situation comedy and soap opera tend to point to American programming as the templates for these genres in Britain.[30] Constanduros was indeed influenced by the American soap opera, *One Man's Family*, when she originated the form in *EFR*. But British situation comedy was not transplanted from America; rather, it was a home-grown invention, starting with the sketch comedy of Constanduros's Buggins Family in 1925. Holding up a mirror to the domestic lives of listening and viewing audiences, the family is the foundational basis of both genres.³¹ As such, Constanduros's invention of the first radio family marked a critical moment in the history of British broadcast entertainment. Her efforts to portray 'ordinary' British families in her writing participated with the BBC's wider claims to represent the nation in the interwar and immediate post-war period. At the same time, her emphasis on the humour of the everyday rhythms of home and relationships are influential in the evolution of both forms in Britain. For instance, the realism with which British soap opera has tended to be viewed can be discerned in *EFR* and its successor, *FLF*.³² It is also instructive that *EFR* has been alternately described as both comedy and soap opera, for later British soap operas also enjoy a similar ambiguity that cannot be said of American soaps.³³ 'Except for the laugh with which they are often dismissed', Nancy Baym has pointed out, '[American] soap operas are rarely taken to evoke humor.'³⁴

The post-war period is often considered the moment in which situation comedy took off in Britain.³⁵ In this period, a profusion of comedies with a domestic focus appeared on the BBC such as *Ray's a Laugh* (1947–61), *Life with the Lyons* (1950–61, and *Meet the Huggetts* (1953–61)). Some of these situation comedies, like *Life with the Lyons* and *Meet the Huggetts*, were set in a home, with a cast of characters coping with day-to-day situations similar to Constanduros's Buggins Family comedy and *EFR*. Others, like *Ray's a Laugh*, followed more in the music-hall tradition as it featured popular comedian Ted Ray cracking one-liners as narrator introducing domestic situations in a cross-talk act with his on-air wife, Kitty, and interspersed throughout with musical interludes.

When Frank Muir and Denis Norden introduced their five-minute comedy sketch, 'The Glums', which began to appear in 1953 on *Take It from Here (TIFH)*, they were responding to the 'cosy family life' portrayed in these post-war sitcoms.³⁶ When the family was introduced to audiences, the writers played on the usual calls to ordinariness seen in *EFR* and *The Huggetts*: 'Our family, the Glums, are very <u>ordinary</u> people. They might be <u>you</u> or <u>you</u> or <u>you</u> … . All five of them are shifty, obstinate, argumentative and dim.'³⁷ But the family name suggests a much longer lineage stretching back to the interwar situation comedy, *The Plums* (1937 and 1942). *The Strange Adventures of Mr. Penny* (1936–7) and wartime series, like Constanduros's *Mr. and Mrs. Sparkes* (1941) and *Down Mangel Street* (1942) as well as the long-running popular Scottish family series written by Helen Pryde, the *McFlannels* (1939–54), should thus be worked into the landscape within which the Glums and subsequent British sitcoms were created.

Working-class characterizations and situations in the Glums are strikingly similar to Buggins sketches. Yet the dysfunctional Glums are considered a 'watershed in the representation of the sitcom family', presaging the Garnett family in *Till Death Us Do Part* and 'the argumentative, less cosy portrayal of the domestic scene ... [in] a whole host of British sitcoms'.[38] Certainly, the line leading to the Garnetts should be extended to include the Bugginses (as well as *The Plums*). Yet, the Glums do represent a critical junction in British sitcom, marking the moment when the feminine and the domestic became increasingly devalued in British sitcom and the primacy of the male perspective took hold: June Whitfield's Eth played the straight woman who rarely spoke, and mother and grandmother (both played by Alma Coogan) were relegated to noises 'off – unintelligible shout' while Ron (Dick Bentley) and Dad (Jimmy Edwards) took centre stage.[39] Thus, the series ushers in the usual British family sitcom dynamic whereby women act as the 'backdrop for the focus on the "real action" of men'.[40]

One reason why Constanduros's influence has escaped much attention in the past is not only due to what Lance Sieveking called 'the ghastly impermanence of the medium' of radio but also because of the domestic and feminine focus of her work.[41] Carolyn Scott-Jeffs has argued that Constanduros's invisibility is the result of situation comedy being a genre largely colonized by men.[42] Gilli Bush-Bailey has pointed to the 'patriarchal assumptions' embedded in the Reithian mission 'as an instance of the careless masculinity that has made and continues to make histories that marginalize or simply forget women, and here forgets their role in laying the foundations of today's broadcasting'.[43] Further, as Maggie Andrews has argued, associations between radio, domesticity and femininity have led to 'the low status of broadcast media'.[44]

Certainly, Constanduros domesticated comedy and light drama on the early BBC: in the family-based entertainment she wrote and performed, Constanduros exercised the power of subjectivity, privileging women's voice, their experiences and their relationships. Her female characterizations both in drama and comedy enabled women to engage with and 'challenge dominant versions of femininity'.[45] Throughout her Buggins material – both on radio and in print – men were often relegated to the periphery. Conversations between her female protagonists – especially in her working-class comedy – rarely failed the Bechdel-Wallace test, which provides a simple guide to gender equality in cultural forms. To pass the test, a text must have '(1) at least two female characters (2) who talk to each other (3) about something other than a man'.[46] While her light drama was less radical, Constanduros nearly always situated her female characters as the main protagonists and privileged their perspective over that of others. In these important aspects, Constanduros prefigures path-breaking Second Wave writers like Carla Lane.

Constanduros's battle to remain relevant over thirty-two years on an ever-changing BBC demonstrates the ways in which women have negotiated male-dominated workplaces and professions. Fiercely protective of her intellectual property and her professional status, Constanduros burnished a maternal and feminine image with BBC staffers, producers and executives in order to gain commissions for herself and others, and to cultivate respect and loyalty. The strategies she employed to manage her public image are instructive for our understandings of the construction of early BBC celebrity and the ways women carved out careers for themselves in the mid-twentieth century. At the same time, these negotiations continue to resonate for women, who continue to be positioned vis-à-vis their femininity and private roles, either using their feminine 'credentials' as a rationale for entering public roles or explaining (to themselves and others) why they exist outside the home and apart from their children (or without children).

In lead acting roles, as writers and creators, and in leadership positions, women remain underrepresented across multiple media;[47] equally the important contributions women have made to these media also remain largely invisible. A cursory scan of *Radio Times* listings across the years discussed in this book reminds us that numerous women have exercised, and continue to exercise, immense, if often unrecognized, influence on the BBC. Following on Kate Murphy's observation of an early BBC that 'burst with women', programme listings and folders at the BBC Written Archives positively bristle with female performers and writers.[48] The names of Hermione Gingold, Ethel Revnell, Helena Millais, Elsie and Doris Waters, Jeanne De Casalis, Nellie Wallace, Tessie O'Shea, Mira B. Johnson, Gladys Young, Francis Kilpatrick, Helen Pryde and Barbara Euphan Todd represent just a fraction of the women who were well known to and beloved by audiences in the 1920s and the 1930s whose work and influence have yet to be written into the history of the BBC. Given the power of broadcasting entertainment to shape ideas of self, family, community and nation, more complex – and necessary – histories of the BBC would include the performers, writers and programmes that women, men and children tuned into every day. As Raphael Samuel noted in the 1990s, 'The BBC is, or ought to be, a researcher's dream.'[49] Then, as now, the history of the BBC remains largely unwritten.

Notes

Introduction

1. *The Performer*, 14 February 1957; *Shields Evening News*, 9 February 1957. Newspaper clippings, Richard Constanduros family archives. Many thanks to Richard and his family for providing access to this material.
2. Collie Knox, 'The Gift of Friendship', *Home Notes*, 11 April 1957. Newspaper clippings, Richard Constanduros family archives.
3. *Birmingham Mail*, 2 May 1957, Robb Wilton's obituary. Newspaper clippings, Richard Constanduros family archives.
4. Personal communication, Anthea Duigan (Constanduros's granddaughter), 5 October 2010. The family retained one diary from 1899, a journal filled with the cramped and detailed writing of a nineteen-year-old's social engagements and potential suitors.
5. David Hendy, 'Biography and the Emotions as a Missing Narrative in Media History: A Case Study of Lance Sieveking and the Early BBC', *Media History*, 18, no. 3–4 (2012): 373.
6. Kate Murphy, *Behind the Wireless: A History of Early Women at the BBC* (London: Palgrave Macmillan, 2016), 10.
7. Gilli Bush-Bailey, 'Mabel Constanduros: Different Voices, Voicing Difference', in Maggie Gale and Kate Dorney, eds., *Stage Women, 1900-1950: Female Theatre Workers and Professional Practice* (Manchester: Manchester University Press, 2019), 279.
8. For instance, Steve Neale and Frank Krutnik, *Popular Film and Television Comedy* (London: Routledge, 1990), especially chapter nine, 209–61; Frances Gray, *Women and Laughter* (Charlottesville, VA: UPVA, 1994).
9. Maggie Andrews, *Domesticating the Airwaves: Broadcasting, Domesticity and Femininity* (London: Continuum, 2012), especially preface and chapter 1, vii–29.
10. Val Gielgud, *Years in a Mirror* (London: The Bodley Head, 1965), 84; Charlotte Brunsdon, 'Text and Audience', in Ellen Seiter, Hans Borchers, Gabriele Kreutzner and Eva-Maria Warth, eds., *Remote Control: Television, Audiences, and Cultural Power* (London: Routledge, 1989), 116.
11. Andrews, *Domesticating the Airwaves*, 18; Brunsdon, 'Text and Audience', 116–17.
12. Gielgud, *Years in a Mirror*, 84–5.

13 Kristin Skoog, "'They're 'Doped' by that Dale Diary": Women's Serial Drama, the BBC and British Post-War Change', in Helen Thornham and Elke Weissmann, eds., *Renewing Feminisms: Radical Narratives, Fantasies and Futures in Media Studies* (London: I.B. Tauris, 2013), 126.
14 Skoog, "'They're 'Doped' by that Dale Diary'", 134 and 126.
15 Judy Giles, *The Parlour and the Suburb: Domestic Identities, Class, Femininities and Modernity* (New York: Berg, 2004), 43; Skoog, "'They're 'Doped' by that Dale Diary'", 128.
16 Andy Medhurst, 'Negotiating the Gnome Zone: Versions of Suburbia in British Popular Culture', in Richard Silverstone, ed., *Visions of Suburbia* (London: Routledge, 1997), 241.
17 J. B. Priestley, *English Humour* (New York: Stein and Day, 1976), 197; Regina Barreca, ed. *Last Laughs: Perspectives on Women and Comedy* (London: Routledge, 1988), 4.
18 Gray, *Women and Laughter*, 83.
19 This is the case in stand-up comedy as well. Dawn French lamented this state of affairs in her memoir, *Dear Fatty* (London: Arrow Books, 2009), 264.
20 Regina Barreca, 'Metaphor-Into-Narrative: Being Very Careful with Words', *Women's Studies* 15 (1988): 254.
21 Gielgud, *Years in a Mirror*, 84.
22 Asa Briggs, *The History of Broadcasting in the United Kingdom, Volume II: The Golden Age of Wireless* (Oxford: Oxford University Press, 1995), 56; for recording on early radio, see 93–5.
23 Murphy, *Behind the Wireless*, 11.
24 Gray, *Women and Laughter*, notes that Carla Lane is often picked out as the exceptional female writer as evidence that women's writing cannot rise to the quality of men, 89.
25 Mabel Constanduros, *Shreds and Patches* (London: Lawson and Dunn, 1946), 7.
26 Mabel Constanduros, 'Where I Found the Bugginses', *Radio Times*, 8 February 1929, 312.
27 Constanduros, *Shreds and Patches*, 10.
28 Mabel Constanduros, 29 May 1899. Richard Constanduros's private collection.
29 Constanduros, *Shreds and Patches*, 31.
30 Constanduros, *Shreds and Patches*, 10.
31 Ath appears as a potential suitor in the 1899 diary.
32 Dick Bower, *The Drama Unfolded: A History of Sutton Amateur Dramatic Club, 1902-2002* (Dick Bower and David Gillespie for the SADC, 2002). Many thanks to Dick Bower for generously sharing this publication with me.
33 Between 1909 and 1925, the couple appeared on stage together seven times; Ath appeared twice without Mabel, and Mabel appeared separately four times.

The SADC was on hiatus during the First World, suspending activities between September 1914 and April 1919. Sutton Local Archives, SADC Box 2, Master Set Programmes to 1957 and Box 3, Meeting Minutes.

34 Sutton Local Archives, SADC Box 6 Programmes 1952–54; 1954–56; 1957–64.
35 'Radio Star's Loss: Mr. A. Constanduros Dies Suddenly', *Sutton and Cheam Advertiser*, 15 July 1937, 6. Sutton Local Archives, SADC Box 4 Newspaper Cuttings 1892–1928.
36 Quoted in Bush-Bailey, 'Different Voices, Voicing Difference', 270.
37 Sutton Local Archives, SADC Box 4 Newspaper Cuttings 1892–1928.
38 Constanduros, *Shreds and Patches*, 38.
39 For music-hall manner of address, see Peter Bailey, 'Conspiracies of Meaning: Music-Hall and the Knowingness of Popular Culture', *Past and Present* 144 (August 1994): 144.

Chapter 1

1 Portions of this chapter appear in Jennifer Purcell, '"Enthusiasm, Experiment and Gallantry in Action": Developing Light Entertainment on the Fledgling BBC, 1922–1932', *Cultural and Social History* 15, no. 3 (2018): 415–32.
2 Murphy, *Behind the Wireless*, 20.
3 Raphael Samuel, 'The Voice of Britain', in Alison Light, ed., *Island Stories: Unravelling Britain* (London: Verso, 1999), 178.
4 Constanduros, *Shreds and Patches*, 38.
5 Collie Knox, *People of Quality* (London: MacDonald and Co, 1947), 113.
6 Constanduros, *Shreds and Patches*, 38.
7 Constanduros, *Shreds and Patches*, 38.
8 Constanduros, *Shreds and Patches*, 39.
9 See 'Programmes', *Times*, 29 May 1925, 9. *The Times Digital Archive*, http://tinyurl.galegroup.com/tinyurl/ABvJ99, accessed 4 June 2019.
10 'Broadcasting', 16 April 1925, 7; 'Broadcasting', *Times*, 16 April 1925, 7. *The Times Digital Archive*, http://tinyurl.galegroup.com/tinyurl/ACEpD8, accessed 5 June 2019. BBC contracts for Constanduros do not exist in this period.
11 *Radio Times* listing for 16 April 1925, http://genome.ch.bbc.co.uk/schedules/2lo/1925-04-16#at-21.15, accessed 11 January 2017.
12 Richard J. Hand, *Listen in Terror: British Horror Radio from the Advent of Broadcasting to the Digital Age* (Manchester: Manchester University Press, 2014), 33–4.
13 Constanduros is not listed in the *Radio Times* as performing in *Squirrel's Cage*. She and Hogan, however, are given first billing in the listing in the *Times*: 'Broadcasting',

Times, 4 March 1929, 23. *The Times Digital Archive*, http://tinyurl.galegroup.com/tinyurl/A9T6z4, accessed 28 May 2019.

14 Hogan wrote the screenplays for *King Solomon's Mines* (1937) and *Rebecca* (1940) and *Tall in the Saddle* (1944), among others. See 'Michael Hogan' on IMDB, https://www.imdb.com/title/tt0037343/?ref_=nm_flmg_wr_8, accessed 1 September 2019.

15 Asa Briggs, *The History of Broadcasting in the United Kingdom, Volume I: The Birth of Broadcasting 1896-1927* (Oxford: Oxford University Press, 1995), 19.

16 Briggs, *The Birth of Broadcasting*, 19; John Reith, quoted in Brian Hennessey, *The Emergence of Broadcasting in Britain* (Lympstone: Southerleigh, 2005), 233.

17 Cecil Lewis, *Broadcasting from Within* (London: George Newnes, 1924), 26.

18 Eric Maschwitz, *No Chip on My Shoulder* (London: H. Jenkins, 1957), 48.

19 Hennessey, *The Emergence of Broadcasting*, 238.

20 Murphy, *Behind the Wireless*, 95–6.

21 Maurice Gorham, *Sound and Fury: Twenty-One Years in the BBC* (London: P. Marshall, 1948), 51, 11.

22 Kate Murphy, *Behind the Wireless*, 19; Briggs, *The Birth of Broadcasting*, 220.

23 Briggs, *The Birth of Broadcasting*, 219–20.

24 Charlotte Higgins, *The New Noise: The Extraordinary Birth and Troubled Life of the BBC* (London: Guardian Books, 2015), 10.

25 Cheryl Tsang, *Microsoft First Generation: The Success Secrets of the Visionaries who Launched a Technology Empire* (New York: Wiley, 2000), xi–xvii. See for instance, Russell Borland, xiii.

26 Tsang, *Microsoft Generation*, xii. The term coined by Scott Oki, former senior VP of Microsoft.

27 Peter Eckersley, *The Power of the Microphone* (London: Scientific Book Club, 1942), 57.

28 Maschwitz, *No Chip on My Shoulder*, 49.

29 Roger Eckersley, *The BBC and All That* (London: Sampson, Low, Marston and Co., 1946), 57–9.

30 Murphy, *Behind the Wireless*, 151. Murphy's focal point is on female staff – not performers or writers, like Constanduros – who were able to find fulfilling and challenging work that sometimes led to promotions beyond what seemed possible for women outside the BBC. See chapters 5 and 6.

31 By the end of 1925, 1.6 million licences had been bought. Briggs, *The Birth of Broadcasting*, 17.

32 Andrew Crisell, *An Introductory History of British Broadcasting* (London: Routledge, 1997), 16.

33 Initially, Plymouth was listed by the committee, but 'for technical reasons', Bournemouth station was established. Briggs, *The Birth of Broadcasting*, 91. See also Hennessey, *The Emergence of Broadcasting*, 269–78 and 380.

34 Briggs, *The Birth of Broadcasting*, 204–5.
35 Crisell, *Introductory History British Broadcasting*, 17.
36 Briggs, *The Birth of Broadcasting*, 212. Illustration 14. A similar cabinet-type BTH wireless set from the same period cost £129, *Catalogue of Radio Receiving Sets, Amplifiers, Components and Accessories* (ND), http://www.valve-radio.co.uk/literature/catalogue-of-radio-receiving-sets/, accessed 22 March 2019.
37 *Popular Wireless* 1926-1929, numerous numbers.
38 David Hendy, 'The Great War and British Broadcasting: Emotional Life in the Creation of the BBC', *New Formations* 82 (2014): 83.
39 Hendy, 'The Great War', 87.
40 Yaron Jean, 'Sonic Mindedness and the Great War: Viewing History Through Auditory Lenses', in Florence Feiereisen and Alexandra Merley Hill, eds., *Germany in the Loud Twentieth Century* (Oxford: Oxford University Press, 2012), 51–62.
41 Hendy, 'The Great War', 88.
42 Hendy, 'The Great War', 90.
43 Reith, *Broadcast over Britain*, quoted in Hendy, 'The Great War'.
44 Programme Board Minutes, 19 January 1925; 26 January 1925; and 12 May 1925. R34/600/2 Policy Progamme Board Minutes, BBC WAC.
45 Programme Board Minutes, 5 January 1925. R34/600/2 Policy Progamme Board Minutes, BBC WAC.
46 Robert Graves and Alan Hodge, *The Long Week-End: A Social History of Great Britain, 1918-1939* (1940; reissue New York: W.W. Norton, 1994), 81–3.
47 Graves and Hodge, *The Long Week-End*, 42–9; See also Jay Winter, *Sites of Memory, Sites of Mourning: The Great War in European Cultural History* (Cambridge: Cambridge University Press, 2009), especially Chapter 3.
48 Winter, *Sites of Memory, Sites of Mourning*, 54–6.
49 Programme Board Minutes, 11 November 1926. R34/600/2 Policy Progamme Board Minutes, BBC WAC.
50 Programme Board Minutes, 11 November 1926. R34/600/2 Policy Progamme Board Minutes, BBC WAC.
51 Briggs, *The Birth of Broadcasting*, 356.
52 Briggs, *The Birth of Broadcasting*, 287.
53 Briggs, *The Birth of Broadcasting*, 354.
54 Briggs, *The Birth of Broadcasting*, 356; for dates, Genome Project. Changing of the Guard, see *Radio Times*, http://genome.ch.bbc.co.uk/3db715079a5e4288bda83e42b2d46be5 and the diver, http://genome.ch.bbc.co.uk/04d39019153843f79e687e17b7d70346, accessed 18 July 2016.
55 Val Gielgud, *British Radio Drama: 1922-1956* (London: George Harrup, 1957), 20.
56 Quoted in Briggs, *The Birth of Broadcasting*, 228.
57 Briggs, *The Birth of Broadcasting*, 65.

58 Eckersley, *The BBC and All That*, 58.
59 Maschwitz, *No Chip on My Shoulder*, 49.
60 Maschwitz, *No Chip on My Shoulder*, 71.
61 Gielgud, *British Radio Drama*, 54.
62 Briggs, *The Birth of Broadcasting*, 229.
63 Martin Dibbs, *Radio Fun and the BBC Variety Department, 1922-1967: Comedy and Popular Music on Air* (London: Palgrave Macmillan, 2019), 27.
64 Ross McKibbin, *Classes and Cultures: England, 1918-1951* (Oxford: Oxford University Press, 2000), 462.
65 Eckersley, *The BBC and All That*, 89.
66 Eckersley, *The BBC and All That*, 84.
67 For instance, Programme Board Minutes, 21 October 1926; Eckersley, *The BBC and All That*, 126 and 153.
68 '"Our Lizzie" Looks Back, 'Introducing Helena Millais, One of Radio's Earliest and Cleverest Comedy Favourites', *Radio Pictorial* clipping from 28 January 1938, RCONTI Helena Millais, BBC WAC 1937–62; Constanduros, *Shreds and Patches*, 37.
69 Joseph Coyne, 'On Broadcast Bent', *Popular Wireless and Wireless Review*, 27 February 1926, 17.
70 Constanduros, *Shreds and Patches*, 47–8.
71 Constanduros, *Shreds and Patches*, 41.
72 A.P. Herbert (known as APH in *Punch*) and 'L du. G' Peach both performed on radio subsequent to this meeting. Peach became an important contributor of radio drama. Gielgud, *British Radio Drama*, 20. *Radio Times*, http://genome.ch.bbc.co.uk/e8c4c6e2e57a4a91b10b6f1ab6a5604a and http://genome.ch.bbc.co.uk/852f3ee6c3d3494fa18dc059453ffb5c, accessed 14 July 2016.
73 Gielgud, *British Radio Drama*, 20.
74 Robert Giddings and Keith Selby, *The Classic Serial on Television and Radio* (Houndmills, Basingstoke and Hampshire: Palgrave, 2001), 6–7; Ian Rodger, *Radio Drama* (London: Macmillan, 1982), vii.
75 See, for instance, *Popular Wireless and Wireless Review*, 20 March 1926, 143.
76 Much of the documentation from the Company period is missing from the archive. What is left are 1925-1926 Programme Board Minutes and brief summaries of Company policies set to paper early on in the Corporation era.
77 Programme Board Minutes, June 1926. R34/600/2 Policy Progamme Board Minutes, BBC WAC.
78 Programme Board Minutes, June 1926. R34/600/2 Policy Progamme Board Minutes, BBC WAC, 23 September and 22 December 1926.
79 Gielgud, *British Radio Drama*, 25.

80 Quoted in Briggs, *The Birth of Broadcasting*, 355–6.
81 Maschwitz, *No Chip on My Shoulder*, 49.
82 Lord Simon of Wythenshawe, *The BBC from Within* (London: Victor Gollancz, 1953), 107.
83 John Mundy and Glyn White, *Laughing Matters: Understanding Film, Television and Radio Comedy* (Manchester: Manchester University Press, 2012), 83–4.
84 *Times* theatre advertisements, January–February 1925; James Ross Moore, *Andre Charlot: The Genius of Musical Revue* (Jefferson, NC: MacFarland and Co., 2005), 114–16.
85 Programme Board Minutes, 26 January 1925. R34/600/2 Policy Progamme Board Minutes, BBC WAC.
86 Hilda Matheson, *Broadcasting* (London: Thornton, Butterworth Ltd., 1933), 159; for more on Matheson's tenure on the BBC, see Murphy, *Behind the Wireless*, especially 168–75.
87 Programme Board Minutes, 26 January 1925. R34/600/2 Policy Progamme Board Minutes, BBC WAC.
88 Quoted in Dibbs, *Radio Fun*, 30.
89 Monroe, *Andre Charlot*, 130.
90 *Radio Times*, http://genome.ch.bbc.co.uk/search/120/20?order=asc&q=charlot#search, accessed 18 July 2016; Dibbs, *Radio Fun*, 29.
91 Matheson, *Broadcasting*, 119.
92 Gielgud, *British Radio Drama*, 20.
93 *Radio Times*, http://genome.ch.bbc.co.uk/aa282f1ba6ab4ca68c673a6b26c7f973; Briggs, *The Birth of Broadcasting*, 191 and *Radio Times*, http://genome.ch.bbc.co.uk/6307c8d01b414af692c52653677296e8, accessed 16 January 2017.
94 Claire Cochrane, *Twentieth-Century British Theatre: Industry, Art and Empire* (Cambridge: Cambridge University Press, 2011), 100.
95 Birmingham station seems to have employed a repertory company for operatic performances a year previously, but Cardiff Repertory Company performed 'King John' in January 1924. 5SC Glasgow followed two months later, in April, performing one-act plays for radio audiences and 5NO established its station repertory company with a performance in July. *Radio Times*, http://genome.ch.bbc.co.uk/search/40/20?order=asc&q=repertory#search, accessed 16 January 2017.
96 Enquiries without appropriate credentials were turned away with a letter of refusal. 'Auditions', 7 August 1925, Staff Policy Auditions 1928-1937, BBC WAC.
97 Brief overview of past policies, n.d. (probably mid-1931) R49/38 Staff Policy Auditions 1928–1937, BBC WAC.
98 Brief overview of past policies, n.d. (probably mid-1931) R49/38 Staff Policy Auditions 1928–1937, BBC WAC.

99 J. Murray Smith, 'Talent Spotters', *Radio Pictorial*, 9 November 1934, 9, gives an excellent sense of the frustration of auditioning poor talent when he confesses that BBC staff often turn off the speakers during bad auditions as 'a means of self-defence'.
100 Programme Board Minutes, 6 April and 14 May 1926. R34/600/2 Policy Progamme Board Minutes, BBC WAC.
101 Constanduros, *Shreds and Patches*, 40.
102 Paddy Scannell and David Cardiff, *A Social History of British Broadcasting, vol. 1: Serving the Nation, 1922-1939* (Oxford: Basil Blackwell, 1991), 225.
103 Crisell, *Introductory History of British Broadcasting*, 33–4.
104 Briggs, *Golden Age*, 87; Crisell, *Introductory History of British Broadcasting*, 34.
105 Gielgud, *British Radio Drama*, 20.
106 Constanduros, *Shreds and Patches*, 41; Briggs, *The Birth of Broadcasting*, 183.
107 Peter Black, *The Biggest Aspidistra in the World: A Personal Celebration of Fifty Years of the BBC* (London: BBC, 1972), 36.
108 Matheson, *Broadcasting*, 112–13.
109 See, for instance, 'Soprano Songs' on 2LO, 14 June 1924. *Radio Times,* https://genome.ch.bbc.co.uk/d69c2927ca0e449d93eb44cedd44936f, accessed 25 March 2019.
110 *Radio Pictorial* clipping from 28 January 1938, RCONTI Helena Millais, 1937–62, BBC WAC
111 Briggs, *The Birth of Broadcasting*, 261.
112 Mundy and White, *Laughing Matters*, 83.
113 *Times*, 15 May 1934. 'John Henry: Death of Wireless Comedian'.
114 Briggs, *The Birth of Broadcasting*, 261–2.
115 Eckersley, *Daily Mail*, 2 March 1932, quoted in Andrews, *Domesticating the Airwaves*, 11.
116 Gielgud, *British Radio Drama*, 63.
117 Matheson, *Broadcasting*, 161.
118 John Henry and Blossom, 'My Wireless Set' (phonograph recording), YouTube (recorded 1925, uploaded 1 September 2012), https://youtu.be/riNiqXUmIiQ, accessed 18 July 2016.
119 David Cardiff, 'Mass Middlebrow Laughter: The Origins of Comedy on the BBC', *Media, Culture and Society* 10 (1988): 44. On 'knowingness', see Bailey, 'Conspiracies of Meaning," 138–70.
120 Michael Bailey, *Narrating Media History* (London, 2009), 53. It should be noted, however, that Michelle Hilmes' analysis of early American radio suggests that many female, African American, and working-class radio amateurs and hobbyists were rendered invisible by the caricature of white, middle-class 'little boys in

short trousers', and therefore, complicates this argument. *Radio Voices: American Broadcasting, 1922-1952* (Minneapolis, MN: University of Minnesota Press, 1997), 37-9 and 132-6.
121 Andrews, *Domesticating the Airwaves*.

Chapter 2

1. According to a 12 April 1934 *Radio Times* listing advertising a programme for the 'First Twelve Years' of entertainment, Constanduros did perform Mrs. Buggins on that fateful day.
2. *Radio Times* listing for 16 June 1925, http://genome.ch.bbc.co.uk/151d2e4f bba74f1cb8449a78716aebdc, accessed 17 January 2017. No contracts exist for Constanduros in 1925 in BBC WAC.
3. See *Radio Times* listings for Constanduros in 1925, http://genome.ch.bbc.co.uk/search/0/20?adv=1&order=asc&q=constanduros&yt=1925#search, accessed 17 January 2017. *Mrs. Smythe-Browne Buys a Book* (London: Samuel French Monologue Series, 1927).
4. See *Radio Times* listing for 29 August, http://genome.ch.bbc.co.uk/75ecb636cbdb4 e6cab6826842a55e89e, accessed 17 January 2017.
5. Mundy and White, *Laughing Matters*), 81.
6. Dibbs, *Radio Fun*, 17.
7. Constanduros, *Shreds and Patches*, 43.
8. The first American radio family were the Goldbergs in *The Rise of the Goldbergs*, who debuted in 1929, Hilmes, *Radio Voices*, 1-4 and 99.
9. John Watt, *Radio Variety* (London: JM Dent and Sons, 1939), 139.
10. Tim Crook, '"The Late Mrs. Buggins"', Radio 4 Special. 5 March 2006, 20:30-21:00.
11. Brett Mills, *Television Sitcom* (London: BFI, 2005), 29.
12. Scott Banville, '"A Bookkeeper, Not an Accountant": Representing the Lower Middle Class from Victorian Novels and Music-Hall Songs to Television Sitcoms', *The Journal of Popular Culture* 44, no. 1 (2011): 16-36.
13. Consider, for instance, the Giles cartoon in the *Express* and Catherine Tate's Nan. Bush-Bailey, 'Mabel Constanduros', 268; Gilli Bush-Bailey, 'Women like Us?' *Comedy Studies* 3, no. 2 (2012): 151-9.
14. Siriol Hugh Jones, 'The Comic Spirit: In Theatre, Cartoon and Column', *Vogue*, February 1952. Carl Giles Trust Collection, University of Kent British Cartoon Archive, https://archive.cartoons.ac.uk/Record.aspx?src=CalmView.Catalog&id=CG%2f2%2f4%2f1%2f16%2f1%2f5, accessed 8 April 2019.

15 Carolyn Scott-Jeffs, 'Voice, Personality and Grandma: Mabel Constanduros and the Buggins Family', *Comedy Studies* 7, no. 2 (2016): 131.
16 See the opening sequence of the pilot episode, 'The School Run', of *Outnumbered* (7 August 2007, BBC One) for family chaos reminiscent of the Bugginses.
17 See for instance, Tim Crook, *Radio Drama: Theory and Practice* (London: Routledge, 1999), chapter 8.
18 Quoted in Rodger, *Radio Drama*, 14.
19 Constanduros, 'Father sweeps the Chimney', in William J. Clark, ed., *Mabel Constanduros* (Windyridge Variety Series, 2009) [Audio CD].
20 Constanduros, *Shreds and Patches*, 46.
21 Susan Douglas, *Listening In: Radio and the American Imagination* (Minneapolis, MN: University of Minnesota Press, 2004), see chapter 5.
22 Gordon Lea, *Radio Drama and How to Write It* (London: George Allen and Unwin, 1926), 47, quoted in D. L. LeMahieu, *A Culture for Democracy: Mass Communication and the Cultivated Mind in Britain between the Wars* (Oxford, 1988), 193.
23 Lea, *Radio Drama*, 40.
24 Robert Silvey, *Who's Listening?* (London: George Allen & Unwin, 1974), 13. It began 1 October 1936.
25 T. H. Pear, *Voice and Personality* (London: Chapman and Hall, 1931), 111.
26 Briggs, *Golden Age*, 235. Class analysis was not done until the creation of Listener Research in 1937. Mark Pegg, *Broadcasting and Society, 1918-1939* (London: Croom Helm, 1983), 122.
27 Pear, *Voice and Personality*, 107.
28 Pear, *Voice and Personality*, 117.
29 Pear, *Voice and Personality*, 117.
30 Pear, *Voice and Personality*, 125. Parentheses in original.
31 Pear, *Voice and Personality*, 125.
32 McKibbin, *Classes and Cultures*, 265.
33 Brett Mills, *TV Genres: The Sitcom* (Edinburgh: Edinburgh University Press, 2009), 79.
34 See Mills, *TV Genres: The Sitcom*, 80.
35 Eckersley, *The BBC and All That*, 74.
36 Filson Young, *Shall I Listen?* (London: Constable, 1933), 244.
37 Quoted in Barry J. Faulk, *Music Hall and Modernity: The Late-Victorian Discovery of Popular Culture* (Athens, OH: Ohio University Press, 2004), 37.
38 Bailey, 'Conspiracies of Meaning', 151.
39 Bailey, 'Conspiracies of Meaning', 153.
40 Young, *Shall I Listen?*, 245.

41 Young, *Shall I Listen?*, 244–5.
42 Young, *Shall I Listen?*, 247.
43 Young, *Shall I Listen?*, 248–9.
44 Phil Wickham, 'The Royle Family', BFI Screenonline, http://www.screenonline.org.uk/tv/id/458640/index.html, accessed 29 May 2019.
45 Sharon Lockyer discusses class-based contempt in her analysis of responses to *Little Britain*'s Vicky Pollard in 'Dynamics of Social Class Contempt in Contemporary British Television Comedy', *Social Semiotics* 20, no. 2 (April 2010): 121–38.
46 Lockyer, 'Dynamics of Social Class Contempt', 130.
47 Faulk, *Music Hall and Modernity*, 3–4.
48 Lucy Delap, *Knowing Their Place: Domestic Service in Twentieth-Century Britain* (Oxford: Oxford University Press 2011), 143.
49 Bailey, 'Conspiracies of Meaning', 153.
50 Mills, *TV Genres: Sitcom*, 80–1.
51 Mabel Constanduros and Michael Hogan, *The Bugginses* (London: Hutchison and Co., 1927), 8.
52 Constanduros, 'Where I Found the Bugginses'.
53 Constanduros, 'Where I Found the Bugginses'.
54 Mabel Constanduros, quoted in Bush-Bailey, 'Different Voices, Voicing Difference', 280. Sylvia Heath, 'A Voice and A Smile You All Know: Mabel Constanduros to Meet Housewives', *Lancashire Daily Post*, 19 April 1937.
55 This would change in wartime sketches, where Grandma often got the better of her social betters. See Wartime Buggins chapter.
56 Mabel Constanduros, 'The Elegant Mr. Fanshawe', in *Down Mangel Street* (London: John Lane, Bodley Head, 1938), 187–96.
57 Mabel Constanduros and Michael Hogan, *Saving Her Face* (London: Samuel French, 1930).
58 Mabel Constanduros and Michael Hogan, *Santa Claus at the Bugginses*, 1930 [phonograph recording], YouTube (recorded 1930, uploaded 15 December 2012), https://www.youtube.com/watch?v=zLDRMtIB2_8, accessed 20 May 2017.
59 Faulk, *Music Hall and Modernity*, 135. See also Gareth Stedman Jones's discussion of literary portrayals of Cockney types from the 1890s onwards, in 'The "Cockney" and the Nation, 1780-1988', in David Feldman and Gareth Stedman Jones, eds., *Metropolis London: Histories and Representations since 1800* (London: Routledge, 1989), especially 302–3.
60 Andrews, *Domesticating the Airwaves*, 152.
61 Constanduros and Hogan, *The Bugginses*, 14.
62 Constanduros, 'Where I Found the Bugginses', 8.
63 LeMathieu, *A Culture for Democracy*, 19.

64 James Drawbell, quoted in LeMatieu, *A Culture for Democracy*, 20; Bailey, 'Conspiracies of Meaning', 153 discusses the authoritative dimension of successful music-hall performance.
65 Mabel Constanduros, 'Where I Found the Bugginses'; Constanduros and Hogan, *The Bugginses*, 7.
66 Ellen Ross, *Slum Travelers: Ladies and London Poverty, 1860-1920* (Berkeley: University of California Press, 2007), 14.
67 Mabel Constanduros, 'Where I Found the Bugginses'; See also Sylvia Heath, 'A Voice and A Smile You All Know', which called Constanduros 'a social worker, who is looking forward to a time when her duties as broadcaster, actress and authoress will allow her to devote herself to the working families', quoted in Bush-Bailey, 'Different Voices, Voicing Difference', 18.
68 See Ross, 'Introduction', in *Slum Travelers*, 1–39.
69 Denis Constanduros, *My Grandfather* (London: Longmans, Green and Co, 1948), 74.
70 Thackeray's Jaemes Yellowplush and *Punch* often used this convention, though William Matthews found this in literary examples reaching as far back as the Elizabethan era. William Matthews, *Cockney Past and Present: A Short History of the Dialect of London* (London: Routledge and Kegan Paul, 1972), 177.
71 L. J. Carter, *Walworth, 1929-1939* (Old Woking: Unwin Brothers Ltd., The Gresham Press, 1985), 78–81. The replacement of 'th' with 'f' is now accepted as common in Cockney dialect, and therefore it is possible that the gradual evolution of the dialect over the course of the twentieth century renders this individual's memory problematic.
72 Matthews, *Cockney Past and Present*, 80.
73 Matthews, *Cockney Past and Present*, 81. Matthews does mention Constanduros as performing 'brilliant' examples of Cockney 'maudlin garrulousness', but does not comment on the authenticity of her accent, 100.
74 Watt, *Radio Variety*, 139.
75 Pear, *Voice and Personality*, 113.
76 Obituary, Thomas Tilling, *Hackney Carriage Guardian*, February 1893, clipping from family archives.
77 This was a common experience among children of the servant-holding classes. See Delap, *Knowing Their Place*, 158.
78 Constanduros, *Shreds and Patches*, 14.
79 Eliza Cook, *The Poetical Works of Eliza Cook* (Philadelphia: Claxton, Remsen, and Haffelfinger, 1870), 40–55.
80 Constanduros, *My Grandfather*, 118.
81 Delap, *Knowing Their Place*, 145.

82 See, for instance, Alison Light, *Mrs. Woolf and the Servants* (London: Penguin Fig Tree, 2007).
83 Lucy Lethbridge, *Servants: A Downstairs History of Britain from the Nineteenth-Century to Modern Times* (New York: W.W. Norton, 2013), 131.
84 Delap, *Knowing Their Place*, 143.
85 Delap, *Knowing Their Place*, 144.
86 Mabel Constanduros, *Aunt Maria's Wireless* (London: Samuel French, 1927), 11.
87 Constanduros, *Down Mangel Street*, 156.
88 Scott-Jeffs, 'Voice, Personality and Grandma', 133.
89 Mabel Constanduros, 'Bugginses Go Gay', 2 July 1942. Script, BBC WAC. *Oxford English Dictionary Online*, s.v. 'winkle', http://www.oed.com/, accessed 20 August 2014.
90 Bailey, 'Conspiracies of Meaning'.
91 Bush-Bailey, 'Different Voices, Voicing Difference', 266.

Chapter 3

1 Portions of this chapter appear in Jennifer Purcell, '"Behind the Blessed Shelter of the Microphone": Managing Celebrity and Career on the Early BBC – Mabel Constanduros, 1925–1957', *Women's History Review* 24, no. 3 (2015): 372–88. doi: 10.1080/09612025.2014.964068.
2 There are various possible reasons for the dearth in material: it is possible that bombing from the Second World War destroyed them, though another explanation is that with the switchover from Company to Corporation in 1927, many documents were destroyed (nothing, for example, remains of John Henry's contracts or correspondence). Thanks to BBC archivists, especially Matthew Chipping, for providing these insights into the state of Constanduros's file. Another plausible reason for this is that the BBC did not begin consciously archiving its material until after the move to Broadcasting House and the setup of an archival department in 1932. On the creation of the archive, see Murphy, *Behind the Wireless*, 11.
3 Constanduros, *Shreds and Patches*, 46.
4 *Radio Times*, https://genome.ch.bbc.co.uk/4d954b19269949408239ef2c98b779d2, accessed 5 June 2019.
5 'Summary', 8 June 1928, R11/27/2 *Children's Hour General Correspondence 1927-1938 File 1B*, BBC WAC.
6 All analysis done through Genome project and *Times* (London) database, https://genome.ch.bbc.co.uk/ and https://www.gale.com/c/the-times-digital-archive. Few 1920s contracts exist for any of the early comedic performers.

7   Briggs, *Golden Age*, 271–314.
8   Briggs, *Golden Age*, 273.
9   Briggs, *Golden Age*, 298. Genome station information for Birmingham and 2LO. For instance, http://genome.ch.bbc.co.uk/schedules/5it/1925-07-22 (5IT) or http://genome.ch.bbc.co.uk/schedules/2lo/1925-07-22#at-21.00 (2LO), accessed 3 February 2017.
10 She also appeared a handful of times on 2BE (Belfast) and 2BD (Aberdeen) in this period. Genome Project, https://genome.ch.bbc.co.uk/search/0/20?adv=1&order=asc&q=constanduros&svc=9371534&yf=1930&yt=1939#search, accessed 30 May 2019.
11 'Tenth Anniversary of the BBC', *Radio Times*, 11 November 1932, vol. 37, no. 476, 412.
12 Dibbs, *Radio Fun*, 52.
13 Constanduros, *Shreds and Patches*, 46.
14 Hennessy, *The Emergence of Broadcasting*, 328; Constanduros, *Shreds and Patches*, 46.
15 Julia Taylor, *From Sound to Print in Pre-War Britain: The Cultural and Commercial Interdependence between Broadcasters and Broadcasting Magazines in the 1930s*, Bournemouth PhD Dissertation, 2013, 138.
16 Andrews, *Domesticating the Airwaves*, 9–10.
17 Andrews, *Domesticating the Airwaves*, 11.
18 'Intrigued', Constanduros, *Shreds and Patches*, 44.
19 *Radio Pictorial*, 1933. Constanduros was the first variety star featured in the magazine. The pilot issues seem only to exist in the British Library Periodicals Collection.
20 Quoted in Taylor, *From Sound to Print*, 154–5.
21 Quoted in Taylor, *From Sound to Print*, 154.
22 Taylor, *From Sound to Print*, 160.
23 Crook, *Radio Drama*, Chapter 8; see specifically, 54.
24 Joshua Gamson, 'The Assembly Line of Greatness: Celebrity in Twentieth-Century America', in Sean Redmond and Su Holmes, eds., *Stardom and Celebrity: A Reader* (Los Angeles: Sage, 2007), 146.
25 Mills, *TV Genres: The Sitcom*, 20.
26 Mills, *TV Genres: The Sitcom*, 20–21.
27 Mills, *TV Genres: The Sitcom*, 21.
28 Andrews, *Domesticating the Airwaves*, 11.
29 Andrews, *Domesticating the Airwaves*, 56.
30 Andrews, *Domesticating the Airwaves*, 14. See also Andrews's discussion of 'pally old friend', 1930s-40s BBC gardener CH Middleton, 55–81.

31 Cardiff, 'Mass Middlebrow Laughter', 42.
32 'Famous Broadcasters Give their Views on the Best Way to Spend Bank Holiday', *Radio Times*, 4 August 1933, 236–7; 'Their Memories of Home', *Radio Times*, 18 November 1938, 13–17.
33 Constanduros, *Shreds and Patches*, 45 mentions his private line. Ted Kavanagh, *Tommy Handley* (London: Hodder and Staughton, 1949), 244–5.
34 Constanduros, *Shreds and Patches*, 45.
35 Mary Douglas and Baron Isherwood, *A World of Goods: Towards an Anthropology of Consumption Volume 6* (London: Routledge, 2003), 70–1.
36 Constanduros, *Shreds and Patches*, 44.
37 Constanduros, *Shreds and Patches*, 44.
38 See Andy Medhurst, 'Every Wart and Pustule: Gilbert Harding and Television Stardom', in Edward Buscombe, ed., *British Television: A Reader* (Oxford: Oxford University Press, 2001), 248–64.
39 Verity Clare, 'The Worst Moment of My Life: Thrills of the Stars, Told by Our Leading Broadcasters', *Radio Pictorial*, 1 November 1935.
40 Constanduros, *Shreds and Patches*, 45–6.
41 P. David Marshall, *Celebrity and Power: Fame in Contemporary Culture* (Minneapolis, MN: University of Minnesota Press, 2004), 86.
42 Andrews, *Domesticating the Airwaves*, 77.
43 'A Pianist's Petition', *Times*, 20 May 1924, 5.
44 Claire Langhamer, 'Adultery in Post-War Britain', *History Workshop Journal* 62 (Autumn 2006): 99.
45 Quoted in Langhamer, 'Adultery in Post-War Britain', 100.
46 'A Pianist's Petition', *Times*, 20 May 1924, 5.
47 Memo from the Organiser of Programmes to the Controller, 23 July 1924. Contract Artists, BBC WAC.
48 Black, *The Biggest Aspidistra in the World*, 17.
49 See *Radio Times*, https://genome.ch.bbc.co.uk/search/20/20?order=asc&q=daisy+kennedy#search, accessed 1 May 2019. Kennedy resumed playing on a regular basis in October 1924. Her last performance was in 1937, but she made several appearances in the 1960s and 70s remembering the early BBC.
50 Briggs, *Golden Age*, 268.
51 Gorham, *Sound and Fury*, 20.
52 Sydney A. Mosley, *Broadcasting in Our Time* (London: Rich and Cowan, Ltd., 1935), 196. Emphasis in original.
53 Dibbs, *Radio Fun*, 16. Eckersley's affair was with Dorothy Clark, wife of Edward Clark.
54 Briggs, *Golden Age*, 269.

55 'Revelations about John Henry: Comedian's Double-Life', *Evening Telegraph and Post*, 16 May 1934.
56 'John Henry's Tragic End', *Nottingham Evening Post*, 14 May 1934.
57 'Revelations about John Henry: Comedian's Double-Life', *Evening Telegraph and Post*, 16 May 1934.
58 Graves and Hodge, *The Long Week-End*, 98.
59 Graves and Hodge, *The Long Week-End*, 362.
60 Carol Smart, 'Good Wives and Moral Lives: Marriage and Divorce, 1937-1951', in Christine Gledhill and Gillian Swanson, eds., *Nationalising Femininity: Culture, Sexuality and British Cinema in the Second World War* (Manchester: Manchester University Press, 1996), 96.
61 Beatrice Lillie with John Philip and James Brough, *Every Other Inch a Lady* (New York: Doubleday, 1972), 233.
62 Jessie Matthews and Muriel Burgess, *Over My Shoulder: An Autobiography* (London: WH Allen, 1974), 107–8.
63 Lillie's husband died at the age of thirty-six, she never remarried. *Every Other Inch a Lady*, 253.
64 Neither Gingold nor Joseph were well known when they divorced.
65 See Hermione Gingold, *The World Is Square* (London: Home and Val Thal Press, 1945); *My Own Unaided Work* (London: W. Laurie, 1952); *Sirens Should Be Seen and Not Heard* (Philadelphia: Lippincott, 1963); and *How to Grow Old Disgracefully* (New York: St. Martin's Press, 1988).
66 Gingold, *How to Grow Old*, 44.
67 Hermione Gingold, 'My BBC Friends', *Radio Pictorial*, 13 May 1938, 10–11 and 36.
68 Gingold, *How to Grow Old*, 41.
69 Purcell, '"Behind the Blessed Shelter of the Microphone"', doi: 10.1080/09612025.2014.964068, 6.
70 Denis Constanduros, 'Rival Households'. Unpublished chapter. Many thanks to Stephanie Down for sharing this copy with me. This last comment about the cakes is particularly humorous when one considers that her most enduring acts was fitting the Buggins characters into the wartime *Kitchen Front* programmes, hawking recipes designed to make the best of wartime rationing.
71 Brenda R. Weber, 'Always Lonely: Celebrity, Motherhood, and the Dilemma of Destiny', *PMLA* 126, no. 4 (2011): 1110–17.
72 Constanduros, *Shreds and Patches*, 75.
73 Constanduros, *Shreds and Patches*, 35 and 75.
74 Bush-Bailey, 'Different Voices, Voicing Difference', 281.
75 Constanduros also dedicated the book to the memory of her mother and Tony.
76 Knox, *People of Quality*, 111–12.

77 Knox, *People of Quality*, 112.
78 Constanduros, *Shreds and Patches*, 35.
79 Weber, 'Always Lonely', 1116.
80 Mabel and the family refer to Athanasius as 'Ath'.
81 Constanduros, *Shreds and Patches*, 64.
82 Knox, *People of Quality*, 112.
83 SADC archive, Box 2, Manilla envelope 'Master Set Programmes to 1957'. Sutton Local Archives.
84 SADC archive, Box 2, Manilla envelope 'Master Set Programmes to 1957'; SADC archive, Box 3, Meeting Minutes, Sutton Local Archives; *Times*, 29 April 1921 and 10 January 1923.
85 SADC Archives, Sutton Local Archives.
86 'Murder on the Second Floor', *Sutton-Epsom Advertiser*, 8–12 November 1932, press clipping Sutton Local Archives.
87 'Radio Star's Loss: Mr. A. Constanduros Dies Suddenly', *Sutton and Cheam Advertiser*, 15 July 1937, 6.
88 Constanduros, *Shreds and Patches*, 64–5.
89 Murphy, *Behind the Wireless*, 85. Though it tightened in the 1930s, the BBC had a fairly liberal policy regarding the marriage bar, even for staffers. See Murphy, Chapter 4.
90 Many thanks to Gilli Bush-Bailey for pointing this out to me. My article, 'Behind the Blessed Shelter of the Microphone' is written on the assumption that Ath signed these documents. Bush-Bailey also discusses this in 'Different Voices, Voicing Difference', 272.
91 Maggie Andrews, *Domesticating the Airwaves*, CH Middleton section.
92 Ath's estate was worth over £5,000 at the time of his death in 1937. Stock certificates, February 1924. Many thanks to Stephanie Down, Denis Constanduros's daughter, for providing these to me from her personal family archives.
93 Roger Mortimore and Andrew Blick, eds., *Butler's British Political Facts* (London: Palgrave, 2018), 467; Stephen Brooke, 'Class and Gender', in Francesca Carnevali and Julie-Marie Strange, eds., *Twentieth-Century Britain: Economic, Cultural and Social Change*, 2nd edn (Harlow: Pearson Longman, 2007), 51.
94 Mabel Constanduros, 'My Story' unpublished extract provided by Richard Constanduros and Anthea Duigan.
95 Ray Strachey, *Careers and Openings for Women: A Survey of Women's Employment and a Guide for Those Seeking Work* (London: Faber and Faber, 1934), 20.
96 Constanduros, *Shreds and Patches*, 54.
97 Constanduros, *Shreds and Patches*, 55.
98 Denis Constanduros, 'Rival Households'. Mr. Pooter is a reference to the main character in George and Weedon Grossman's (1892) *Diary of a Nobody* and suggests a provincial, narrow-minded and unimaginative individual.

99 Interview of Hilda Constanduros. 'Beagling' refers to hunting with beagles. Richard Constanduros's private collection.
100 Smart, 'Good Wives and Moral Lives', 94.
101 J 77/3060/4305 Divorce Court File: 4305, Appellant: Stephanos Constanduros. Respondent: Gertrude Norah Constanduros. Co-respondent: Oscar Fiedler, The National Archives. Norah was living with Mabel at the time.
102 Constanduros, *Shreds and Patches*, 39.

Chapter 4

1 Murphy, *Behind the Wireless*, 151.
2 Val Gielgud quoted in Dibbs, *Radio Fun*, 90.
3 Briggs, *Golden Age*. *Daily Mail* poll cited in LeMahieu, *A Culture for Democracy*, 285.
4 David Cardiff, 'Time, Money and Culture: BBC Programme Finances, 1927-1939', *Media, Culture, and Society* 5 (1983): 382.
5 LeMahieu, *A Culture for Democracy*, 152.
6 Briggs, *Golden Age*, 326.
7 Jennifer Spohrer, 'Ruling the Airwaves: Radio Luxembourg and the Origins of European National Broadcasting, 1929-1950', Columbia University PhD dissertation, 2008, 2.
8 Briggs, *Golden Age*, 326–35.
9 Dibbs, *Radio Fun*, 33.
10 Gerald Cock quoted in Cardiff, 'Time, Money and Culture', 383.
11 Dibbs, *Radio Fun*, 7.
12 Cardiff, 'Time, Money and Culture', 384.
13 Briggs, *Golden Age*, 84–5.
14 Dibbs, *Radio Fun*, 33.
15 Briggs, *Golden Age*, 87; Higgins, *This New Noise*, 16.
16 Black, *The Biggest Aspidistra in the World*, 55. Maschwitz, *No Chip on My Shoulder*, 49; Briggs, *The Birth of Broadcasting*, 279.
17 Quoted in Briggs, *Golden Age*, 97.
18 LeMahieu, *A Culture for Democracy*, 285. See also Dibbs, *Radio Fun*, 49.
19 Briggs, *Golden Age*, 87; Dibbs, *Radio Fun*, 42.
20 Cardiff, 'Time, Money and Culture', 384.
21 Cardiff, 'Time, Money and Culture', 384.
22 Mosley, *Broadcasting in Our Time*, 192.
23 Briggs, *Golden Age*, 100; Dibbs, *Radio Fun*, 53.

24 Cardiff, 'Time, Money and Culture', 387; see also Herbert Harris, 'The Concert Party Route to Fame', *Radio Pictorial*, 15 July 1938, 11.
25 Briggs, *Golden Age*, 98.
26 Maschwitz, *No Chip on My Shoulder*, 66. Briggs, *Golden Age*, 98–100.
27 Maschwitz, *No Chip on My Shoulder*, 67–9.
28 Cardiff, 'Time, Money and Culture', 385; Dibbs, *Radio Fun*, 68.
29 *Radio Times*, http://genome.ch.bbc.co.uk/search/0/20?adv=0&q=mr.+penny&media=all&yf=1923&yt=2009&mf=1&mt=12&tf=00%3A00&tt=00%3A00#search, accessed 1 August 2015.
30 Maurice Moisewitsch, *The Strange Adventures of Mr. Penny* episode 1, season 1, BBC WAC.
31 Maurice Moiseiwitsch, season 1 and 2 scripts, BBC WAC; I would like to thank the participants at the Montreal British History Seminar at McGill in January 2016, for their encouragement and helpful remarks regarding a paper about the development of British situation comedy in the 1930s.
32 Maurice Moiseiwitsch, *Moiseiwitsch: Biography of a Concert Pianist* (London: Frederick Muller, 1965), 126. Benno Moiseiwitsch was Maurice Moiseiwitsch's uncle.
33 Features and Drama Executive (Play Library) to Programme Copyright, 23 July 1937. COPYRIGHT R12/125 'MR PENNY' AGREEMENT 1937-1938, BBC WAC.
34 Max Kester to DV, Internal memo, 'The Strange Adventures of Mr. Penny – The History of the Series from the beginning and some notes on the existing position', 8 September 1937, 2. Copyright R12/125 'MR PENNY' AGREEMENT 1937-1938, BBC WAC.
35 Max Kester to DV, Internal memo, 'The Strange Adventures of Mr. Penny – The History of the Series from the beginning and some notes on the existing position', 8 September 1937. Copyright R12/125 'MR PENNY' AGREEMENT 1937-1938, BBC WAC.
36 Max Kester and Edwin Collier, with a forward by Eric Maschwitz, *Writing for the BBC: Practical Hints on How to Write Successfully for the Light Entertainment Department of the BBC* (London: Sir Isaac Pitman and Sons, Ltd., 1937), 10–11.
37 Kester and Collier, *Writing for the BBC*, 14.
38 Max Kester to DV, Internal memo, 'The Strange Adventures of Mr. Penny – The History of the Series from the beginning and some notes on the existing position', 8 September 1937, 6. Copyright R12/125 'MR PENNY' AGREEMENT 1937-1938, BBC WAC.
39 Howgill to Copyright department, 15 September 1937. Copyright R12/125 'MR PENNY' AGREEMENT 1937-1938, BBC WAC.
40 R. Jardine Robbins letter to Maurice Moiseiwitsch, 21 September 1937. Copyright R12/125 'MR PENNY' AGREEMENT 1937-1938, BBC WAC.

41 E. A. Davis letter to R. Jardine Brown, 5 October 1937. Copyright R12/125 'MR PENNY' AGREEMENT 1937-1938, BBC WAC. The BBC had corresponded with British National Film to understand the nature of the agreement between them and Moiseiwitsch. BNF executives seemed incensed by Moiseiwitsch's seeming breach of contract and withheld payment.
42 R. Jardine Robbins to Variety Executive MM Dewar, 7 October 1937. Copyright R12/125 'MR PENNY' AGREEMENT 1937–1938, BBC WAC.
43 E. A. Davis letter to R. Jardine Brown, 5 October 1937. Copyright R12/125 'MR PENNY' AGREEMENT 1937-1938, BBC WAC.
44 MM Dewar to Maschwitz, 8 October 1937. Copyright R12/125 'MR PENNY' AGREEMENT 1937–1938, BBC WAC.
45 Dibbs, *Radio Fun*, 84.
46 Arthur Brown to Constanduros, 31 July 1936. FILE 1B ARTISTS, Constanduros July 1936–1937, BBC WAC.
47 Constanduros to Arthur Brown, 4 August 1936. FILE 1B ARTISTS, Constanduros July 1936–1937, BBC WAC.
48 Kester to DV, Internal memo, 'The Strange Adventures of Mr. Penny', 8 September 1937, 6, BBC WAC.
49 Maschwitz to R. Jardine Brown, 27 September 1937. Copyright R12/125 'MR PENNY' AGREEMENT 1937–1938, BBC WAC.
50 Some scholars, such as Steve Neale and Frank Krutnik, *Popular Film and Television Comedy*, 221, have suggested that Robb Wilton's series, *Mr. Muddlecombe J.P.*, which took to the air in 1937 was the first BBC situation comedy. However, *Mr. Penny* actually preceded it by several months and initially, *Muddlecombe* was not a regular series like either *The Plums* or *Mr. Penny*; instead, the programme appeared on different nights at different times sporadically throughout 1937. In 1939, Wilton's character was reprised and shifted to a regular, weekly series entitled *Public Futilities*, produced by Max Kester. Perhaps to avoid the copyright minefield experienced in the *Penny* case, the *Radio Times* listings in the first year of *Muddlecombe* clearly state that the programme was based on an 'idea suggested by Barry Bernard' and written by Adrian Thomas. In contrast to *Mr. Penny* and *The Plums*, *Muddlecombe* enjoyed unusual longevity: Wilton reprised the role in various weekly series spanning a decade. The irregular appearances were advertised in the *Radio Times* as follows: 'The Bench will sit at irregular intervals till the circuit is cut off.' For instance, *Radio Times*, https://genome.ch.bbc.co.uk/542effb220e242bc95c030533f7e8d39, accessed 13 May 2019. *Muddlecombe J.P.* appeared sporadically through 1937, ending in January 1938; after *Public Futilities*, Muddlecombe returned for several series during the war and then once again in 1948. Muddlecombe was also a popular character on the 1952–53 programme,

The Leisure Hour. See *Radio Times*, https://genome.ch.bbc.co.uk/search/120/20?order=asc&q=muddlecomb#search, accessed 14 May 2019.

51 Correspondence, Millais to Robinson, 2 May 1938. RCONT1 Helena Millais, 1937–62, BBC WAC.
52 RCONT1 Helena Millais, 1937–62, BBC WAC and *Radio Times* listings.
53 Constanduros, *Shreds and Patches*, 49.
54 Bush-Bailey, 'Different Voices, Voicing Difference', 262–3.
55 Mabel Constanduros, 'Through the Stage Door' script, 21 December 1954, BBC WAC.
56 Constanduros, 'Through the Stage Door'.
57 Arthur Askey, *Before Your Very Eyes* (London: Woburn Press, 1975), 99.
58 Bush-Bailey, 'Different Voices, Voicing Difference', 2.
59 Mabel Constanduros, 'My Story II', 14, draft chapter. Constanduros family archives, many thanks to Anthea Duigan for access to this material.
60 Constanduros, 'Through the Stage Door'.
61 Constanduros, 'My Story II', 12.
62 Constanduros, *Shreds and Patches*, 69.
63 See 'New Films in London', *Times*, 19 August 1935 and '£100,000 Appeal for Papworth Village', *Times*, 12 December 1935.
64 *Three for Luck* was written by Violet M. Methley and *Cold Comfort Farm* by Stella Gibbons.
65 Bush-Bailey, 'Different Voices, Voicing Difference', 275.
66 Bush-Bailey, 'Different Voices, Voicing Difference', 275.
67 'Grandma Buggins was a Great Friend of the Little Theatre', *Bristol Evening News*, 9 February 1957. Cutting from Constanduros family archives.
68 Knox, *People of Quality*, 114.
69 Anthea Duigan and Richard Constanduros, Personal Communication, October 2011. Amanda Swift's 1991 Radio 2 Programme about early BBC comediennes, *Writing Jokes in Bed*, was also based on this observation about Constanduros. Many thanks to Swift for sending me a copy of this programme.
70 For instance, 'Twas a Dear Little Song' (London: Boosey & Co., 1933) and 'Sam's Medal' (London: Francis, Day and Hunter, 1933) with Hogan and 'Well, I Didn't' (London: Reynolds & Co., 1941). Her earliest copyrighted song was published in 1915. Library of Congress Copyright Office, Catalogue of Copyright Entries, Part 3: Musical Compositions; last half of 1915, nos. 8–13, with annual index, entry 12529, p. 806. Musical Compositions. 'June's in my garden', words by Mabel, music by A. Healey Foster. Chappell and Co., https://archive.org/details/catalogofcopyrig102libr/page/806.
71 See Nicola Wilson, *Home in British Working-Class Fiction* (Farnham: Ashgate, 2015), 20–7.

72 Ross, *Slum Travelers*, 1–29.
73 Carter, *Walworth, 1929-1939*, 38. Joanna Bourke, *Working-Class Cultures in Britain, 1890-1960* (London: Routledge, 1994), discusses the phases of post-war rehousing schemes and their impact on working-class life, 155–9.
74 On tentpole tactics, see M. J. Clarke, *Transmedia Television: New Trends in Network Serial Production* (London: Bloomsbury, 2013).
75 Clarke, *Transmedia Television*, 4. Henry Jenkins, *Convergence Culture: Where Old and New Media Collide* (New York: New York University Press, 2006) explores the concept of 'transmedia storytelling' over multiple media platforms in ways the develop a complex fictional world surrounding the original film or media story; see in particular, chapter 3 'Searching for the Origami Unicorn'. For a brief explanation of the concept, see http://henryjenkins.org/2007/03/transmedia_storytelling_101.html, accessed 12 May 2017.
76 Mabel Constanduros and Michael Hogan, *The Bugginses* (London: Hutchinson and Co., 1928), 63.
77 Constanduros and Hogan, *The Bugginses*, 8.
78 Elizabeth Roberts, *A Woman's Place: An Oral History of Working-Class Women 1890-1940* (Oxford: Blackwell, 1995), 184.
79 Constanduros and Hogan, *The Bugginses*, 110.
80 Constanduros and Hogan, *The Bugginses*, 111.
81 Constanduros and Hogan, *The Bugginses*, 119–20. William Willing was shortened to Billy Willing in the novel much as Thomas Tilling was often shortened to Tommy Tilling (also Cockney slang for shilling).
82 Constanduros did pen a poem for *Radio Times* 1936 Humour number which hints at Grandma's injury scam, but does not flesh it out, 'Mrs. Jones's Operation', 6 October 1936, 5.
83 In the forward, Constanduros acknowledges Denis's assistance in helping her write several of the sketches that constitute the core of the stories in the novel for radio, and thanks Hogan for permission to use their original Whale sketch.
84 John Rorke would later play father in a handful of sketches on *Children's Hour* in 1937. He also played opposite Constanduros and Young in *Down Mangel Street* performances.
85 24 September 1937 to Charles, Mabel Constanduros scriptwriter 1935–1942 file, BBC WAC. *Down Mangel Street* series appeared in 1942.
86 For instance, 'Ghost Poison' was performed by Constanduros and John Rorke in late-1938.
87 30 October 1935 memo Max Kester to Eric Maschwitz; 11 December 1935 letter EM to Constanduros; 30 August 1938 Pifford to Constanduros Mabel Constanduros scriptwriter 1935–1942 file, BBC WAC.

Chapter 5

1. Asa Briggs, *The History of Broadcasting in the United Kingdom, Volume III: The War of Words* (Oxford: Oxford University Press, 1970), 29; Val Gielgud, *Years of the Locust* (London: Nicholson and Watson, 1947), 167; Gorham, *Sound and Fury*, 89; Siân Nicholas, *The Echo of War: Home Front Propaganda and the Wartime BBC, 1939-45* (Manchester: Manchester University Press, 1996), 25.
2. Constanduros to Val Gielgud, 1 September 1939, Constanduros Scriptwriter 1935–1942, BBC WAC.
3. Constanduros to John Watt, 1 September 1939, Constanduros Artists File 2A 1938–1939, BBC WAC.
4. 2 September 1939, Artists file 2A 1938–1939, BBC WAC.
5. Jennifer Purcell, *Domestic Soldiers: Six Women's Lives in Wartime* (London: Constable and Robinson, 2010), especially Chapter One.
6. Constanduros to Watt, 1 September 1939, Artists file 2A 1938–1939, BBC WAC.
7. Constanduros to Gielgud, 10 September 1939, Scriptwriter File 1935–1942.
8. Constanduros to Arthur Brown, n.d., most likely early September 1939, Artists file 2A 1938–1939, BBC WAC.
9. Dibbs, *Radio Fun*, 111.
10. Nicholas, *Echo of War*, 16.
11. Nicholas, *Echo of War*, 17–18; 'BBC's Wartime Plans', *Radio Pictorial*, 17 June 1938, 7.
12. Nicholas, *Echo of War*, 20.
13. Briggs, *War of Words*, 29; Norman Longmate, *How We Lived Then: A History of Everyday Life During the Second World War* (London: Pimlico, 2002), 67; Val Gielgud, quoted in John Snagge and Michael Barsley, *Those Vintage Years of Radio* (London: Pitman, 1972), 109.
14. Briggs, *War of Words*, 29; Tom Hickman, *What Did You Do in the War, Auntie?* (London: BBC Books, 1995), 43; Longmate, *How We Lived Then*, 66.
15. Hickman, *What Did You Do in the War?*, 45.
16. Briggs, *War of Words*, 29.
17. Gorham, *Sound and Fury*, 42.
18. Nicholas, *The Echo of War*, 27.
19. Briggs, *War of Words*, 107. Hickman, *What Did You Do in the War?*, 45.
20. John Watt quoted in Briggs, *War of Words*, 111.
21. Hickman, *What Did You Do in the War?*, 45.
22. Hickman, *What Did You Do in the War?*, 45. Denham would later become part of the cast of the hugely popular *ITMA*. Many of the twenty-two would also do so: Vera Lennox, Sam Costa, Horace Percival, and Jack Train are a few of the VRC members who later became famous on the show.

23 Nicholas, *Echo of War*, 54–5.
24 Briggs, *War of Words*, 107. *Band Waggon* remained on air only through November 1939. Tired out by requirements to write new material every week, the cast left to tour with a successful stage show based on the programme. Dibbs, *Radio Fun*, 126.
25 Briggs, *War of Words*, 107.
26 *Radio Times*, 12 February 1940, 'Revival by Public Demand of *Adolf in Blunderland*', https://genome.ch.bbc.co.uk/8eece4c0f68745f6a084e4857cf6e54a, accessed 6 June 2019; 'Broadcasting', *Times*, 9 October 1939, 2. *The Times Digital Archive*, http://tinyurl.galegroup.com/tinyurl/ACd9a3, accessed 6 June 2019.
27 Robert Douglas-Fairhurst, *The Story of Alice* (Harvard: Harvard University Press, 2015), 228.
28 Douglas-Fairhurst, *The Story of Alice*, 228.
29 'Broadcasting', *Times*, 9 October 1939, 2. *The Times Digital Archive*, http://tinyurl.galegroup.com/tinyurl/ACd9a3, accessed 6 June 2019.
30 Briggs, *War of Words*, 110.
31 Nicholas, *Echo of War*, 28; Hickman, *What Did You Do in the War?*, 45.
32 Juliet Gardner, *Wartime Britain: 1939-1945* (London: Review, 2004), 6.
33 Arthur Greenwood, House of Commons Debate, 11 October 1939, vol. 352 cc376-484. https://hansard.parliament.uk/Commons/1939-10-11/debates/421fae5a-afda-48e5-9244-4a3f762c3dff/MinistryOfInformationAndBroadcasting?highlight=greenwood#contribution-20796f7b-6d2b-49e3-ada4-e8dba5a09a9a, accessed 6 June 2019.
34 Quoted in Nicholas, *Echo of War*, 31. See above listed parliamentary debate for further detail.
35 Gardiner, *Wartime Britain*, 140.
36 Dibbs, *Radio Fun*, 111.
37 Joe Moran, *Armchair Nation: An Intimate History of Britain in Front of the TV* (London: Profile, 2014), 48.
38 Moran, *Armchair Nation*, 48.
39 Briggs, *War of Words*, 102.
40 Briggs, *War of Words*, 106.
41 Dibbs, *Radio Fun*, 112; See also Briggs, *War of Words*, 102.
42 See contracts dated 19 September, 6 October and 13 November 1939, Constanduros Artists File 2A 1938–1939, BBC WAC. Constanduros was dividing her time between BBC work and touring with her own company playing Gower's *Ma's Bit o' Brass*.
43 Contract letter, 5 June 1940, Constanduros Copyright file 1B 1939–1940, BBC WAC.
44 Quoted in Johanna Alberti, 'A Time for Hard Writers: The Impact of War on Women Writers', in Nick Hayes and Jeff Hill, eds., *'Millions Like Us'? British Culture in the Second World War* (Liverpool: Liverpool University Press, 1999), 163.

45 Constanduros to Arthur Brown, n.d., most likely early September 1939, Artists file 1939–1940, BBC WAC. See also Lucy D. Curzon, 'Visualising the Home Front: Evelyn Dunbar and Wartime Citizenship', *Oxford Art Journal* 41, Issue 3 (December 2018): 341–60, on Evelyn Dunbar and wartime female artists.
46 2 October 1939, *Daily Herald*, 3.
47 Genome listings for each performer(s) during the war. Constanduros's efforts as a writer make her very competitive in this field. She is listed in over 150 acting parts and over 35 original or adapted works during the war. One of the novels, '*Anging Round the Pubs* (London: Methuen, 1940), was explicitly war-related and not used on the BBC. The others were based off BBC plays or characters. She published nineteen acting editions during the war.
48 Quoted in Longmate, *How We Lived Then*, 184.
49 Gert and Daisy, Freddie Grisewood, and 'the Radio Doctor' Charles Hill are the other broadcasters most often linked to the programme.
50 Nicholas, *Echo of War*, 72–3.
51 Nicholas, *Echo of War*, 74; *Express and Echo*, 'Feeding the Berts and Wallys: Cooking Advice by "Gert" and "Dais"' 1 November 1940, 4.
52 Nicholas, *Echo of War*, 75–6; Tom Harrisson, 'Report from Mass-Observation on Gert and Daisy's BBC Talks', 23 April 1940, MO-A.
53 Harrisson, 'Gert and Daisy's BBC Talks'.
54 *Radio Times*, Kitchen Front listing, for example, 25 June 1940; Nella Last, 8 September 1940, MO-A Diary. Last mentions sending a tip on boiling potatoes to Heath in this entry.
55 Nicholas, *Echo of War*, 76–7.
56 Nicholas, *Echo of War*, 78.
57 Nicholas, *Echo of War*, 77; Jennifer Purcell, *Beyond Home: Housewives and the Nation, Private and Public Identities 1939-1949*, DPhil Dissertation, University of Sussex 2008, 189; 14 October 1940 *Kitchen Front* script, BBC WAC.
58 Briggs, *War of Words*, 301; Nicholas, *Echo of War*, 82; Angus Calder claims that Dr. Charles Hill, 'the Radio Doctor', amassed as many as 14 million listeners, *The People's War: Britain, 1939-1945* (London: Jonathan Cape, 1969), 383.
59 *Radio Times* listings, October 1940–April 1941, https://genome.ch.bbc.co.uk/search/0/20?adv=1&mf=10&mt=4&order=asc&q=kitchen+front&yf=1940&yt=1941#search, accessed 6 June 2019.
60 Nicholas, *Echo of War*, 78.
61 See, for instance, *Radio Times* listings June–October 1941, https://genome.ch.bbc.co.uk/search/0/20?adv=1&q=kitchen+front&media=all&yf=1941&yt=1941&mf=6&mt=10&tf=00%3A00&tt=00%3A00#search, accessed 6 June 2019; Nicholas, *Echo of War*, 78.

62 Nella Last, 5 October 1940 diary, MO-A.
63 Nicholas, *Echo of War*, 83.
64 Fielden to Quigley, 17 December 1940, *Kitchen Front* R51/178/3, BBC WAC.
65 See Winifred Holmes's (assistant producer from 1942) angry letter regarding Westerby's overreaching his role in Nicholas, *Echo of War*, 78.
66 Rowntree to Barnes, 7 October 1941, Constanduros Artists File 3A 1941, BBC WAC.
67 Rowntree sent the invitation to Constanduros on the same day that she requested Barnes's approval, Constanduros Artists File 3A 1941, BBC WAC.
68 Sometimes Constanduros appeared fortnightly instead of weekly. The day change was requested 1 May 1945, Bridgeman to Constanduros, Constanduros Artists File 5A 1945, BBC WAC.
69 Rowntree to Bridgemont, 27 October 1941, regarding the possible booking of variety act Kenway and Young, R51/178/5, BBC WAC.
70 Constanduros to Rowntree, 10 October 1941, Constanduros Artists File 3A, BBC WAC.
71 Nicholas, *Echo of War*, 82.
72 Gardner, *Wartime Britain*, 187. Constanduros to Rowntree, 25 November 1941 and Rowntree to Constanduros, 28 November 1941, Constanduros Artists File 3A, BBC WAC.
73 Mabel Constanduros, 'Kitchen Front', in Joanna Bourke, *Eyewitness 1939-1949*, narrator Tim Piggot-Smith, [CD] (London: BBC, 2005), disc 1 track 12.
74 Constanduros, 'Kitchen Front'; Grandma's response about parsnips is also found in Gardner, *Wartime Britain*, 187.
75 Correspondence between Rowntree and Constanduros in January 1942 regarding the issue. In an undated letter, Constanduros asks Rowntree to find out diseases that can be contracted as a result of deprivation. Constanduros Artists File 3B, 1942.
76 10 February 1942 script, Kitchen Front Broadcasts, MAF 102/4 1942, The National Archives.
77 10 July 1943 script, Kitchen Front Broadcasts, MAF 102/5 1943, The National Archives.
78 5 May 1942 script, Kitchen Front Broadcasts, MAF 102/4 1942, The National Archives.
79 BBC correspondence asks for Constanduros's photo for the campaign, Watt to Constanduros, 5 February 1942; Constanduros accepts on 13 February, saying she collected in her village, Constanduros Artists File 3B, BBC WAC. Nicholas, *Echo of War*, 108.
80 Purcell, *Domestic Soldiers*, 2.
81 12 October 1943, Kitchen Front Broadcasts, MAF 102/5, The National Archives.
82 'Miss M. Constanduros praises women', *Surrey Advertiser*, 30 October 1943.

83 17 November 1942 script, Kitchen Front Broadcasts, MAF 102/4, The National Archives.
84 23 November 1943 script, Kitchen Front Broadcasts, MAF 102/5, The National Archives.
85 15 August 1944 script, Kitchen Front Broadcasts, MAF 102/6, The National Archives.
86 23 May 1944 script Kitchen Front Broadcasts, MAF 102/6, The National Archives.
87 Correspondence and internal memos, 23 May 1944 to 30 May 1944, Constanduros Artist 1944 File, BBC WAC.
88 Max Kester to Eric Maschwitz, internal memorandum, 22 October 1935. Constanduros Scriptwriter 1935–1942, BBC WAC.
89 Dibbs, *Radio Fun*, 143.
90 Though Variety producers sought an official code, nothing was established until the 1948 *Green Book*. Dibbs, *Radio Fun*, 146.
91 Correspondence and internal memos, 23 May 1944 to 30 May 1944, Constanduros 1944 Artist File 4B, BBC WAC.
92 Nicholas, *Echo of War*, 5; see also Anselm Heinrich, *Entertainment, Propaganda, Education: Regional Theatre in Germany and Britain between 1918 and 1945* (Hatfield: University of Hertfordshire Press, 2007), 47.
93 Briggs, *War of Words*, 110; Siân Nicholas, 'The People's Radio: The BBC and Its Audience, 1939-1945', in Nick Hayes and Jeff Hill, eds., *'Millions like Us'?: British Culture and the Second World War* (Liverpool: Liverpool University Press, 1999), 63.
94 Nicholas, *Echo of War*, 83.
95 Andrews, *Domesticating the Airwaves*, 100–1.
96 Andy Medhurst, *A National Joke: Popular Comedy and English Identities* (London: Routledge, 2007), 69.
97 See Thomas Hajkowski, *The BBC and National Identity in Britain, 1922-1953* (Manchester: Manchester University Press, 2010), especially chapters 5–7, for discussions regarding tensions between London and the regions as well as the role of regional broadcasts in supporting national identity.
98 Purcell, *Domestic Soldier*, 275–6; Gardiner, *Wartime Britain*, 177.
99 Gardiner, *Wartime Britain*, 177.
100 Gardiner, *Wartime Britain*, 177; Calder, *The People's War*, 386.
101 Constanduros, 'Bugginses Go Gay', 2 July 1942. Script, BBC WAC.
102 For varying reactions to these loopholes, see Purcell, *Domestic Soldiers*, 275–6.
103 Nicholas, *Echo of War*, 1–6.
104 Nicholas, *Echo of War*, 3.

Chapter 6

1. See the 19 March 1932 *Radio Times* listing for *Conversation* for description, https://genome.ch.bbc.co.uk/2c4684773ea940628c0d9753f5aeb100; for *Decision* see 8 October 1935 listing, https://genome.ch.bbc.co.uk/cd33a83346b74ea492b60a2566fe3d4b, accessed 31 May 2019. One of Denis Constanduros's first solo writing efforts was his contribution to *Decision* on 31 March 1936.
2. Constanduros to Gielgud, 11 March 1936, BBC WAC Scriptwriter 1935–1942. Constanduros is not credited in *Radio Times* for *Conversation*, but she wrote and performed the last instalment of the 1935 series on 3 May, Constanduros File 1A 1935–June 1936 Artists, BBC WAC.
3. Gielgud to Constanduros, 5 May 1936, BBC WAC Scriptwriter 1935–1942.
4. Constanduros to Gielgud, 20 May 1938, BBC WAC Scriptwriter 1935–1942.
5. Val Gielgud, *Years in the Mirror* (London: Bodley Head, 1965), 84.
6. Constanduros to Gielgud, 11 March 1936, BBC WAC Scriptwriter 1935–1942.
7. *Radio Times*, http://genome.ch.bbc.co.uk/44de479e518b45cca03449fe2124e285, accessed 16 February 2017. Though the play was one of two originally written when she approached Gielgud about writing radio plays, it was not aired until 1939.
8. Alison Light, *Forever England: Femininity, Literature and Conservatism between the Wars* (London: Routledge, 1991), 138.
9. See, for instance, Nick Hubble, *Mass Observation and Everyday Life: Culture, History, Theory* (London: Palgrave Macmillan, 2006) and James Hinton, *The Mass Observers: A History, 1937-1949* (Oxford: Oxford University Press, 2013).
10. Light, *Forever England*, 146. In her afterword, Light considers the importance of radio and other forms of mass entertainment in these processes, arguing that much work has to be done in understanding their contributions to our understandings of the interwar period, 215–17.
11. Briggs, *Golden Age*, 236, statistics approximate 6 million of 9 million licence-holders earned less than £5 a week; Pegg, *Broadcasting and Society*, estimates about 66 per cent of the population as working class, 118.
12. Pegg, *Broadcasting and Society*, 144–5; Nicholas, *Echo of War*, 13.
13. Gordon Stowell, 'Meet Denis Constanduros', *Radio Times*, 4 August 1939. Many thanks to Stephanie Down for providing this material from her family archives. Denis's personal diary bemoans a number of factual errors in the piece, and the family copy has a handwritten note that corrects the caption for the embedded picture of Denis in front of a cottage, listed as Mabel's, but corrected here as being Denis's cottage in Wiltshire. Though there are numerous errors in this piece, based on his diaries and his oft-expressed desire to write serious material, it is most likely that Guthrie's inspirational influence is entirely accurate.

14 Denis contributed six posters to the 'Visit Britain's Landmarks' and 'Everywhere You Go' series. 'Constanduros', http://www.nationalmotormuseum.org.uk/Explore_shell, accessed 24 March 2017. For more on artists in the Shell marketing campaigns, see John Hewitt, 'The "Nature" and "Art" of Shell Advertising in the Early 1930s', *Journal of Design History* 5, no. 2 (1992): 121–39.
15 Bush-Bailey, 'Mabel Constanduros', 274. For instance, Denis was known for his adaptation of *The Railway Children* (in which Bush-Bailey acted) and a number of highly acclaimed Jane Austen adaptations.
16 Constanduros to Gielgud, 20 May 1938, BBC WAC Scriptwriter 1935–1942; Michele Hilmes, 'Front Line Family: "Women's Culture" Comes to the BBC', *Media, Culture and Society* 29, no. 5 (2007): 7.
17 Constanduros to Gielgud, 20 May 1938, BBC WAC Scriptwriter 1935–1942.
18 Gielgud to Constanduros, 8 June 1938, BBC WAC Scriptwriter 1935–1942.
19 *Radio Times Fiftieth Anniversary Souvenir: 1923-1973* (London: BBC, 1973), 38.
20 One of her first successful radio sketches that was published in the amateur market was also set in Strutham, and entitled *The Strutham Amateurs Rehearse Dick Whittington*. Constanduros, *Shreds and Patches*, 36.
21 Jörg Dürrschmidt, *Everyday Lives in the Global City: The Delinking of Locale and Milieu* (London: Routledge, 2001), chapter six, 'Streatham – the Reluctant Suburb: The Metropolis Extends', 91–114.
22 H. W. Bromhead, *Streatham's Beginnings* (London: Streatham Ratepayers Association and Streatham Antiquarian and Natural History Society, 1936), quoted in Dürrschmidt, *Everyday Lives in a Global City*, 110.
23 Dürrschmidt, *Everyday Lives in a Global City*, 105–6.
24 J. B. Priestley, *English Journey* (London: William Heinemann, 1934).
25 David Kynaston, *Austerity Britain, 1945-1951* (London: Bloomsbury, 2007), 30.
26 Kynaston, quoting Welsh architect Sir Clough Williams-Ellis in 1928, *Austerity Britain*, 29–30.
27 Paddy Scannell, 'Broadcasting and the State', *The State and Society* D209, Unit 11 (Milton Keynes: Open University Press, 1984), 49–103. Sincerest thanks to Leah Clark, Paddy Scannell, and numerous staff and faculty at the Open University, who helped me find the appropriate bibliographic information for an extract of this chapter given me by Stephanie Constanduros.
28 Scannell, 'Broadcasting and the State', 61–2.
29 Light, *Forever England*, 215.
30 Scannell, 'Broadcasting and State', 61.
31 N.A., 'The English Family Robinson: New Serial Play for Everybody Begins on Friday Next', *Radio Times*, 30 September 1938, 11.
32 N.A., 'The English Family Robinson', 11.

33 N.A., 'The English Family Robinson', 11.
34 Skoog, '"They're 'Doped' by that Dale Diary"', 126.
35 Mabel Constanduros, *A Nice Fire in the Drawing Room: A Story about Ordinary People* (London: The Bodley Head, 1939), 27–8.
36 Constanduros, *A Nice Fire*, 119–20.
37 Constanduros, *A Nice Fire*, 124.
38 Constanduros, *A Nice Fire*, 125.
39 Light, *Mrs. Woolf and the Servants*, 180.
40 Light, *Forever England*, 141.
41 Gielgud to Constanduros, 6 September 1939, Scriptwriters file 1935–42, BBC WAC.
42 Gielgud to Constanduros, 27 September 1939, Scriptwriters file 1935–42, BBC WAC.
43 Rose to Gielgud, 30 January 1940, Scriptwriters file 1935–42, BBC WAC. Laurence Gilliam, assistant director of features, also recorded interest in a wartime series structured around the family in February 1940, Hilmes, 'Front Line Family', 14.
44 Constanduros to Rose, 13 July 1940, Scriptwriter file 1935–1942, BBC WAC.
45 Director of Drama and Features, Gielgud was most resistant to the model, and remained an opponent of *FLF* after its inception. Hilmes, 'Front Line Family', 16.
46 Quoted in Hilmes, 'Front Line Family', 14.
47 Quoted in Hilmes, 'Front Line Family', 18.
48 Hilmes, 'Front Line Family', 18.
49 For Constanduros's account, see *Shreds and Patches*, 129.
50 See Constanduros Copyright Files 1B, 1939–1940 and 2A, 1941–1942, BBC WAC.
51 Howard Agg to Gilliam, 15 February 1942; Internal Memorandum, 20 February 1942, Constanduros Copyright File 2A, 1941–2, BBC WAC.
52 Internal Memorandum, 25 February 1942, Constanduros Copyright File 2A, 1941–2, BBC WAC.
53 Internal Memoranda, 27 February, 14 March and 21 March 1942, letter dated 7 March to Agg, Constanduros Copyright File 2A, 1941–2, BBC WAC.
54 Bush-Bailey, 'Different Voices, Voicing Difference', 276; note in 6 October 1941 contract states that Agg can negotiate higher fees when working with Constanduros. Otherwise, he receives Staff fees. Constanduros Copyright File 2A, 1941–2, BBC WAC.
55 Bush-Bailey, 'Different Voices, Voicing Difference', *fn* 27, 284.
56 Howard Agg to Mary Allen, 9 August 1941, Howard Agg Scriptwriter File 1, 1939–1944, BBC WAC.
57 Howard Agg to Val Gielgud, 1 October 1940, Howard Agg Scriptwriter File 1939–1944, BBC WAC.

58 Internal Memorandum regarding Agg and Constanduros submission of 'The Three Year Plan', handwritten note, 27 January 1945, Constanduros Scriptwriter File 2, 1943–1950.
59 Gilli Bush-Bailey, unpublished draft, 'Different Voices, Voicing Difference', 16. Many thanks to Gilli for sharing this draft in advance of the final publication.
60 Mabel Constanduros and Howard Agg, *Mr and Mrs Sparkes* (London: Samuel French Ltd., 1941).
61 Constanduros and Agg, *Mr and Mrs Sparkes*, 3.
62 Bush-Bailey, 'Different Voices, Voicing Difference', 276.
63 Constanduros and Agg, *Mr and Mrs Sparkes*, 4.
64 Constanduros and Agg, *Mr and Mrs Sparkes*, 3–4.
65 Denis Constanduros, 'Rival Households', extract from *Father, Dear Father*, Stephanie Down's (nee Constanduros) private collection. Many thanks to Stephanie for this document.
66 Denis Constanduros, 'Rival Households'.
67 Constanduros and Agg, *Mr and Mrs Sparkes*, 4.
68 Constanduros and Agg, *Mr and Mrs Sparkes*, 4.
69 Bush-Bailey, 'Different Voices, Voicing Difference', 265.
70 Light, *Forever England*, 217.
71 Light, *Forever England*, 218.
72 Light, *Forever England*, 218.
73 'Mrs. Buggins Tells Her Story!' *Radio Pictorial*, 18 October 1935, 10.
74 'Mrs. Buggins Tells Her Story!' *Radio Pictorial*, 18 October 1935, 10.
75 SADC clippings, 1925. Sutton Local Archive.
76 SADC clippings, 1925. Sutton Local Archive.
77 Constanduros, *Shreds and Patches*, 39.
78 See Maggie Andrews, 'Butterflies and Caustic Asides: Housewives, Comedy and the Feminist Movement', in Stephen Wagg, ed., *Because I Tell a Joke or Two: Comedy, Politics and Social Difference* (London: Routledge, 1998), 50–64.
79 Claire Langhamer, 'Feelings, Women and Work in the Long 1950s', *Women's History Review* 26, no. 1 (2017): 10–11.
80 Jill Seddon, 'Mentioned, but Denied Significance: Women Designers and the Professionalization of Design in Britain, c. 1920-1951', *Gender and Society* 12, no. 2 (July 2000): 426.
81 Strachey, *Careers and Openings for Women*, 46.
82 Strachey, *Careers and Openings for Women*, 61.
83 Beverly Thiele, 'Vanishing Acts in Social and Political thought: Tricks of the Trade', in Linda McDowell and Rosemary Pringle, eds., *Defining Women: Social Institutions and Gender Divisions* (London: Polity Press, 1992), 27.

84 Quoted in Dibbs, *Radio Fun*, 52.
85 Constanduros, *Shreds and Patches*, 43.
86 Thiele, 'Vanishing Acts', 29.
87 Seddon, 'Mentioned, but Denied Significance', 428.
88 Judith Hubback, *Wives Who Went to College* (London: William Heinemann, 1957), 159, quoted in Langhamer, 'Feelings, Women and Work', 6.
89 Constanduros to Copyright, 2 September 1937, Copyright File 1A, 1926–1938, BBC WAC.
90 Constanduros to Candler, 23 February 1943, Copyright File 2B, 1943–44, BBC WAC.
91 Constanduros to Copyright, 7 February 1936, Copyright File 1A, 1926–1938, BBC WAC.
92 Constanduros to Candler, 23 February 1943, Copyright File 2B, 1943–44, BBC WAC.
93 Candler to Constanduros, 4 March 1943, Copyright File 2B, 1943–44, BBC WAC.
94 Constanduros to Bray, 9 May 1954, Scriptwriter files 5, 1954–1962, BBC WAC.
95 See, for instance, correspondence between Constanduros and Lefeaux June 1951–December 1952. Scriptwriter files 3A and B, 1951 and 1952, BBC WAC.
96 Constanduros continues to refer to her as 'Mrs. Bray' throughout their professional relationship. See, for instance, correspondence between Constanduros and Bray, June 1954. Scriptwriter file 5, 1954–62.
97 Barbara Bower, Children's Hour, 1939–1950, File II, BBC WAC.
98 See, for instance, correspondence between Charles Brewer and Constanduros October 1937, Scriptwriter file 1934–1942. See also, *Shreds and Patches*, where she refers to cocktail parties for one hundred people arranged by her faithful housekeeper, Bina, 77.
99 Knox, *People of Quality*, 114–15.
100 For instance, Constanduros to Howard Rose 20 February 1940, Scriptwriter File 1935–1942, BBC WAC.
101 See, for instance, Constanduros to Gielgud 6 January 1943, Scriptwriter 1943–1950 File 3, BBC WAC.
102 Ursula Bloom, *No Lady with a Pen* (London: Chapman and Hall, 1947), 156.

Chapter 7

1 Clipping, 'What's On', 21 April 1944 in Sydney and Muriel Box Diary, 1943–1947, Item 15 BFI; 'Mabel Constanduros', *The Stage*, 14 February 1957, 13. Richard Constanduros private collection.

2. Denis Constanduros, unpublished diary, 4 July 1943. Many thanks to Stephanie Down for generously providing access to her father's diary.
3. Denis Constanduros, unpublished diary, 16 October 1943.
4. Mabel and Denis Constanduros, *Acacia Avenue: A Comedy* (London: Samuel French, 1944).
5. 8 February 1945, Sydney and Muriel Box Diary, 1943–1947, Item 15 BFI.
6. 8 February 1945, Sydney and Muriel Box Diary, 1943–1947, Item 15 BFI.
7. 26 September 1944, Sydney and Muriel Box Diary, 1943–1947, Item 15 BFI.
8. Sue Aspinall, 'Women, Realism and Reality in British Films, 1943-1953', in James Curran and Vincent Porter, eds., *British Cinema History* (London: Weidenfeld and Nicolson, 1983), 272–93.
9. 16 March 1945, Sydney and Muriel Box Diary, 1943–1947, Item 15 BFI.
10. Aspinall, 'Women, Realism and Reality in British Films', 293.
11. Andrew Spicer, *Sydney Box* (Manchester: Manchester University Press, 2006), 50.
12. 'Film Reviews – 29 Acacia Avenue', *Today's Cinema* v71 n5729, 19 November 1948, BFI.
13. 'Reviews for showmen', *Kinematograph Weekly*, 14 June 1945, BFI.
14. 'Film Reviews – 29 Acacia Avenue', *Today's* Cinema v71 n5729, 19 November 1948, BFI.
15. 'Film Reviews – *29 Acacia Avenue*', *Today's Cinema* v71 n5729, 19 November 1948. See also '29 Acacia Avenue', *Monthly Film Bulletin* 12, no. 139 (July 1945), 84 and 'Reviews for Showmen', *Kinematograph Weekly*, 14 June 1945, BFI.
16. 'Reviews for showmen', *Kinematograph Weekly*, 14 June 1945, BFI.
17. 22 January 1945, Sydney and Muriel Box Diary, 1943–1947, Item 15 BFI.
18. Spicer, *Sydney Box*, 50.
19. Searle Kochberg, 'Cinema as Institution', in Jill Nelmes, ed., *Introduction to Film Studies*, 3rd edn (London: Routledge, 2003), 42.
20. Marcia Landy, *British Genres: Cinema and Society, 1930-1960* (Princeton: Princeton University Press, 1991), 443.
21. Claire Langhamer, *The English in Love: The Intimate Story of a Revolution* (Oxford: Oxford University Press, 2013), 7.
22. Simon Szreter and Kate Fisher, *Sex before the Sexual Revolution: Intimate Life in England, 1918-1963* (Cambridge: Cambridge University Press, 2010), 162. For further detail regarding respondents' specific attitudes, see chapter three. Ross McKibbin points out that individuals in the early surveys may not have necessarily seen sex prior to marriage as 'premarital sex' if marriage was intended, thus making reportage of the practice problematic. McKibbin, *Classes and Cultures*, 297–98.
23. Kinematograph Weekly, 7 June 1945.

24 Clipping, 'Acacia Avenue', n.d. in Sydney and Muriel Box Diary, 1943–1947, Item 15 BFI.
25 Leonard Maltin, *Classic Movie Guide: From the Silent Era to 1965* (New York: Plume, 2005), 20.
26 Christine Geraghty, *British Cinema in the Fifties: Gender, Genre and the New Look* (London: Routledge, 2000), 137.
27 *Picturegoer* quoted in *Vote for Huggett* large press book for overseas. BEB/5 VOTE FOR HUGGETT (GB, 1948), Betty Box collection, BFI.
28 Denis Constanduros diary, 17 July 1946.
29 Spicer, *Sydney Box*, 111.
30 Spicer, *Sydney Box*, 110.
31 Robert Murphy, *Realism and Tinsel: Cinema and Society in Britain, 1939-1949* (London: Routledge, 2016), 214; Spicer, *Sydney Box*, 80.
32 Charles Drazin, 'Anglo-American Collaboration: Korda, Selznick and Goldwyn', in Paul Cooke, ed., *World Cinema's 'Dialogues' with Hollywood* (London: Palgrave, 2007), 57.
33 Hubert Griffith, Review of *Holiday Camp* in *Sunday Graphic*, 1947 (day/month illegible). In *Holiday Camp* press cuttings, p113753, BFI. The film did do well in America, see Box diary, 14 February 1948.
34 Quoted in Spicer, *Sydney Box*, 111.
35 See 'A Week at Billy Butlin's', 27 September to 4 October 1947. Mass-Observation Archive, Topic Collection 58/2/G 'Butlin's Holiday Camp'; and Kynaston, *Austerity Britain*, 218–20.
36 Murphy, *Realism and Tinsel*, 215.
37 Jeffrey Richards, *Film and British National Identity: From Dickens to Dad's Army* (Manchester: Manchester University Press, 1997), 129 and Geraghty, *British Cinema in the Fifties*, 15.
38 Geraghty, *British Cinema in the Fifties*, 136.
39 Geraghty, *British Cinema in the Fifties*, 136–7.
40 Evening News Review of *Holiday Camp*, 4 August 1947. In *Holiday Camp* press cuttings, p113753, BFI.
41 Quoted in Spicer, *Sydney Box*, 112.
42 Claire Langhamer, 'The Meanings of Home in Postwar Britain', *Journal of Contemporary History* 40, no. 2 (2005): 345. Langhamer quotes one Mass-Observer as arguing that 'a happy home and family life is the bulwark of the Nation'. Emphasis in original.
43 His character in the previous film was also Jimmy Gardner.
44 Sonya Rose, *Which People's War? National Identity and Citizenship in Wartime Britain, 1939-1945* (Oxford: Oxford University Press, 2003), 80.

45 For a discussion of the film, see Murphy, *Realism and Tinsel*, 89–93.
46 Rose, *Which People's War?*, 83.
47 Kynaston, *Austerity Britain*, 97.
48 Spicer, *Sydney Box*, 112.
49 Richards, *Film and British National Identity*, 142.
50 Both wartime and post-war *ITMA* episodes regularly featured healthy scepticism of government officials, their promises and self-serving agendas, as well as corruption. For a discussion of immediate post-war politics, see Kenneth O. Morgan, *The People's Peace: British History since 1945*, 2nd edn (Oxford: Oxford University Press, 1999), especially chapter one 'The Façade of Unity'.
51 Phillip Gillett, *The British Working Class in Postwar Film* (Manchester: Manchester University Press, 2003), 86.
52 J. B. Priestley, 20 October 1940, *Postscripts* (London: W. Heinemann, 1940), 98.
53 Gillett, *British Working Class*, 86, uses the term amateurish to describe Huggett's electioneering. In wartime, it was often asserted that British amateurism would prevail against Nazi efficiency – see Priestley 5 June 1940 *Postscript* and Orwell's wartime essay, 'The Lion and the Unicorn: Socialism and the English Genius', in *Why I Write* (London: Penguin Books, 2004, originally published 1940), 18.
54 21 July 1949, Box Diary.
55 Andrew Spicer, *Typical Men: Representations of Masculinity in Popular British Culture* (London: IB Taurus, 2003), 85.
56 'New Films In London', *Times*, 4 July 1949, 7. The Times Digital Archive, http://tinyurl.galegroup.com/tinyurl/ACjHnX, accessed 6 June 2019.
57 Brian MacFarlane, *An Autobiography of British Cinema: As Told By the Filmmakers and Actors Who Made It* (London: Methuen, 1997), 23.
58 Richards, *Film and British National Identity*, 142–3.
59 For instance, Flossie is a recurring Constanduros character who is often portrayed as having stolen the hearts of young men during Mrs. Buggins's and other female protagonists' courting years. When Joe remembers his first look at Ethel when they were young in *Here Come the Huggetts*, she retorts that he described his ex-girlfriend Flossie, not her.
60 Spicer, *Typical Men*, 84.
61 *Vote for Huggett*, Small press book BFI.
62 Quoted in Kynaston, *Austerity Britain*, 102. See also 72, 248 and 595.
63 Kynaston, *Austerity Britain*, 72.
64 Langhamer, 'Meanings of Home', 350.
65 Mary Douglas and Baron Isherwood, *A World of Goods: Towards an Anthropology of Consumption* (London: Routledge, 1979/1996), 70–1.
66 See Langhamer, 'Meanings of Home', 346–7.

67 Gillett, *British Working Class*, 82.
68 Richards, *Films and British National Identity*, 141.
69 Gillett, *British Working Class*, 83–5, superbly analyses these features.
70 Many thanks to Stephen Laing, Curator of the British Motoring Museum, for identifying the car and dates of production. While the Prefect was made through 1949, the touring car was not made after the war and the registration plate firmly dates the car as a 1938 model. Personal communication, 28–30 June 2017.
71 See 1939 brochure, http://www.fordprefecttourer.co.uk/ford-prefect-brochures, accessed 29 June 2017. Stephen Laing, personal communication, 30 June 2017.
72 Sean O'Connell, *The Car and British Society: Class, Gender and Motoring, 1896-1939* (Manchester: Manchester University Press, 1998), 37.
73 O'Connell, *The Car and British Society*, 30.
74 O'Connell, *The Car and British Society*, 21.
75 Gillett, *British Working Class*, 81.
76 Gillett, *British Working Class*, 82, 86 and 89.
77 Jon Lawrence, 'Class, "Affluence," and the Study of Everyday Life in Britain, c. 1930-1964', *Cultural and Social History* 10, no. 2 (2013): 273–99.
78 Spicer, *Typical Men*, 84.
79 Richards, *Film and British National Identity*, 142–3.
80 Lawrence, 'Class, "Affluence," and Everyday Life', 282.
81 Lawerence, 'Class, "Affluence," and Everyday Life', 283.
82 Gillett, *British Working Class*, mentions Leeds and Sheffield as being lukewarm to the Huggett films.
83 Denis Constanduros Diary, 13 August 1947.
84 Letter to Val Gielgud, 1 January 1947. Constanduros Scriptwriter File 2, 1943–50.
85 RG Walford (Copyright) to Mabel Constanduros, 29 September 1948. Constanduros Scriptwriter File 2, 1943–50, BBC WAC.
86 15 October 1948, Memo from Alick Hayes to Script Editor Variety. Constanduros Scriptwriter File 2, 1943–50. A handwritten note dated 15 November reveals that Constanduros had sold the rights to the Huggett name to Betty Box, and Sydney Box now threatened the BBC to sue if the radio series plagiarized the movie scripts or plots. BBC WAC.
87 Constanduros to Standing, 9 November 1948. Constanduros Scriptwriter File 2, 1943–50, BBC WAC.
88 10 December 1948, Standing to Constanduros, Constanduros Copyright File 2, 1943–50, BBC WAC; Meet the Huggetts R19/720 Entertainment 1948–1954, especially memorandum from Gale Pedrick 4 November 1952, BBC WAC.
89 Contract, 25 August 1949; Constanduros to Chalmers, 4 August 1949, Constanduros Scriptwriter File 2, 1943–50, BBC WAC.

90 9 July 1952 Memo to Pedrick. Constanduros Scriptwriter File 2, 1943–50, BBC WAC.
91 There are no explanations in the BBC WAC files as to why Maguire was engaged instead of Constanduros.
92 *Meet the Huggetts* scripts, BBC WAC.
93 The 1945 version was produced by Howard Rose and the 1948 *AA*'s producer was John Richmond. *Radio Times*, https://genome.ch.bbc.co.uk/bb4080cdf5e345718 508ed5b5ca7b107 and https://genome.ch.bbc.co.uk/fafaad3e48ba41afacc670 0db4b495e6, accessed 14 January 2019. Hubert Gregg, who played the film and stage version's Michael, reprised the role in the 1948 production. For the television broadcast, see https://genome.ch.bbc.co.uk/2f9024dfe5cd41ee801dbae3aa22dc0b, accessed 19 March 2019.
94 3 September 1945, BBC memo Tom Roland to Director of Variety, Constanduros Scriptwriter File 2, 1943–50.
95 Asa Briggs, *History of Broadcasting in the United Kingdom, Volume IV: Sound and Vision* (Oxford: Oxford University Press, 1995), 53.
96 Dibbs, *Radio Fun*, 173.
97 Kynaston, *Austerity Britain*, 81.
98 Briggs, *Sound and Vision*, 53–5.
99 William Haley in 1944, quoted in Briggs, *Sound and Vision*, 63.
100 Dibbs, *Radio Fun*, 174.
101 Dibbs, *Radio Fun*, 175.
102 Dibbs, *Radio Fun*, 171.
103 Briggs, *Sound and Vision*, 364; Dibbs, *Radio Fun*, 219–21.
104 Briggs, *Sound and Vision*, 364–5. The numbers were contested, however, by advertisers on Radio Luxembourg as too low.
105 Kynaston, *Austerity Britain*, 305.
106 Kynaston, *Austerity Britain*, 357.
107 Dibbs, *Radio Fun*, 178–80.
108 Dibbs, *Radio Fun*, 196; Briggs, *Sound and Vision*, 710.
109 Kynaston, *Austerity Britain*, 293.
110 Dibbs, *Radio Fun*, 175.
111 Briggs, *Sound and Vision*, 61.
112 Archie Campbell to Martyn Webster, 20 May 1949. Constanduros Scriptwriter File 2, 1943–50, BBC WAC.
113 For instance, Mollie Greenhalgh, Reader's Report on Constanduros's idea to adapt *The Mollusc*, 4 April 1952. Constanduros Scriptwriter Files.
114 Briggs, *Sound and Vision*, 688; Val Gielgud, *One Year of Grace: A Fragment of Autobiography* (London: Longmans, 1951).
115 Constanduros to Gielgud, 4 August 1949. Constanduros Scriptwriter Files, BBC WAC.

116 See August 1949 correspondence in Constanduros Scriptwriter Files, BBC WAC.
117 Pedrick to Constanduros, 28 April 1953. Constanduros Scriptwriter File, BBC WAC.
118 Pederick to Lefeaux, 22 April 1953. Constanduros Scriptwriter File, BBC WAC.
119 Lefeaux to Pedrick, 24 April 1953. Memo, no author, to Pedrick, 9 July 1952. Constanduros Scriptwriter File 3B, 1952, BBC WAC.
120 Dibbs, *Radio Fun*, 196–7.
121 Cynthia Pughe, 'Readers Report – Feathers in the Wind', 22 February 1951. Constanduros Scriptwriter File 3A, 1951, BBC WAC.
122 Charles Lefeaux to Constanduros, 5 December 1951. Constanduros Scriptwriter File 3A, 1951, BBC WAC. Famous architect Francis Rattenbury was murdered by either his wife Alma or her lover, George Stoner in 1935.
123 Constanduros to Harding, 10 May 1949. Constanduros Scriptwriter File 2, 1943–50, BBC WAC.
124 Harding to Constanduros, 20 June 1949. Constanduros Scriptwriter File 2, 1943–50, BBC WAC.
125 Constanduros to Gielgud, 10 December 1946. Constanduros Scriptwriter File 2, 1943–50, BBC WAC.
126 Giddings and Selby, *The Classic Serial*, 4. Dates of adaptations: Gielgud, *British Radio Drama*, 21.
127 *Radio Times* listings, 28 September 1923, 23. The programme aired on 6 October, https://genome.ch.bbc.co.uk/page/49df10011e5c40c1a906f4a00d343749, accessed 11 March 2019.
128 *Radio Times* listings, https://genome.ch.bbc.co.uk/search/0/20?order=asc&q=adaptation#search, accessed 11 March 2019; Jeffrey's appointment, Gielgud, *British Radio Drama*, 20.
129 Giddings and Selby, *The Classic Serial*, 10.
130 Black, *The Biggest Aspidistra in the World*, 122.
131 Siân Nicholas argues that the BBC protected national culture, but does not apply it to these radio adaptations of literature. See 'The People's Radio: The BBC and Its Audience, 1939-1945', 62-92.
132 Constanduros mentions receiving many appreciative fan letters about *Bleak House* and that the Dickens Society invited the writers to a luncheon, *Shreds and Patches*, 130.
133 Frank A. Gibson, '*Great Expectations* on the Air', *The Dickensian* XLV, part 2 (Spring 1949): 109.
134 Gielgud to Constanduros, 10 August 1949. Constanduros Scriptwriter File 2, 1943–50, BBC WAC.
135 E. A. Harding to Gielgud, 8 June 1950. Constanduros Scriptwriter File 2, 1943–50, BBC WAC.

136 Gielgud to AHD, 9 June 1950. Constanduros Scriptwriter File 2, 1943–50, BBC WAC.
137 Hugh Stewart to Constanduros, 5 July 1950. Constanduros Scriptwriter File 2, 1943–50, BBC WAC.
138 Frank Gibson, 'Another Dickens Serial', *The Dickensian* XLVIII (Spring 1951): 79.
139 Sean Grass, *Charles Dickens's Our Mutual Friend: A Publication History* (Routledge, 2016), 153.
140 For an overview of this debate regarding visual adaptations, see Deborah Cartmell and Imelda Whelehan's edited volume, *Adaptations: From Text to Screen, Screen to Text* (London: Routledge, 1999), especially Imelda Whelehan, 'Adaptations: Some Contemporary Dilemmas', 3–19 and Julian North, 'Conservative Austen, Radical Austen: *Sense and Sensibility*, from Text to Screen', 38–50.
141 In regards to cinematic adaptations, Brian McFarlane, *Novel to Film: An Introduction to the Theory of Adaptation* (Oxford: Clarendon Press, 1996), 14 and Whelehan, 'Adaptations: Some Contemporary Dilemmas', 10.
142 Gibson, 'Another Dickens Serial', 80.
143 Gielgud to AHD, 9 June 1950. Constanduros Scriptwriter File 2, 1943–50, BBC WAC.
144 She had asked for the commission two years previously. 23 June 1950 Constanduros to EA Harding, Constanduros Scriptwriter File 2, 1943–50, BBC WAC.
145 Agg to Constanduros, copy sent to BBC. Agg Scriptwriter File 2, 1945–1952, BBC WAC.
146 Lefeaux to Constanduros, 29 January 1952. Constanduros Scriptwriter File 3B, 1952, BBC WAC.
147 See, for instance, correspondence regarding the adaptation of *Wives and Daughters* in June 1953. Constanduros Scriptwriter File 4B, 1953, BBC WAC.
148 Lefeaux to Constanduros, 2 December 1952. Constanduros Scriptwriter Files, File 3B 1952; Layton to Constanduros, 12 December 1952. Constanduros Copyright File 4, 1951–1962, BBC WAC.
149 Deirdre David, *Olivia Manning: A Woman at War* (Oxford: Oxford University Press, 2012), 206 fn.
150 Lefeaux to Constanduros, 4 February 1953. Constanduros Scriptwriter File 4, 1953, BBC WAC.
151 Layton to Constanduros, 19 March 1954. Constanduros Scriptwriter File 5, 1954–62, BBC WAC.
152 Constanduros to Bray, 4 May 1956; Bray to Constanduros, 22 May 1956. Constanduros Scriptwriter File 5, 1954–62, BBC WAC.
153 Genome data for WD; Cynthia Pughe, Reader's report for 'Undying Flame', 29 June 1962. Constanduros Scriptwriter File 5, 1954–62, BBC WAC.

Conclusion

1 See 1957 BBC memoranda, Constanduros Artists File 9, 1956–57, BBC WAC. Seemingly in line with this decision, when Robb Wilton passed away later that year in May, the BBC do not seem to have commemorated his BBC career on air either.
2 *The Laughing Mirror* aired posthumously in July 1957, but was accepted in 1951. Lefeaux to Constanduros, 12 December 1951. BBC Scriptwriter 3A File, 1951, BBC WAC. See *Radio Times* listing, https://genome.ch.bbc.co.uk/64a4d7c0192e482cb 33dc40cba165310, accessed 20 March 2019.
3 Briggs, *Sound and Vision*, 56–7.
4 Andrews, *Domesticating the Airwaves*, 118–19.
5 27 November 1956 was her last appearance on *Woman's Hour*. See *Radio Times* listings, https://genome.ch.bbc.co.uk/6aac845097a84326a535bb93847eae9b, accessed 5 June 2019.
6 Monica Simms (Talks) to Constanduros, 7 September 1953. Constanduros Artists File 8, 1953–1954, BBC WAC. The Buggins Coronation sketch appeared 1 June 1953. See *Radio Times* listing, https://genome.ch.bbc.co.uk/8f8975e3c3f2434c8 3117cc76f32bb26, accessed 5 June 2019.
7 *Radio Times* listings, see for instance, 6 November 1953, https://genome.ch.bbc.co.uk/596b8052c5e844709d3801bdb1084b86, accessed 20 March 2019.
8 Monica Simms to Constanduros, 16 December 1954. Constanduros Artists File 8, 1953–1954, BBC WAC.
9 Mabel Constanduros, 'Settling Down', 12 September 1955. Script, BBC WAC.
10 Moran, *Armchair Nation*, 62; See also Mass Observation Topic Collection 69, Royalty, Folders 69-3-D and 69-6-C.
11 Briggs, *Sound and Vision*, 718; Dibbs, *Radio Fun*, 230.
12 Dibbs, *Radio Fun*, 230.
13 Moran, *Armchair Nation*, 81.
14 Briggs, *Sound and Vision*, 12.
15 Moran, *Armchair Nation*, 84. VHF was introduced in 1954. Briggs, *Sound and Vision*, 9.
16 Brian Willey, quoted in Dibbs, *Radio Fun*, 216.
17 Quoted in Asa Briggs, *Sound and Vision*, 9.
18 Constanduros to Harding, 26 December 1950. Constanduros Scriptwriter File 2, 1943–1950, BBC WAC.
19 Harding to Constanduros, 9 January 1951, Constanduros Scriptwriter File 3A, 1951, BBC WAC.
20 Gielgud, *One Year of Grace*, 159. Emphasis in original.
21 Gielgud, *One Year of Grace*, 157.

22 Gielgud, *Years of the Locust*, 191.
23 Briggs, *Sound and Vision*, 688; Val Gielgud discusses his concerns in detail in *Years in a Mirror*, 131–5. Largely, he was disgusted by the fact that producers were unable to rehearse sufficiently in front of the camera.
24 Constanduros to Walford, 18 November 1949. Constanduros Copyright File 3, 1945–1950, BBC WAC. For this television appearance and her original piece, she received £13 instead of the usual £21 she received for radio.
25 Constanduros to Gielgud, 13 March 1953. Constanduros Scriptwriter File 4, 1953, BBC WAC.
26 Gielgud to Constanduros, 16 March 1953. Constanduros Scriptwriter File 4, 1953, BBC WAC.
27 Dibbs, *Radio Fun*, 231–6.
28 Dibbs, *Radio Fun*, 236–7.
29 See, for instance, 'common characteristics' of sitcom in Stephen Wagg, '"At Ease, Corporal": Social Class and the Situation Comedy in British Television, from the 1950s to the 1990s', in Stephen Wagg, ed., *Because I Tell a Joke or Two: Comedy, Politics and Social Difference* (London: Routledge, 1998), 3 and Mills, *TV Genres: The Sitcom*, 28.
30 Neale and Krutnik, *Popular Film and Television Comedy*, especially chapter nine; Mundy and White, *Laughing Matters*, 82–8.
31 Mills, *TV Genres: Sitcom*, 20; Scott-Jeffs, 'Voice, Personality and Grandma', 125.
32 Su Holmes, *Entertaining Television: The BBC and Popular Television Culture in the 1950s* (Manchester: Manchester University Press, 2008), 40–1.
33 See, for instance, the 1950s Grove Family and some interpretations of *Coronation Street*. Holmes, *Entertaining Television*, 54; Andrews, *Domesticating the Airwaves*, 156.
34 Nancy K. Baym, 'Interpreting Soap Operas and Creating Community: Inside an Electronic Fan Culture', in Sara Kiesler, ed., *Culture of the Internet* (New York: Psychology Press, 2014), 112.
35 Wagg, *Because I Tell a Joke or Two*; Dibbs, *Radio Fun*, 200.
36 Dibbs, *Radio Fun*, 200.
37 Frank Norden and Denis Muir, *Take It From Here (TIFH)*, 12 November 1953, BBC WAC.
38 Mills, *TV Genres: The Sitcom*, 20.
39 Norden and Muir, *Take It From Here (TIFH)*.
40 Andrews, 'Butterflies and Caustic Asides", 52.
41 Quoted in Briggs, *Golden Age*, 56.
42 Scott-Jeffs, 'Voice, Personality and Grandma', 126; Mills, *TV Genres: The Sitcom*, 21.
43 Bush-Bailey, 'Different Voices, Voicing Difference', 279.

44 Andrews, *Domesticating the Airwaves*, viii and Chapter one.
45 Andrews, 'Butterflies and Caustic Asides', 50.
46 Carolyn Coccia, *Superwomen: Gender, Power, and Representation* (New York: Bloomsbury, 2016), 4; Megan Garber, 'Call It the Bechel-Wallace Test', *The Atlantic*, 25 August 2015, https://www.theatlantic.com/entertainment/archive/2015/08/call-it-the-bechdel-wallace-test/402259/, accessed 21 March 2019.
47 Coccia, *Superwomen*, 6; French, *Dear Fatty*.
48 Murphy, *Behind the Wireless*, 10.
49 Samuel, 'The Voice of Britain', 186.

Bibliography

BBC Written Archives Centre, Caversham

Radio files

R8/38 Artists' Policy Booking of Artists (1927–39)
R12/125, Copyright 'Mr Penny' Agreement (1937–1938)
R19/281 Entertainment, Drama Repertory Company (1929–1937)
R19/310, Entertainment, English Family Robinson (1940)
R19/720 Entertainment, Meet the Huggetts (1948–1954)
R34/600/2 Policy Programme Board Minutes File 2 (1925)
R49/481, Staff Policy, Payment of Artists (1922–1937)
R49/38 Staff Policy Auditions (1928–1937)
R49/57 Staff Policy Booking of Artists (1922–1935)
R51/178/3 Kitchen Front (1940)
R51/178/5 Kitchen Front (1941)

Artist files

Mabel Constanduros, Artists 1A (1935–June 1936)
Mabel Constanduros, Artists 1B (July 1936–37)
Mabel Constanduros, Artists 2A (1938–39)
Mabel Constanduros, Artists 2B (1940)
Mabel Constanduros, Artists 3A (1941)
Mabel Constanduros, Artists 3B (1942)
Mabel Constanduros, Artists 4A (1943)
Mabel Constanduros, Artists 4B (1944)
Mabel Constanduros, Artists 5A (1945)
Mabel Constanduros, Artists 5B (1946–47)
Mabel Constanduros, Artists 6 (1948–50)
Mabel Constanduros, Artists 7 (1951–52)
Mabel Constanduros, Artists 8 (1953–54)
Mabel Constanduros, Artists 9 (1956–57)
Richard Goolden, Artists (1948–1962)
Richard Goolden, Rcont1 (1941–47)
Helena Millais, Rcont1 (1937–62)
Jack Warner, Artists 1 (1937–1941)
Jack Warner, Artists 2 (1942–1951)

Copyright files

Mabel Constanduros, Copyright 1A (1926–1938)
Mabel Constanduros, Copyright 1B (1939–1940)
Mabel Constanduros, Copyright 2A (1941–1942)
Mabel Constanduros, Copyright 2B (1943–1944)
Mabel Constanduros, Copyright 3 (1945–1950)
Mabel Constanduros, Copyright 4 (1951–1962)
Barbara Bower, Copyright (1950–57)
Eddie Maguire, Rcont1 Copyright 2 (1951–1956)

Scriptwriter files

Mabel Constanduros, Scriptwriter (1935–1942)
Mabel Constanduros, Scriptwriter 2 (1943–1950)
Mabel Constanduros, Scriptwriter 3A (1951)
Mabel Constanduros, Scriptwriter 3B (1952)
Mabel Constanduros, Scriptwriter File 4 (1953)
Mabel Constanduros, Scriptwriter File 5 (1954–1962)
Howard Agg, Scriptwriter 1 (1939–1944)
Howard Agg, Scriptwriter 2 (1945–1952)

Program files

Children's Hour, Barbara Bower File II (1939–1950)
Mrs. Dale's Diary (1947–1951)
Robinsons File 3 (1947–1948)

Scripts

Mabel and Denis Constanduros, 'Cruising Family Robinson' (30 June 1939)
Mabel and Denis Constanduros, 'Private Robinson' (30 April 1940)
Mabel and Denis Constanduros, 'Red Warning at the Robinsons' (7 August 1940)
Mabel Constanduros, 'Bugginses Go Gay' (2 July 1942)
Mabel and Denis Constanduros, 'Lido Ladd' (2 January 1947)
Mabel Constanduros, 'A Victorian Childhood' (5 April 1951)
Mabel Constanduros, 'Bygone Holidays' (14 May 1951)
Mabel Constanduros, *Through the Stage Door* (21 December 1954)
Maurice Moisewitsch, *The Strange Adventures of Mr. Penny* (1936–1937)
Frank Norden and Denis Muir, *Take It From Here* (1953)

British Film Institute, Southbank, London

Sydney box collection diaries

ITM-2359 (1943–47)
ITM-2360 (1947–1954)

Betty Box collection

BEB/5 Vote For Huggett (GB, 1948)
BEB/6 Here Come the Huggetts (GB, 1948)
BEB/7 Huggetts Abroad (GB, 1949)

Scripts

SCR-9473 Here Come the Huggetts, Script # S14273
SCR-9831 Huggetts abroad, Script # S13353
Mass Observation Archive, university of sussex
File Report, "Gert and Daisy's BBC Talks." 23 April 1940
Topic Collection 58, "Holidays, 1937-51." 2/G Butlins Holiday Camp
Topic Collection 69, "Royalty, 1942-64." 3 Children's Essays
Nella Last, Diarist 5353

National Archives, Kew

1942 Kitchen Front Broadcasts, MAF 102/4
1943 Kitchen Front Broadcasts, MAF 102/5
1944 Kitchen Front Broadcasts, MAF 102/6

Sutton local archives

Sutton Amateur Dramatic Club Collection

Box 2, Master Set of Programmes to 1957
Box 3, Meeting Minutes
Box 4, Newspaper Cuttings
Box 6, Programmes

Constanduros family archival collections

Anthea Duigan personal collection
Richard Constanduros personal collection
Stephanie Down personal collection:
Denis Constanduros Diary

Periodicals

Popular Wireless Weekly (3 June 1922–26 January 1924)
Popular Wireless and Wireless Review (1924–1925)
Popular Wireless (1926–1933)
Radio Pictorial (1933–1938)
Radio Times, BBC Genome Project. https://genome.ch.bbc.co.uk/
The Times, Gale Database. https://www.gale.com/c/the-times-digital-archive

Published works by Mabel Constanduros

Shreds and Patches. London: Lawson and Dunn, 1946.
A Nice Fire in the Drawing Room: A Story about Ordinary People. London: The Bodley Head, 1939.
Grandma. London: Frederick Muller, 1939.
Down Mangel Street. London: John Lane, Bodley Head, 1938.
Mrs. Buggins Calls. London: George Routledge, 1936.
Aunt Maria's Wireless. London: Samuel French, 1927.
A Family Group. London: Samuel French, 1927.
With Howard Agg, *On the Run*. London: Hammond, Hammond and Co., 1943.
With Howard Agg, *Mr and Mrs Sparkes*. London: Samuel French, 1941.
With Michael Hogan, *Saving Her Face*. London: Samuel French, 1930.
With Michael Hogan, *The Bugginses*. London: Hutchison and Co., 1927.
With Denis Constanduros. *Acacia Avenue: A Comedy*. London: Samuel French, 1944.
With Denis Constanduros. *The Cruising Family Robinson: A Comedy in One Act*. London: Samuel French, 1939.

Audio/video

Annakin, Kenneth, dir. *The Huggetts Abroad*. 1949; London: ITV Studios, 2007. [DVD]
Annakin, Kenneth, dir. *Vote for Huggett*. 1949; London: ITV Studios, 2007. [DVD]

Annakin, Kenneth, dir. *Here Come the Huggetts*. 1948; London: ITV Studios, 2007. [DVD]
Annakin, Kenneth, dir. *Holiday Camp*. 1947; London: ITV Studios, 2007. [DVD]
Bourke, Joanna. *Eyewitness 1939-1949*, narrator Tim Piggot-Smith [CD]. London: BBC, 2005.
Mabel Constanduros. *Mabel Constanduros*. Editor William J. Clark (Windyridge Variety Series, 2009). [Audio CD]
Mabel Constanduros and Michael Hogan, 'Santa Claus at the Bugginses', [phonograph recording], YouTube (recorded 1930, uploaded 15 December 2012). https://www.youtube.com/watch?v=zLDRMtIB2_8 (accessed 20 May 2017).
Norman Clapham (John Henry) and Gladys Horridge. My Wireless Set [phonograph recording], YouTube (recorded 1925, uploaded 1 September 2012). https://youtu.be/riNiqXUmIiQ (accessed 18 July 2016).
Crook, Tim. 'The Late Mrs. Buggins', Radio 4 Special. 5 March 2006, 20:30-21:00.
Swift, Amanda. "Writing Jokes in Bed: Mabel Constanduros." Radio 2, Third Episode. 4 July 1991, 21:45-22:00.

Books and articles

Alberti, Johanna. 'A Time for Hard Writers: The Impact of War on Women Writers'. In Nick Hayes and Jeff Hill (eds), *'Millions Like Us'? British Culture in the Second World War*, 156–78. Liverpool: Liverpool University Press, 1999.
Andrews, Maggie. 'Butterflies and Caustic Asides: Housewives, Comedy and the Feminist Movement'. In Stephen Wagg (ed.), *Because I Tell a Joke or Two: Comedy, Politics and Social Difference*, 50–64. London: Routledge, 1998.
Andrews, Maggie. *Domesticating the Airwaves: Broadcasting, Domesticity and Femininity*. London: Continuum, 2012.
Askey, Arthur. *Before Your Very Eyes*. London: Woburn Press, 1975.
Aspinall, Sue. 'Women, Realism and Reality in British Films, 1943-1953'. In James Curran and Vincent Porter (eds), *British Cinema History*, 272–93. London: Weidenfeld and Nicolson, 1983.
Bailey, Michael. *Narrating Media History*. London: Routledge, 2009.
Bailey, Peter. 'Conspiracies of Meaning: Music-Hall and the Knowingness of Popular Culture', *Past and Present* 144 (August 1994): 138–70.
Banville, Scott. '"A Bookkeeper, Not an Accountant": Representing the Lower Middle Class from Victorian Novels and Music-Hall Songs to Television Sitcoms'. *The Journal of Popular Culture* 44, no. 1 (2011): 16–36.
Barreca, Regina, ed. *Last Laughs: Perspectives on Women and Comedy*. London: Routledge, 1988.
Barreca, Regina. 'Metaphor-into-Narrative: Being Very Careful with Words', *Women's Studies* 15 (1988): 243–56.

Baym, Nancy K. 'Interpreting Soap Operas and Creating Community: Inside an Electronic Fan Culture'. In Sara Kiesler (ed.), *Culture of the Internet*. New York: Psychology Press, 2014.

Black, Peter. *The Biggest Aspidistra in the World: A Personal Celebration of Fifty Years of the BBC*. London: BBC, 1972.

Bloom, Ursula. *No Lady with a Pen*. London: Chapman and Hall, 1947.

Bourke, Joanna. *Working-Class Cultures in Britain, 1890-1960*. London: Routledge, 1994.

Bower, Dick. *The Drama Unfolded: A History of Sutton Amateur Dramatic Club, 1902-2002*. Dick Bower and David Gillespie for the SADC, 2002.

Briggs, Asa. *The History of Broadcasting in the United Kingdom, Volume I: Birth of Broadcasting 1896-1927*. Oxford: Oxford University Press, 1995.

Briggs, Asa. *The History of Broadcasting in the United Kingdom, Volume II: The Golden Age of Wireless*. Oxford: Oxford University Press, 1995.

Briggs, Asa. *The History of Broadcasting in the United Kingdom, Volume III: The War of Words*. Oxford: Oxford University Press, 1970.

Brooke, Stephen. 'Class and Gender'. In Francesca Carnevali and Julie-Marie Strange (eds), *Twentieth-Century Britain: Economic, Cultural and Social Change*, 2nd edn, 42–57. Harlow: Pearson Longman, 2007.

Brunsdon, Charlotte. 'Text and Audience'. In Ellen Seiter, Hans Borchers, Gabriele Kreutzner and Eva-Maria Warth (eds), *Remote Control: Television, Audiences, and Cultural Power*, 116–29. London: Routledge, 1989.

Bush-Bailey, Gilli. 'Mabel Constanduros: Different Voices, Voicing Difference'. In Maggie Gale and Kate Dorney (eds), *Stage Women, 1900-1950: Female Theatre Workers and Professional Practice*, 262–85. Manchester: Manchester University Press, 2019.

Bush-Bailey, Gilli. 'Women Like Us?' *Comedy Studies* 3, no. 2 (2012): 151–9.

Calder, Angus. *The People's War: Britain, 1939-1945*. London: Jonathan Cape, 1969.

Cardiff, David. 'Mass Middlebrow Laughter: The Origins of Comedy on the BBC', *Media, Culture and Society* 10 (1988): 41–60.

Carter, L. J. *Walworth, 1929-1939*. Old Woking, Surrey: Unwin Brothers Ltd., The Gresham Press, 1985.

Cartmell, Deborah and Imelda Whelehan. *Adaptations: From Text to Screen, Screen to Text*. London: Routledge, 1999.

Clarke, M. J. *Transmedia Television: New Trends in Network Serial Production*. London: Bloomsbury, 2013.

Coccia, Carolyn. *Superwomen: Gender, Power, and Representation*. New York: Bloomsbury, 2016.

Cochrane, Claire. *Twentieth-Century British Theatre: Industry, Art and Empire*. Cambridge: Cambridge University Press, 2011.

Constanduros, Denis. *My Grandfather*. London: Longmans, Green and Co., 1948.

Cook, Eliza. *The Poetical Works of Eliza Cook*. Philadelphia: Claxton, Remsen, and Haffelfinger, 1870.

Crisell, Andrew. *An Introductory History of British Broadcasting*. London: Routledge, 1997.

Crook, Tim. *Radio Drama: Theory and Practice*. London: Routledge, 1999.

Curzon, Lucy D. 'Visualising the Home Front: Evelyn Dunbar and Wartime Citizenship', *Oxford Art Journal* 41, Issue 3 (December 2018): 341–60.

David, Deirdre. *Olivia Manning: A Woman at War*. Oxford: Oxford University Press, 2012.

Delap, Lucy. *Knowing Their Place: Domestic Service in Twentieth-Century Britain*. Oxford: Oxford University Press, 2011.

Dibbs, Martin. *Radio Fun and the BBC Variety Department, 1922-1967: Comedy and Popular Music on Air*. London: Palgrave MacMillan, 2019.

Douglas, Mary and Baron Isherwood. *A World of Goods: Towards an Anthropology of Consumption Volume 6*. London: Routledge, 2003.

Douglas, Susan. *Listening In: Radio and the American Imagination*. Minneapolis, MN: University of Minnesota Press, 2004.

Douglas-Fairhurst, Robert. *The Story of Alice*. Harvard: Harvard University Press, 2015.

Drazin, Charles. 'Anglo-American Collaboration: Korda, Selznick and Goldwyn'. In Paul Cooke (ed.), *World Cinema's 'Dialogues' with Hollywood*, 52–68. London: Palgrave, 2007.

Dürrschmidt, Jörg. *Everyday Lives in the Global City: The Delinking of Locale and Milieu*. London: Routledge, 2001.

Eckersley, Peter. *The Power of the Microphone*. London: Scientific Book Club, 1942.

Eckersley, Roger. *The BBC and All That*. London: Sampson, Low, Marston and Co., 1946.

Faulk, Barry J. *Music Hall and Modernity: The Late-Victorian Discovery of Popular Culture*. Athens, OH: Ohio University Press, 2004.

French, Dawn. *Dear Fatty*. London: Arrow Books, 2009.

Gamson, Joshua. 'The Assembly Line of Greatness: Celebrity in Twentieth-Century America'. In Sean Redmond and Su Holmes (eds), *Stardom and Celebrity: A Reader*, 141–55. Los Angeles: Sage, 2007.

Garber, Megan. 'Call It the Bechdel-Wallace Test', *The Atlantic* (25 August 2015). https://www.theatlantic.com/entertainment/archive/2015/08/call-it-the-bechdel-wallace-test/402259/ (accessed 21 March 2019).

Gardiner, Juliet. *Wartime Britain: 1939-1945*. London: Review, 2004.

Geraghty, Christine. *British Cinema in the Fifties: Gender, Genre and the New Look*. London: Routledge, 2000.

Gibson, Frank A. 'Another Dickens Serial', *The Dickensian* XLVIII (Spring 1951): 79.

Gibson, Frank A. '*Great Expectations* on the Air', *The Dickensian* XLV, part 2 (Spring 1949): 109.

Giddings, Robert and Keith Selby. *The Classic Serial on Television and Radio.* Houndmills, Basingstoke and Hampshire: Palgrave, 2001.
Gielgud, Val. *British Radio Drama: 1922-1956.* London: George Harrup, 1957.
Gielgud, Val. *One Year of Grace: A Fragment of Autobiography.* London: Longmans, 1951.
Gielgud, Val. *Years of the Locust.* London: Nicholson and Watson, 1947.
Gielgud, Val. *Years in a Mirror.* London: The Bodley Head, 1965.
Giles, Judy. *The Parlour and the Suburb: Domestic Identities, Class, Femininities and Modernity.* New York: Berg, 2004.
Gillett, Philip. *The British Working Class in Postwar Film.* Manchester: Manchester University Press, 2003.
Gingold, Hermione. *How to Grow Old Disgracefully.* New York: St. Martin's Press, 1988.
Gingold, Hermione. *My Own Unaided Work.* London: W. Laurie, 1952.
Gingold, Hermione. *Sirens Should Be Seen and Not Heard.* Philadelphia: Lippincott, 1963.
Gingold, Hermione. *The World Is Square.* London: Home and Val Thal Press, 1945.
Gorham, Maurice. *Sound and Fury: Twenty-One Years in the BBC.* London: P. Marshall, 1948.
Grass, Sean. *Charles Dickens's Our Mutual Friend: A Publication History.* London: Routledge, 2016.
Graves, Robert and Alan Hodge. *The Long Week-End: A Social History of Great Britain, 1919-1939.* New York: WW Norton, 1994.
Gray, Frances. *Women and Laughter.* Charlottesville, VA: University Press of VA, 1994.
Hajkowski, Thomas. *The BBC and National Identity in Britain, 1922-1953.* Manchester: Manchester University Press, 2010.
Hand, Richard J. *Listen in Terror: British Horror Radio from the Advent of Broadcasting to the Digital Age.* Manchester: Manchester University Press, 2014.
Heinrich, Anselm. *Entertainment, Propaganda, Education: Regional Theatre in Germany and Britain Between 1918 and 1945.* Hatfield: University of Hertfordshire Press, 2007.
Hendy, David. 'Biography and the Emotions as a Missing Narrative in Media History: A Case Study of Lance Sieveking and the Early BBC', *Media History* 18, no. 3-4 (2012): 361-78.
Hendy, David. 'The Great War and British Broadcasting: Emotional Life in the Creation of the BBC', *New Formations* 82 (2014): 82-99.
Hennessey, Brian. *The Emergence of Broadcasting in Britain.* Lympstone: Southerleigh, 2005.
Hewitt, John. 'The "Nature" and "Art" of Shell Advertising in the Early 1930s', *Journal of Design History* 5, no. 2 (1992): 121-39.
Hickman, Tom. *What Did You Do in the War, Auntie?* London: BBC Books, 1995.

Higgins, Charlotte. *The New Noise: The Extraordinary Birth and Troubled Life of the BBC*. London: Guardian Books, 2015.

Hilmes, Michele. 'Front Line Family: "Women's Culture" Comes to the BBC', *Media, Culture and Society* 29, no. 5 (2007): 5–29.

Hilmes, Michelle. *Radio Voices: American Broadcasting, 1922-1952*. Minneapolis, MN: University of Minnesota Press, 1997.

Hinton, James. *The Mass Observers: A History, 1937-1949*. Oxford: Oxford University Press, 2013.

Hubble, Nick. *Mass Observation and Everyday Life: Culture, History, Theory*. London: Palgrave MacMillan, 2006.

Jean, Yaron. 'Sonic Mindedness and the Great War: Viewing History Through Auditory Lenses'. In Florence Feiereisen and Alexandra Merley Hill (eds), *Germany in the Loud Twentieth Century*, 51–62. Oxford: Oxford University Press, 2012.

Jones, Gareth Stedman. 'The "Cockney" and the Nation, 1780-1988'. In David Feldman and Gareth Stedman Jones (eds), *Metropolis London: Histories and Representations since 1800*, 272–324. London: Routledge, 1989.

Jones, Siriol Hugh. 'The Comic Spirit: In Theatre, Cartoon and Column', *Vogue* (February 1952). Carl Giles Trust Collection, University of Kent British Cartoon Archive. https://archive.cartoons.ac.uk/Record.aspx?src=CalmView.Catalog&id=CG%2f2%2f4%2f1%2f16%2f1%2f5 (accessed 8 April 2019).

Kavanagh, Ted. *Tommy Handley*. London: Hodder and Stoughton, 1949.

Kester, Max and Edwin Collier. *Writing for the BBC: Practical Hints on How to Write Successfully for the Light Entertainment Department of the BBC* with a forward by Eric Maschwitz. London: Sir Isaac Pitman and Sons, Ltd., 1937.

Knox, Collie. *People of Quality*. London: MacDonald and Co, 1947.

Kochberg, Searle. 'Cinema as Institution'. In Jill Nelmes (ed.), *Introduction to Film Studies*, 3rd edn. London: Routledge, 2003.

Kynaston, David. *Austerity Britain, 1945-1951*. London: Bloomsbury, 2007.

Landy, Marcia. *British Genres: Cinema and Society, 1930-1960*. Princeton: Princeton University Press, 1991.

Langhamer, Claire. 'Adultery in Post-War Britain', *History Workshop Journal* 62 (Autumn 2006): 86–115.

Langhamer, Claire. *The English in Love: The Intimate Story of a Revolution*. Oxford: Oxford University Press, 2013.

Langhamer, Claire. 'Feelings, Women and Work in the Long 1950s', *Women's History Review* 26, no. 1 (2017): 77–92.

Langhamer, Claire. 'The Meanings of Home in Postwar Britain', *Journal of Contemporary History* 40, no. 2 (2005): 341–62.

Lawrence, Jon. 'Class, "Affluence", and the Study of Everyday Life in Britain, c. 1930-1964', *Cultural and Social History* 10, no. 2 (2013): 273–99.

Lea, Gordon. *Radio Drama and How to Write It*. London: George Allen and Unwin, 1926.

LeMahieu, D. L. *A Culture for Democracy: Mass Communication and the Cultivated Mind in Britain between the Wars*. Oxford: Oxford University Press, 1988.

Lethbridge, Lucy. Servants: *A Downstairs History of Britain from the Nineteenth-Century to Modern Times*. New York: W.W. Norton, 2013.

Lewis, Cecil. *Broadcasting from Within*. London: George Newnes, 1924.

Light, Allison. *Forever England: Femininity, Literature and Conservatism between the Wars*. London: Routledge, 1991.

Light, Alison. *Mrs. Woolf and the Servants*. London: Penguin, 2007.

Lillie, Beatrice with John Philip and James Brough. *Every Other Inch a Lady*. New York: Doubleday, 1972.

Lockyer, Sharon. 'Dynamics of Social Class Contempt in Contemporary British Television Comedy', *Social Semiotics* 20, no. 2 (April 2010): 121–38.

Longmate, Norman. *How We Lived Then: A History of Everyday Life During the Second World War*. London: Pimlico, 2002.

Maltin, Leonard. *Classic Movie Guide: From the Silent Era to 1965*. New York: Plume, 2005.

Marshall, P. David. *Celebrity and Power: Fame in Contemporary Culture*. Minneapolis, MN: University of Minnesota Press, 2004.

Maschwitz, Eric. *No Chip on My Shoulder*. London: H. Jenkins, 1957.

Matheson, Hilda. *Broadcasting*. London: Thornton, Butterworth Ltd., 1933.

Matthews, Jessie and Muriel Burgess. *Over My Shoulder: An Autobiography*. London: WH Allen, 1974.

Matthews, William. *Cockney Past and Present: A Short History of the Dialect of London*. London: Routledge and Kegan Paul, 1972.

McFarlane, Brian. *An Autobiography of British Cinema: As Told By the Filmmakers and Actors Who Made It*. London: Methuen, 1997.

McFarlane, Brian. *Novel to Film: An Introduction to the Theory of Adaptation*. Oxford: Clarendon Press, 1996.

McKibbin, Ross. *Classes and Cultures: England, 1918-1951*. Oxford: Oxford University Press, 2000.

Medhurst, Andy. 'Every Wart and Pustule: Gilbert Harding and Television Stardom'. In Edward Buscombe (ed.), *British Television: A Reader*, 248–64. Oxford: Oxford University Press, 2001.

Medhurst, Andy. *A National Joke: Popular Comedy and English Identities*. London: Routledge, 2007.

Medhurst, Andy. 'Negotiating the Gnome Zone: Versions of Suburbia in British Popular Culture'. In *Visions of Suburbia*, 240–67. London: Routledge, 1997.

Mills, Brett. *Television Sitcom*. London: BFI, 2005.

Mills, Brett. *TV Genres: The Sitcom*. Edinburgh: Edinburgh University Press, 2009.

Moiseiwitsch, Maurice. *Moiseiwitsch: Biography of a Concert Pianist*. London: Frederick Muller, 1965.

Moore, James Ross. *Andre Charlot: The Genius of Musical Revue*. Jefferson, NC: McFarland and Co., 2005.

Moran, Joe. *Armchair Nation: An Intimate History of Britain in Front of the TV*. London: Profile, 2014.

Morgan, Kenneth O. *The People's Peace: British History since 1945*, 2nd edn. Oxford: Oxford University Press, 1999.

Mortimore, Roger and Andrew Blick, eds. *Butler's British Political Facts*. London: Palgrave, 2018.

Mosley, Sydney A. *Broadcasting in Our Time*. London: Rich and Cowan, Ltd., 1935.

Mundy, John and Glyn White. *Laughing Matters: Understanding Film, Television and Radio Comedy*. Manchester: Manchester University Press, 2012.

Murphy, Kate. *Behind the Wireless: A History of Early Women at the BBC*. London: Palgrave Macmillan, 2016.

Murphy, Robert. *Realism and Tinsel: Cinema and Society in Britain, 1939-1949*. London: Routledge, 2016.

Neale, Steve and Frank Krutnik. *Popular Film and Television Comedy*. London: Routledge, 1990.

Nicholas, Siân. *The Echo of War: Home Front Propaganda and the Wartime BBC, 1939-45*. Manchester: Manchester University Press, 1996.

Nicholas, Siân. 'The People's Radio: The BBC and Its Audience, 1939-1945'. In Nick Hayes and Jeff Hill *'Millions like Us'?: British Culture and the Second World War*, 62–92. Liverpool: Liverpool University Press, 1999.

North, Julian. 'Conservative Austen, Radical Austen: *Sense and Sensibility*, from Text to Screen'. In Deborah Cartmell and Imelda Whelehan (eds), *Adaptations: From Text to Screen, Screen to Text*, 38–50. London: Routledge, 1999.

O'Connell, Sean. *The Car and British Society: Class, Gender and Motoring, 1896-1939*. Manchester: Manchester University Press, 1998.

Pear, T. H. *Voice and Personality*. London: Chapman and Hall, 1931.

Pegg, Mark. *Broadcasting and Society, 1918-1939*. London: Croom Helm, 1983.

Priestley, J. B. *English Humour*. New York: Stein and Day, 1976.

Priestley, J. B. *English Journey*. London: William Heinemann, 1934.

Priestley, J. B. *Postscripts*. London: W. Heinemann, 1940.

Purcell, Jennifer. '"Behind the Blessed Shelter of the Microphone": Managing Celebrity and Career on the Early BBC—Mabel Constanduros, 1925–1957', *Women's History Review* 24, no. 3 (2015): 372–88.

Purcell, Jennifer. *Beyond Home: Housewives and the Nation, Private and Public Identities 1939-1949*. DPhil Dissertation, University of Sussex, 2008.

Purcell, Jennifer. *Domestic Soldiers: Six Women's Lives in Wartime*. London: Constable and Robinson, 2010.

Purcell, Jennifer. '"Enthusiasm, Experiment and Gallantry in Action": Developing Light Entertainment on the Fledgling BBC, 1922–1932', *Cultural and Social History* 15, no. 3 (2018): 415–32.

Radio Times Fiftieth Anniversary Souvenir: 1923-1973. London: BBC, 1973.

Richards, Jeffrey. *Film and British National Identity: From Dickens to Dad's Army*. Manchester: Manchester University Press, 1997.

Roberts, Elizabeth. *A Woman's Place: An Oral History of Working-Class Women 1890-1940*. Oxford: Blackwell, 1995.

Rodger, Ian. *Radio Drama*. London: Macmillan, 1982.

Rose, Sonya. *Which People's War? National Identity and Citizenship in Wartime Britain, 1939-1945*. Oxford: Oxford University Press, 2003.

Ross, Ellen. *Slum Travelers: Ladies and London Poverty, 1860-1920*. Berkeley: University of California Press, 2007.

Samuel, Raphael. 'The Voice of Britain'. In Alison Light (ed.), *Island Stories: Unravelling Britain*, 172–93. London: Verso, 1999.

Scannell, Paddy. *The State and Society*. Milton Keynes: Open University Press, 1984.

Scannell, Paddy and David Cardiff. *A Social History of British Broadcasting, vol. 1: Serving the Nation, 1922-1939*. Oxford: Basil Blackwell, 1991.

Scott-Jeffs, Carolyn. 'Voice, Personality and Grandma: Mabel Constanduros and the Buggins Family', *Comedy Studies* 7, no. 2 (2016): 124–36.

Seddon, Jill. 'Mentioned, But Denied Significance: Women Designers and the Professionalization of Design in Britain, c. 1920-1951', *Gender and Society* 12, no. 2 (July 2000): 426–47.

Silvey, Robert. *Who's Listening?* London: George Allen & Unwin, 1974.

Skoog, Kristin. '"They're 'Doped' by that Dale Diary": Women's Serial Drama, the BBC and British Post-War Change'. In Helen Thornham and Elke Weissmann (eds), *Renewing Feminisms: Radical Narratives, Fantasies and Futures in Media Studies*, 124–39. London: IB Tauris, 2013.

Smart, Carol. 'Good Wives and Moral Lives: Marriage and Divorce, 1937-1951'. In Christine Gledhill and Gillian Swanson (eds), *Nationalising Femininity: Culture, Sexuality and British Cinema in the Second World War*, 91–105. Manchester: Manchester University Press, 1996.

Snagge, John and Michael Barsley. *Those Vintage Years of Radio*. London: Pitman, 1972.

Spicer, Andrew. *Sydney Box*. Manchester: Manchester University Press, 2006.

Spicer, Andrew. *Typical Men: Representations of Masculinity in Popular British Culture*. London: IB Taurus, 2003.

Spohrer, Jennifer. 'Ruling the Airwaves: Radio Luxembourg and the Origins of European National Broadcasting, 1929-1950'. PhD dissertation, Columbia University, 2008.

Strachey, Ray. *Careers and Openings for Women: A Survey of Women's Employment and a Guide for Those Seeking Work*. London: Faber and Faber, 1934.

Szreter, Simon and Kate Fisher. *Sex before the Sexual Revolution: Intimate Life in England, 1918-1963*. Cambridge: Cambridge University Press, 2010.

Taylor, Julia. *From Sound to Print in Pre-War Britain: The Cultural and Commercial Interdependence between Broadcasters and Broadcasting Magazines in the 1930s*. PhD Dissertation, Bournemouth, 2013.

Thiele, Beverly. 'Vanishing Acts in Social and Political thought: Tricks of the Trade'. In Linda McDowell and Rosemary Pringle (eds), *Defining Women: Social Institutions and Gender Divisions*, 26–35. London: Polity Press, 1992.

Tsang, Cheryl. *Microsoft First Generation: The Success Secrets of the Visionaries Who Launched a Technology Empire*. New York: Wiley, 2000.

Wagg, Stephen. '"At Ease, Corporal": Social Class and the Situation Comedy in British Television, from the 1950s to the 1990s'. In Stephen Wagg (ed.), *Because I Tell a Joke or Two: Comedy, Politics and Social Difference*, 1–31. London: Routledge, 1998.

Watt, John. *Radio Variety*. London: JM Dent and Sons, 1939.

Weber, Brenda R. 'Always Lonely: Celebrity, Motherhood, and the Dilemma of Destiny', *PMLA* 126, no. 4 (2011): 1110–17.

Whelehan, Imelda. 'Adaptations: Some Contemporary Dilemmas'. In Deborah Cartmell and Imelda Whelehan (eds), *Adaptations: From Text to Screen, Screen to Text*, 3–19. London: Routledge, 1999.

Wickham, Phil. 'The Royle Family', BFI Screenonline. http://www.screenonline.org.uk/tv/id/458640/index.html (accessed 29 May 2019).

Wilson, Nicola. *Home in British Working-Class Fiction*. Farnham: Ashgate, 2015.

Winter, Jay. *Sites of Memory, Sites of Mourning: The Great War in European Cultural History*. Cambridge: Cambridge University Press, 2009.

Wythenshawe, Lord Simon of. *The BBC from Within*. London: Victor Gollancz, 1953.

Young, Filson. *Shall I Listen?* London: Constable, 1933.

Index

29 Acacia Avenue   13, 134–8, 151
2LO   15–17, 26, 29, 31, 50–1, 156

abdication crisis   61
Acacia Avenue   13, 131–4, 137, 151
Adolf in Blunderland   92
adultery   58, 61, 134–5
Agg, Howard   12, 95, 119–20, 126, 129, 151, 154, 156–9, 161
Aherne, Caroline   6, 41
Alexandra Palace   52, 93
Algiers   145
Alhambra, The   26, 81
amateurs   144, 166
   performers   9–10, 22, 27–9, 83, 123, 126
   and theatre   1, 83, 119
America   3–5, 10, 25, 32, 111, 118, 139, 163–4, 166
Andrews, Maggie   3, 30, 52, 104, 168
Annakin, Ken   145
announcers (BBC)   52, 55
Archer, William   39
Archers, The   1, 163
artists, see performers
Askey, Arthur   55, 81, 92
As the World Goes By   96
Astoria Odeon   136
Attenborough, Richard   157–8
At the Billet Doux   91
audience   49, 52, 55–7, 74, 87, 102–6, 111, 115, 134–5, 152–4, 166
   class   11, 36, 41–5, 47–8, 97, 104–6, 111, 113, 135, 137, 145, 149, 152, 163
   expectations   13, 63
   identification   41–2, 44, 52, 104–5, 113–14, 137, 141, 145–7
   responses   10, 36–8, 41–2, 98, 136, 145, 149
auditory slapstick, see linguistic slapstick

aural imagination, see theatre of the mind
Austen, Jane   5, 48
austerity   144
automobile ownership   148

Bailey, Michael   30
Bailey, Peter   39–41
Band Waggon   92–4
Banville, Scott   32
Barnes, George   97, 103
Barreca, Regina   5–6
Baxter, Clive   114
Baym, Nancy   167
BBC Theatre   74
BBC Yearbook   125
Bechdel-Wallace Test   168
Bentley, Dick   166, 168
Berkeley, Reginald   8, 16
Birkinshaw, D. J.   163
Black, George   73–4
Black, Peter   58, 157
Bleak House   120, 157
Bloom, Ursula   129
Blossom   30–2
Blunt, Bruce   96
Blythe, John   142
Bognor Regis   116, 131
Bott, Elizabeth   148
Box, Muriel   13, 131, 134–5, 138–9, 144, 150
Box, Sydney   13, 131, 134–5, 138–9, 142, 144, 150
Bray, Barbara   127, 160
Bread   33
Brewer, Charles   128
Bridgeman, Dorothy   103
Bridson, D. G.   161
Brief Encounter   135
Briggs, Asa   2, 17, 60, 72
Brighton quickie   58
Bristol   83, 89–91, 94

Index

Britain
  interwar 7, 10, 124–5
  post-war 1, 13, 124, 131, 135, 138, 140–9, 167
    and housing 145–8
    and politics 143–4
British Broadcasting Company 8, 15–18, 24, 27
  London Radio Repertory Company 16, 26
British Broadcasting Corporation (BBC) 1, 4, 8–9, 17
  Alexandra Palace 52, 93
  amateurs 9–10, 27–9, 126, 166
  Americanization 72–4, 118, 163–4, 166
  announcers 52, 55
  artist pay 24–5
  audience demand 72, 111, 152–4
  audience statistics 36, 95–6, 103, 111, 152–3, 162–3
  auditions 22–3, 26–7
  BBC Drama Repertory Company 90
  BBC Orchestra 90
  BBC Written Archives (BBC WAC) 2, 6, 169
  Bristol 89–91, 94
  Broadcasting House 8, 17, 52, 74, 77, 91, 128
  broadcast tours 49–51, 64
  celebrity 9–11, 28, 49, 52–7, 60, 68–71, 83
  censorship 16
    and vulgar or "blue" content 103
  centralisation 51
  class 12, 41–4, 47–8, 68, 97, 104–6, 109–16, 118, 150, 152, 163, 168
  comedy 39, 42, 51, 87, 91, 99–107, 109–10, 167–8
  commercial broadcasting 24, 71–3, 75, 79, 153, 163–5
  competition 72–3, 153
  copyright 75–80, 126
  divorce 57–62, 69, 154
  domestication of 3–4, 30, 55, 166, 168
  Drama and Features 90–1, 118–19
  Drama department 89–90, 97, 154, 159

Drama Script Readers 153–5
Empire Service 119
Evesham 89
experimentation 10, 16–18, 20–2, 27–8, 33, 166
First BBC Repertory Company 9
Forces Programme *or* General Forces Programme (GFP) 104, 120, 151
gender 3, 12, 30, 54, 101, 114, 119–28, 168–9
history of 3, 6–9, 15–22, 27, 166–9
Home Broadcasting Committees 93
Home Service 89, 120, 151–3, 156, 160, 162, 165
Huggetts 13, 150–1
jokes about 30, 47, 91
licenses 18, 162
light entertainment 2–13, 16, 21, 27–8, 51–2, 71–4, 81, 92, 111, 129, 151, 156, 165–8
Light Programme 151–2, 154, 161, 165
Listener Research 36, 98, 111, 153
microphone technique 10, 23, 26–30, 32–5, 47–8, 98, 166
morality 57–62, 69, 85–6
national identity 11, 112–13, 157
nostalgia programmes 13, 73, 81, 161
and ordinariness 109–14, 117–18, 129, 137, 146, 167
Overseas Service or North American Service 118
paternalism 32
performers 9, 24, 50–60, 74–5, 91–4
post-war programming 151–4, 156, 165, 167
productions department 73
  revue and vaudeville section 51, 73
Programme Board 19–21, 24–5, 27, 36
programming 3, 7, 10, 19–21, 23–5, 52, 74, 91–5, 97, 109, 111, 118–20, 151–4, 156
propaganda 12, 92, 99–102, 104, 106–7, 117, 119
public service 4
pyramid of culture 152, 165

recruitment of performers   22–7, 29, 74, 125
regional scheme   49, 51, 59
Reith, (Sir) John   9, 17–19, 21, 32, 52, 58–60, 72, 90, 165
Reithian principles   47, 49, 57, 152–3, 165, 168
religious broadcasting   90
repertory companies   9
Savoy Hill   15, 17–18, 22, 27
scheduling   10, 74–5, 84, 96–7
scriptwriters   119–20, 155
Second World War   11–13, 89–99, 117–20, 129, 151, 157
serialization   10, 74–5, 84, 156–7, 166
situation comedy   75, 80, 87, 121, 168
staffers   3, 9, 13, 17–18, 24–5, 27, 30, 52–3, 57, 59–60, 71, 76–80, 89–91, 119–20, 127–9, 154–5, 158, 160, 169
stations   19, 26, 50–1
  Aberdeen (2BD)   19, 26, 50
  Belfast (2BE)   19, 50
  Birmingham (5IT)   19, 26, 50–1
  Bournemouth (6BM)   19, 50
  Cardiff (5WA)   19, 50–1
  Daventry (5XX)   19, 31, 50–1
  Experimental (5GB)   51
  Glasgow (5SC)   19, 31, 50, 156
  Liverpool (6LV)   50–1
  London (2LO)   15–17, 19, 26, 29, 31, 50–1, 156
  Manchester (2ZY)   19, 51
  Newcastle (5NO)   19, 26, 50
  Nottingham (5NG)   51
  Plymouth (5PY)   50–1
  Sheffield (6SL)   19
Talks department   97
Third Programme   151–2, 161
tripartite system   152
variety   10, 21, 29, 50, 60, 81–2, 91, 93–5, 98, 103
Variety department   2, 10–11, 25, 27–8, 52, 73–80, 89–91, 97, 125, 153–5
Variety Repertory Company (VRC)   90–1, 94
Variety Script Section   153

wartime programming   91–7, 116–20, 151, 157
women
  and careers   3, 11, 169
  and humour   5–7, 10
  invisibility of   3, 168–9
  performers   3, 7, 13
  staffers   3, 13, 17, 71, 129, 169
  writers   3, 6–7, 13, 119, 124, 126–7, 155–60
Wood Norton Hall   90
British film industry   135–6
British National Film Company   78
Britishness   11, 110, 112–13, 138–48, 157
British Post Office   17, 30
Broadcasting House   8, 17, 52, 74, 77, 91, 128
Brooklands   110, 114, 132
Brown, Arthur   89–90
Bugginses   1–2, 4, 10, 12, 16, 31–45, 47–8, 50, 52, 74, 79, 81, 83–7, 92, 94–107, 109–11, 123–4, 145–6, 151, 161–2, 166–8
Burrows, Arthur   20–1
Bush-Bailey, Gilli   3, 48, 64, 81, 121–2, 168
Bushnell, Ernie   118
Butlins   139–40
Butt, Clara   24
Butterflies   6, 33

Café Collette   74
Calling all Women   97
Cannon, Esma   139
Cardiff, David   27, 30, 55, 74
Carpendale, Adm. C. D.   58
Carroll, Lewis   7
celebrity
  divorce   57–62, 69
  film   52, 54–5, 61–2, 149
  photography   52–4
  radio   9–11, 28–9, 38, 49, 52–7, 63–5, 68, 71, 81, 83, 161, 169
  scandal   60–2
  television   54–5
censorship   16
  and vulgar or "blue" content   103
Central School for Speech and Drama (CSSD)   8

Chaplin, Charlie 91
Charity Organisation Society 56
Charlot, Andre 25-6
Charlot's Hour 25
Children's Hour 15, 50, 81, 83, 90, 92, 128, 153, 161
Choice, The 123
Churchill, Sir Winston 144
cinema, *see* film
Clapham, Norman, *see* John Henry
Clapham and Dwyer 29
Clark, Petula 13, 142, 150
class 12, 19, 38-48, 56, 68, 97, 111-16, 118, 122, 124, 132, 134, 136-8, 140, 146-50, 152, 168
  accent 37-8, 134, 148-9
  audience 11, 36, 41-4, 104-6, 113, 135, 137, 149, 152, 163
  representation of 7, 10, 12, 31, 33, 36-48, 109-10, 114
  Cock, Gerald 72-3
Cockney 15, 40-1, 45, 134, 150
  representation of 7, 10, 31-2, 37-9, 43, 45, 81, 95, 123
Cockney Past and Present 45
Cold Comfort Farm 82
Coliseum, The 26, 81
Colley, Mrs. Ronnie 119
Collier, Frederick
Collins, Norman 154
Columbia Studios 76, 135-6
comedy 7, 12, 87, 91, 98-104, 109-10, 145, 166-9
  female perspective 6, 43, 124, 129, 168-9
  radio 10, 30-2, 39, 42-3, 51, 87
Coming Up For Air (Orwell) 5
communality 140-1, 144
companion novels 83-7, 115, 120
Conrad, Joseph 156
Constanduros, Athanasius 8, 65-9, 121-2
Constanduros, Denis 12, 45-6, 63, 69, 95, 111, 116-17, 121-2, 126, 129, 131-3 (image 133), 138-9, 149-51, 161
Constanduros, Hilda 64, 69

Constanduros, Mabel 4, 23, 27, 60, 63, 92, 94, 114, 155, 166-8 (images 53, 65, 133)
and adaptations 1, 13, 127, 134-5, 137, 150-1, 153-61
audience response 36-8, 42, 44, 102, 104, 157-9
BBC 66-7, 81
  audition 8, 15-16
  broadcast tours 49-51, 64
  contract negotiations 119-20, 126-7
  copyright 79-80, 126-7
  correspondence 2, 12, 89, 94, 102-3, 124-9, 139, 149, 155
  "star" status 9, 49
Bugginses 1-2, 4, 10, 12, 16, 31-45, 47-8, 50, 52, 74, 79, 81, 83-7, 92, 94-107, 109-11, 123-4, 145-6, 151, 161-2, 166-8
career management 11-13, 63, 68, 71, 81-7, 89, 94, 109-10, 124-9, 131, 149-60, 165, 169
celebrity 9-11, 49, 52-7, 63-71, 81, 83, 149, 161, 169
children's books 2, 83
comedy 3, 5, 10, 12, 30-3, 39, 51, 80, 87, 99-107, 109-10, 120-1, 124, 145-6, 166-8
death 1, 161
early life 7-9
Earthy Mangold 164
female perspective 6, 43, 114-15, 124, 129
film 1, 11, 13, 131, 134-5, 138-9, 149, 156
Grandma Buggins 1, 33, 40, 42, 85-7, 92, 98-107, 123-4, 145, 162
marriage 8, 65-9, 101-2, 121-2
microphone technique 10, 32-5, 47-8, 98, 166
motherhood 64-5, 69, 128-9, 169
music hall 11, 22, 28, 50, 81-2
musical scores 83
novels 2, 11, 83-7, 111, 115, 120, 151
Pix 63, 132, 149
Samuel French Acting Editions 2, 31, 82, 94-5, 121

Second World War   89–90, 94–107, 116–20, 129
servants   46–7
situation comedy   6, 32–3, 80, 87, 120–1, 166–8
Smith, Bina (housekeeper)   57, 64, 98
stage/theatre   11, 82, 119
Sussex, H. M. (pseudonym)   158–9
Sutton Amateur Dramatics Club (SADC)   8, 66–8, 123
Woman's Hour   13, 161–2
works
   29 Acacia Avenue   13, 134–8, 151
   Acacia Avenue   13, 131–4, 137, 151
   Aunt Maria's Wireless   47
   Baby and the Silkworm   86
   Browns of Brixton, The   150
   Bugginses, The   43–4, 83–6
   Bugginses at the Zoo, The   33
   Bugginses Go Gay, The   104–6
   Bugginses Make a Christmas Pudding, The   36–9
   Buggins's Day Out, The   33
   Come Out to Play   83
   Cruising Family Robinson   116, 131
   Down Mangel Street   86–7, 111, 167
   English Family Robinson (EFR)   4–5, 12–13, 110–18, 122, 131, 137, 146, 166–7
   family group, The   82, 86
   Father Sweeps the Chimney   33–5
   Feathers in the Wind   155
   Grandma   87
   Holiday Camp   13, 138–43, 146–7, 149
   Horti-Mania   151
   Lido Ladd   151
   Mr. and Mrs. Sparkes   121–2, 128, 167
   Mrs. Buggins Calls   86
   Mrs. Buggins Chooses a Hat   31
   Mrs. Smythe-Brown Buys a Book   31, 109
   A Nice Fire in the Drawing Room: A Story about Ordinary People (1939)   115
   Ogboddy's Outing   103
   One Saturday Afternoon   110–11
   On the Run   120
   Portugal Lady   164
   Red Alert at the Robinson's   117–18
   Santa Claus at the Bugginses   43
   Saving Her Face   43
   Shreds and Patches (autobiography)   2, 7–8, 23, 52, 56–7, 63–9, 81–2, 98, 125, 128–9
   Smalls at Home, The   150–1, 154–5
   Sweep and the Daffodil, The   83
   Wives and Daughters (Gaskell)   1, 160
Constanduros, Michael   57, 64, 66, 68, 81, 89, 128
Constanduros, Norah   69
Constanduros, Stephanos   69
Constanduros, Tony   64
Conversation in the Train   109, 126
Coogan, Alma   168
Cook, Eliza   46
cookery talks   95–104
copyright   75–80, 126–7
Count of Monte Cristo, The   156
Court, Hazel   139, 141
Coyne, Joseph   23
critics   39, 59, 72
Crook, Tim   32, 35, 54
cross-media adaptations   11, 84, 131–2, 137, 151
cross-talk routine   10, 26, 29, 167
cultural tourism   43
Curtain Up!   154

Daily Graphic   139
Daily Herald, The   94
Daily Mail, The   29, 72, 128
David Copperfield   161
Davies, Margaret Llewellyn   110
Dawson, Basil   5
Deane, Tessa   82
De Casalis, Jeanne   74, 84, 96, 169
Decision   109, 111
Delap, Lucy   41, 46
demobilisation   142–3
Denham, Maurice   91–2
Derby Day   82
Designed for Women   164

dialect humour   32, 36-8, 81
Diary of a Nobody   69, 134
Dibbs, Martin   2, 32, 52, 79, 93-4, 153-5, 165
Dickens, Charles   7, 45, 84, 120, 155-8
divorce   57-62, 69, 134-6, 154
Dixon, Sophie   21
domesticity   5, 112, 115, 122-3, 129, 166, 168
Dors, Diana   142
Douglas, Susan   35
Down Mangel Street   86-7, 111, 167
Doyle, Sir Arthur Conan   20
Drama department (BBC)   89-90, 97, 154, 159
Draper, Ruth   24
Drinkwater, J. D.   58
Dunkirk   94
Dweller in the Darkness (Reginald Berkeley)   16
Dyrenforth, James   92

Eckersley, Peter   18, 21, 30, 51, 59-60
Eckersley, Roger   18, 21, 25, 39
Edward VIII   61
Edwards, Jimmy   166, 168
Elizabeth II   143, 162, 165
emigration   143-5
emotional communities   2
emotional labour   128
English Family Robinson (EFR)   4-5, 12-13, 110-18, 122, 131, 137, 146, 166-7
Englishness, *see* Britishness
entertainers, *see* performers
Ever Decreasing Circles   121
everyday, the   4-5, 110, 112, 117, 129, 167
Evesham   89, 91
experimentation   10, 16-18, 20-2, 27-8, 33, 36-7, 166

Facts of Love, The   136
family   4, 136
    alternative   141, 143
    and "ordinary"   12-13, 110-14, 117-18, 129, 131, 138, 142, 146, 148, 167

and radio   10-11, 30, 32-3, 42-3, 71, 83-4, 110-18, 129, 150, 162, 166-8
fan magazines, *see* magazines, fan
fans   56-7
Farino, Julian   158
Father Knows Best   150
Faulk, Barry J.   41
Fawlty Towers   6
Feed the Brute   95
female visitors   44-5
femininity   4, 63, 67-8, 101-2, 115, 122-4, 126, 131, 168-9
    performance of   3, 9, 63-4, 68-9, 102, 122-4, 128-9, 169
    and the popular   4, 129
    and sexuality   132, 138, 140, 142
feminism   122, 169
Fielden, Lionel   97
fifth dimension   35
film   1, 5, 11-13, 84, 131, 134-49
    adaptations   131, 134, 137, 158
    America   136, 138-9
    and critics   135-6, 138
    and morality   135-7, 142
    and national identity   138-48
First BBC Repertory Company   9
First Royal Scots Fusiliers Military Band   156
First World War or World War I   9, 62, 69, 94, 121
Fisher, Kate   137
Flotsam and Jetsam   24
Flowers Are Not for You to Pick, The (Tyrone Guthrie)   111
Fogerty, Elsie   8, 68
For Amusement Only   91
Forces programme   120, 151
Ford   148
fourth wall   10
Fox's Mask, The (Denis Constanduros)   111
Frankau, Ronald   74
Frederick Muller   84
French, Dawn   6
French Leave (Reginald Berkeley)   8, 16, 66
Front Line Family (FLF)   118-20, 167
Fuller, Walter   73
Future of Sound Broadcasting, The   165

Gainsborough Pictures   138–9
Garrick Theatre   24
Gaskell, Elizabeth   1, 156, 160
Gaumont Theatre   149
gender   3, 9, 11–12, 30, 54, 101–2, 114, 119–28, 136, 138, 140, 168–9
General Electric Company   17
General Theatres Corporation (GTC)   73
generational conflict   44, 133–4
George VI   23
Gert and Daisy (Elsie and Doris Waters)   29, 51, 95, 97–8, 104, 169
Giddings, Robert   24, 156–7
Gielgud, Val   1, 4–6, 13, 21–2, 24, 26, 28–9, 73, 89–90, 109–10, 112, 116, 120, 128, 149, 154–9, 163–5
Gilbert, Elizabeth   114
Giles, Carl   33
Gillett, Phillip   147–8
Gilliam, Laurence   119
Gilmore, Doris   75
Gingold, Hermione   62–3, 169
Glums, The   167–8
Goering, Hermann   92
Goldbergs, The   10, 32
Good Time Girl   142
Goolden, Richard   75, 121, 150, 154–5
Goon Show, The   163
Gorham, Maurice   17, 59
Gourley, Ronald   50
Gower, Roland   94
Grandma Buggins   1, 33, 40, 42, 85–7, 92, 98–107, 123–4, 145, 162
Grant, Elspeth   139
Grass, Sean   158
Graves, Robert   20, 61
Gray, Francis   6
Great Expectations   157
Greenwood, Arthur   93
Gregg, Hubert   132, 143
Grisewood, Freddie   96–7
Grossmith, George Jr.   23, 25
Grove Family, The   1, 33, 145–6
Guthrie, Tyrone   16, 111

Hale, Sonny   61–2, 91
Haley, Sir William   103, 152, 165
Hamilton, Dorothy   132
Hammond, Peter   139, 141, 158
Hancock, Tony   166
Handley, Tommy   1, 4, 29, 56, 91, 95, 161
Hanley, Jimmy   134, 138, 140, 142
Hard Cash   155
Harding, E. A.   155–7, 159, 163
Hardy, Andy   138
Harker, Gordon   82, 132, (image 133), 134
Harrison, Kathleen   13, 139, 141, 150
Hart, Miranda   6
Hawthorne, Nathaniel   48
Haye, Helen   8
Heath, Ambrose   96–7
Heath, Neville   140
Hendy, David   2, 19
Henry, John (Norman Clapham)   10, 29–32, 47, 50, 60–1, 80, 166
Henry, Leonard   91
Herbert, A. P.   58, 82
Here Come the Huggetts   141–2, 146–7, 150
Hervey, Grizelda   128
Higgins, Charlotte   18
Hillyard, Pat   154–5
Himmler, Heinrich   92
hire-purchase   148, 163
Hitler, Adolf   6, 91, 102
Hodge, Alan   20, 61
Hoffe, Monckton   128
Hogan, Michael   16, 34, 38, 44, 52, 82–4, 86, 149
Holiday Camp   13, 138–43, 146–7, 149
Holloway, Stanley   82
Hollywood   16, 86, 139, 149
Holy Deadlock   58
Home Guard   117
Hood, Miki   132
Horridge, Gladys   60–1
housewives   96, 98, 104, 122–3
housing   83, 141, 145–8
Howard, Leslie   8
Howard, Sydney   82
Huggetts   13, 138–51, 167
Huggetts Abroad   144–5
Humorist   39
Hurlstone, William   16
Hylton, Jane   141

imagination, *see* "theatre of the mind"
In Town Tonight 74
intellectual property 127, 169
Intimate Theatre 151
It's That Man Again (ITMA) 29, 56, 91, 93, 95
ITV 162
Ivy Restaurant 128

Jacob, Sir Ian 162
Jean, Yaron 19
Jefferies, Stanton 17
Jeffrey, R. E. 26, 28, 156
Jenkins, Megs 114
Johnson, Celia 135
Johnson, Mira B. 169
Johnson, Phillip 120
Johnston, Sue 6
Jones, Emrys 140
Joseph, Michael 62

Kennedy, Daisy 57–60
Kentucky Minstrels, The 73
Kester, Max 76–80, 92, 103
Kilpatrick, Francis 169
Kinematograph Weekly 136
Kitchen Front (KF) 12, 81, 95–104
knowingness 30, 39–41, 44, 47–8
Knox, Collie 1–2, 64, 66, 83, 128
Kossoff, David 129, 150, 154
Kynaston, David 143

Lady Precious Stream 82
Lambeth 7, 45
Lancashire Daily Post 42
Lane, Carla 6, 169
Langhamer, Claire 124, 141
Last, Nella 97
Laughing Mirror, The 161
Law of Property Act (1925) 68
Lawrence, Jon 148–9
Laye, Evelyn 61–2
Lea, Gordon 35
Lefeaux, Charles 127, 155, 159–60
legitimate theatre 11, 82
Lehmann, Carla 134
LeMathieu, D. L. 44, 72
Lewis, Cecil 17, 33, 58–9
Life with the Lyons 167

Light, Alison 110, 113, 122
light entertainment 2–13, 16, 21, 27–8, 51–2, 71–4, 81, 92, 111, 129, 151, 156, 165–8
Lillie, Beatrice 61–2
linguistic slapstick 30, 35
Little Englandism 134, 144
Little Man 75–7
Liverbirds, The 6
Lloyd's Dramatic Society 8, 66
London 37–8, 42, 44–5, 57, 68, 82–7, 112, 128, 146, 148
London Radio Repertory Company 15, 26
Lord Jim 156

McDermott, Hugh 144
McFlannels, The 167
McKay, Iver 7
McKibbin, Ross 22
McLaren, Moray 118
magazines 39, 59
 amateur wireless 19, 24, 54
 fan 11, 52–4
 women's 19
Magnet House 17
Maguire, Eddie 150–1
Mais, S. P. B. 96
malapropisms 47–8, 145
Manning, Olivia 160
Marconi Company 16–17
Marconi House 17, 22
marriage 8, 65–9, 101–2, 121–2, 124, 132, 134, 136–7, 140, 142–3
marriage bar 17, 124
Ma's Bit o' Brass 94
Maschwitz, Eric 18, 21–2, 24–5, 27–8, 60, 62, 73–4, 76, 80, 125
masculinity 126, 168
Mass-Observation 96–7, 110, 146
Matheson, Hilda 25–6, 28
Matrimonial Causes acts 58
Matthews, Jessie 61–2, 91
Matthews, William 45
Maugham, Somerset 120, 154–6
Mayhew, Henry 45
Medhurst, Andy 5
Mediterranean Merry Go Round 152
Meet Mr. Penny 78

Meet the Huggetts   150–1, 167
Melville, Alan   118–19
microphone technique   10, 23, 26–30, 32–5, 47–8, 98, 166
Microsoft Corporation   18
middle classes   4–5, 19, 36, 39, 41–8, 56, 68, 83, 97, 104–6, 109–16, 120, 122–3, 134–8, 140, 146–50
  representation of   31, 109–10, 114, 118, 123
middlebrow   47–8
Mid-Morning Story   151
Millais, Helena ("Our Lizzie")   11, 23, 28–9, 32, 50, 60, 80–1, 87, 169
Mills, Brett   32, 42, 54
Milton, John   16
Ministry of Food (MoF)   12, 95–101, 105–6
Ministry of Information (MoI)   91
Mitchison, Naomi   94
modernisation   147
Moiseiwitsch, Benno   58
Moiseiwitsch, Maurice   76–80, 84
Monday Night at Seven   75, 80
monologue   10, 15, 28, 30, 32–3, 42, 80, 82, 84, 109
morality   57–62, 69, 85–6, 134–6, 142
Morning Story   161
Moseley, Sydney   59, 74
motherhood   64–5, 99, 128–9, 169
mother-in-laws   33
Mrs. Dale's Diary   1, 4–5, 110, 119, 162–3
Mrs. Feather   79, 84
Mrs. Miniver   110, 115–16
Much Binding in the Marsh   152
Muir, Frank   166–7
Mundy, John   32, 35
Munich Crisis   90, 115–16
Murdoch, Richard   92
Murgatroyd, Joe   31
Murphy, Kate   2, 17–18, 71, 169
Murphy, Robert   140
Music Hall   73
music hall   11, 24–5, 29, 30, 60, 80–2, 166–7

Nash, Paul   111
national identity   11, 110, 112–13, 138–48, 157

National Savings Campaign   100
NBC (America)   111
Nicholas, Sîan   95
Nichols, Dandy   6, 142
Norden, Denis   166–7
nostalgia   13, 36, 57, 73, 81, 161
novel adaptation   1, 13, 127, 153–61
Novello, Ivor   61

One Man's Family   111, 166
Orde, Beryl   74
ordinariness   12–13, 52, 55, 57, 69, 75, 109–14, 117–18, 129, 131, 137–8, 142, 145–8, 167
Orwell, George   5, 147
Oscar, Henry   16
O'Shea, Tessie   169
Our Lizzie, *see* Helena Millais
Our Mutual Friend   157–9
Owen, Yvonne   132, 139

Painted Veil, The (Somerset Maugham)   156
Palmer, Rex   21
Panting, Phyllis   15
paternalism   32, 46
Peach, L. Du Garde   24
Pear, T. H.   20, 36–40, 45
Pearce, Ashton   16
Peckham   7, 112
Pedrick, Gale   154–5
People's War, the   12, 94–107, 117–18
performers   3, 7, 9, 24, 39, 53–60, 74–5, 91–4
Plums, The   80, 111, 167–8
Pooter, Mr.   69, 134
popular entertainment, *see* light entertainment
popular psychology   9
Popular Wireless and Wireless Review   19, 23
Popular Wireless Weekly   19, 24
Portman, Eric   150
Postscripts   144
Potter, Gillie   74, 90
Price, Dennis   140
Price, Nancy   82
Priestley, J. B.   5, 94, 112–13, 144
Prince of Wales Theatre, The   25

Prisoner of Zenda, The 156-7
professionalism 3, 67, 124-7, 155, 169
propaganda 12, 92, 99-102, 104, 106-7
Pryde, Helen 167, 169
pseudoinclusion 125
psychologising age 19-20
public service 80
Pughe, Cynthia 155
Punch 24, 39, 46-7

Quigley, Janet 96-8

radio 163-5
  family 10-11, 30, 32-3, 42-3, 71, 83-4, 110-14
  novels 83-7, 151, 156-8
  serials 74-5, 84, 112-14, 118, 156-7, 166
  technology 49, 51, 59, 163
  theory 33-5
  "transmedia extensions" 84
  variety 10-11, 50, 60, 81-2, 91, 93-5, 98, 103
Radio Doctor, the 96
radiogenic 27, 29, 81
Radio Luxembourg 72, 75, 153
Radio Manufacturer Association 72
Radio Newsreel 154
Radio Normandie 72, 79
Radio Pictorial 7, 11, 28, 52-4, 57, 62, 80, 90, 123
Radio Radiance 29
radio repertory companies 26
Radio Times 7, 17, 42, 44, 49-51, 55, 73, 87, 93, 110, 112-14, 161, 169
Rank, Arthur 135-6, 150
rationing 96-101, 104-6
Rattenbury murder 155
Ray, Ted 22, 166-7
Raymond, Ernest 1
Ray's a Laugh 150, 167
Reade, Charles 155
realism 12, 136, 138-9
Reese, Harold 114
Reith, (Sir) John 9, 17-19, 21, 32, 47, 52, 58-60, 72, 90, 165
Reithian principles 47, 49, 57, 152-3, 165, 168
remediation 32-3, 166

re-runs, literary 86
respectability 43, 59, 82, 123, 134, 136-7, 140, 144, 148
Revnell, Ethel 169
Revue and Vaudeville section (BBC) 51, 73
Richards, Jeffrey 145, 147-8
Roberts, Elizabeth 85
Roberts, Nancy 33
Robey, George 22
Robinsons, the 12-13, 117-19, 131
Rob Roy 156
Robson, Flora 139
Rogers, Peter 139
Ronald, Tom 151
Rooney, Mickey 138
Rorke, John 129
Rose, Howard 27, 116, 118, 128
Rosenstein, Barbara 2
Rose without a Thorn, The 82
Ross, Herbert 16
Rowntree, Jean 97-8
Royal Air Force (RAF) 117, 140
Royle Family, The 6, 40, 47

St. George's Hall 74
Sam's Medal 82
Samuel, Raphael 15, 169
Samuel French acting editions 2, 31, 82, 94-5, 121
Sarabande for Dead Lovers 153
Saturday Night Theatre 151, 157
Saunders, Jennifer 6
Savoy Hill 15, 17-18, 22, 27, 128
Scales, Prunella 6
Scannell, Paddy 27, 113
Scheduling 10, 74-5, 84, 96-7
Scott, Sir Walter 156
Scott-Jeffs, Carolyn 168
Scrapbook 80
scriptwriting 77, 119-20, 155
seaside resorts 22
Second World War 6, 11-13, 89, 116-17
  and BBC 89-99, 117-20, 129, 151, 157
  and changing attitudes 132, 134-6
  and entertainment 93
  and evacuation 116
  morality 134-6

National Savings Campaign 100
  and rationing 96–101, 104–6
  and women 90, 94, 101
Seddon, Jill 125–6
Selby, Keith 24, 156–7
serials 74–5, 84, 112–14, 118, 156–7, 166
servants 46–7, 64, 114–15, 147
  and jokes 41, 46
sexuality 132, 134–7, 140, 142
Shakespeare, William 16, 26, 48
Shameless 33
Shaw, Susan 141
Shoemaker's Holiday, The 82
Shreds and Patches 2, 7–8, 23, 52, 56–7, 63–9, 81–2, 98, 125, 128–9
Sieveking, Lance 6, 73, 127, 168
silence 19
Simpson, Helen 153
Sing it Through 92
situation comedy (sitcom) 3, 6, 10, 32–3, 40, 75, 80, 84, 120–1, 129, 166–8
  and family 10, 31–3, 129, 150, 166–8
slum clearances 83
Smith, Bina (housekeeper) 57, 64, 98
soap opera 3–5, 12, 32, 109–11, 114, 119, 129, 166–7
social explorers 44–5, 83
Society for Psychical Research 20–1
Songs from the Shows 73
sonic-mindedness 19
sound effects 28, 33
South Africa 143–5
Spicer, Andrew 148
spiritualism 9, 20
spivs 139–42
Spring-Rice, Margery 110
Squirrel's Cage (Tyrone Guthrie) 16, 111
Stage, The 81
Standing, Michael 150, 154
stations, *see* British Broadcasting Corporation and Stations
Stewart, Hugh 158
Stoll, (Sir) Oswald 26
Stone, Christopher 55
Story of Papworth Village, The 82
Strachey, Ray 68, 124
Strange Adventures of Mr. Penny, The 75–80, 84, 111, 121, 167

Streatham 112–13
Streatham Anomalies 112
Strube, Sidney 75, 77
Strutham 112–13, 146
Struther, Jan 110, 115–16
suburbia 31, 110–16, 121–3, 136–7, 145–6, 148
  criticism of 5, 113, 121, 123
superiority theory of humour 39, 41–2, 48, 105–6
Surrey 7
Survivor, The (Mabel Constanduros and Michael Hogan) 16
Sussex, H. M. 158–9
Sutherland, Graham 111
Sutton 8, 23, 68–9, 111–12, 121, 123
Sutton Amateur Dramatic Club (SADC) 8, 23, 66–8, 123
Sutton Coldfield transmitter 153
Swiss Family Robinson, The 112
Szreter, Simon 137

Take it from Here (TIFH) 167
Tate, Catherine 33
Taylor, Julia 54
technology companies 9
telephone ownership 56, 147
television 5–7, 9, 13, 33, 43, 47, 54–5, 84, 93, 145, 153, 158, 162–6
  criticism of 47, 164–5
  licenses 18, 153, 162
tentpole tactics 84
Thackeray, W. M. 45
theatre 22, 24, 33, 131
  amateur 1, 11, 15, 82–3, 112, 119, 123, 126, 154, 166
  "legitimate" 11, 82
theatre of the mind 33–5, 54
These Radio Times 73, 81, 161
Thiele, Barbara 125
Three for Luck 82
Through the Stage Door 161
Til Death Us Do Part 6, 33, 42, 168
Tilling, Richard 7, 68
Tilling, Sophia 7
Tilling, Thomas 7
Tilling Omnibus Company 7, 45–6, 85–6
Times, The 49, 110, 115

Index

Times Square 136
Today's Cinema 136
Todd, Barbara Euphan (Bower) 128, 169
Tomlinson, David 143
Tomlinson, Ricky 6
Train, Jack 92
transmedia extensions 84
Tregarthen, Jeanette 140
Truman, Ralph 114

Union Internationale de Radiophonie 21

Vaness, Amy 142
Variety Department (BBC) 2, 10–11, 25, 27–8, 52, 73–80, 89–91, 97, 125, 153–5
Variety Repertory Company (VRC) 90–1, 94
vaudeville 50, *see also* variety
Vaudeville, The 131
Vote for Huggett 143–4, 146–7, 151

Walker, Rhoderick 132
Wallace, Nellie 169
Walworth 36, 44–5, 83–6, 146
Warner, Jack 8, 13, 66, 139, 141, 150, 166
Warner Brothers 135
Waters, Doris, *see* Gert and Daisy
Waters, Elsie, *see* Gert and Daisy
Watt, John 32, 45, 73, 89, 92
Weber, Brenda 65
Wembley Exhibition 22
Westerby, Robert 97, 99
Westminster Abbey 143
Westward Ho! 156
Where's George? 82
White, Glyn 32, 35
Whitfield, June 168
Wickham, Phil 40
Willis, Ted 139
Wilton, Robb 1, 4, 95
Wimbledon 111
Winn, Godfrey 139
Winter, Jay 20
Wireless Constructor, The 19
wireless manufacturers 17, 72
wireless sets 19

Wireless Sub-Committee of the Imperial Communications Committee 18
Woman and Beauty 16
Woman's Hour 13, 98, 161–2
women 5, 85, 94, 101–2, 109, 114, 119, 124
  amateurs 83, 123, 126
  and BBC 3, 13, 169
  and careers 3, 11, 68, 124–6
  and celebrity 3, 9, 11, 63–9, 81, 169
  and comedy 5–7, 30–2, 99–107, 109–10, 168–9
  and entertainment 7, 13, 168–9
  and marriage 68, 101–2, 124, 140, 142–3
  and pay inequality 126–7
  performers 3, 7, 13, 28, 169
  professionalism 3, 67, 124–7, 155, 169
  and situation comedy 6, 32–3
  social explorers 44–5, 83
  writers 6–7, 13, 94, 110, 119, 124, 126–7, 155, 169
Wood, Victoria 6
Woolley, Dr. V. J. 20–1
Woolton, Lord Frederick Marquis 100
Woon, Basil 119–20
Worker's Educational Association (WEA) 36
working classes 4, 12, 36, 38, 42–8, 84–7, 97, 104–6, 110, 113, 123, 135–7, 147–50, 163
  and affluence 138, 147–9
  representation of 10, 31, 33, 36–48, 83–7, 109–11, 115, 118, 123, 168
Worthing 83
Worzel Gummidge 128, 164
Writing for the BBC 77
Writtle Experimental Station 16, 21
Wyss, Johann David 112

Young, Filson 39–42
Young, Gladys 8, 86–7, 129, 169
Young, William 8
youth 132, 134–7